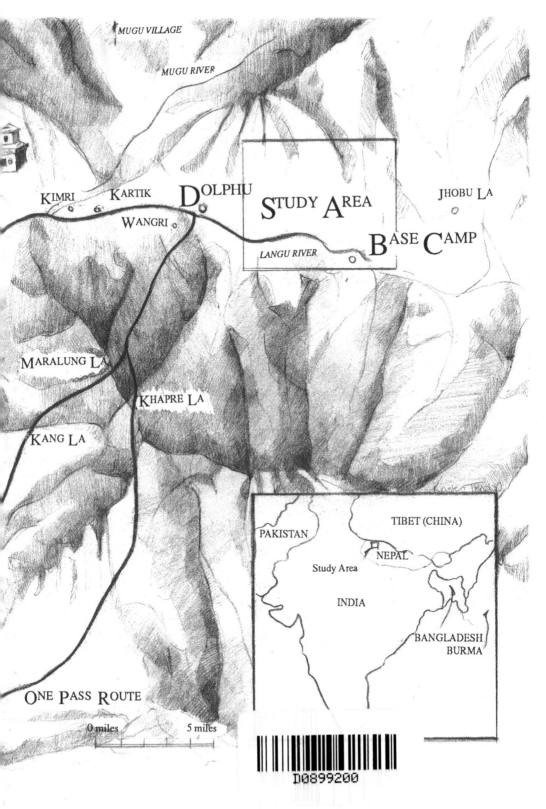

MUGU VILLAGE

MUGU RIVER

KIMRI   KARTIK   DOLPHU   STUDY AREA   JHOBU LA

WANGRI

BASE CAMP

LANGU RIVER

MARALUNG LA

KHAPRE LA

KANG LA

PAKISTAN   TIBET (CHINA)

NEPAL

Study Area

INDIA

BANGLADESH
BURMA

ONE PASS ROUTE

0 miles   5 miles

JUMLA TO DOLPHU

Vanishing Tracks

To Jane
with best wishes

Darla Hillard

Rodney Jackson

Vanishing Tracks

*Four Years Among the
Snow Leopards of Nepal*

DARLA HILLARD

Arbor House/William Morrow
New York

Library of Congress Cataloging-in-Publication Data

Hillard, Darla.
    Vanishing tracks: four years among the snow leopards of Nepal/
Darla Hillard.
        p.   cm.
    Bibliography: p.
    Includes index.
    ISBN 0-87795-972-2
    1. Snow leopard—Nepal.   2. Mammals—Nepal.   I. Title.
QL737.C23H55   1989
599.74′428—dc19   89-8
                                                   CIP

Printed in the United States of America

First Edition

1 2 3 4 5 6 7 8 9 10

BOOK DESIGN BY BRIAN MALOY

For Rodney
For the Bhotes of Dolphu and Wangri
And in memory of my father

ACKNOWLEDGMENTS

The Snow Leopard Project, and thus this book, would never have been possible without those who made the first vital commitments, supporting Rod's vision on the one hand with governmental approvals and on the other with the cash to begin.

For the joy of discovery, for our lives' most valuable educational experience, and for the intense personal satisfaction in living and working in Nepal, we must express our deepest appreciation to His Royal Majesty Birendra Bir Bikram Shah Dev, King of Nepal. To His Highness Prince Gyanendra Bir Bikram Shah, Royal Nepalese Patron of Wildlife; to B. N. Upreti, Director General, His Majesty's Government, Department of National Parks and Wildlife Conservation; and to Hemanta Mishra, Member-Secretary to the Board of Trustees, King Mahendra Trust for Nature Conservation, we extend also our deep appreciation for the opportunity to work with the Nepalese government and the kingdom's remarkable people.

Since 1978, Rolex of Geneva has provided one of the few opportunities worldwide for researchers, explorers, inventors, and dreamers to breathe life into designs for humanity and the environment that are often considered unfundable by traditional sources. As such, the Snow Leopard Project was one of five submittals selected out of over five thousand for the 1981 Rolex Awards for Enterprise. The award funded most of the first year's study. To all the members of the Selection Committee and the Rolex supporting staff, particularly Mr. André J. Heiniger and Mlle. C. Ricou, we extend our abiding gratitude. Here, too, I must give a special thanks to John and Joy Hunt, also known as Lord and Lady Hunt of Llanfair Waterdine. Lord Hunt was a member of "our" Rolex Selection Committee. He is better known for having led the first successful ascent of Mount Everest, when Edmund Hillary and Tensing Norgay reached the top. In our minds, Lord Hunt was a key player in Rod's being selected for the Rolex Award.

The National Geographic Society made it possible for us to continue by becoming our primary funding source. By publishing our article in *National Geographic* magazine, the society not only generated worldwide recognition for the Snow Leopard Project but also gave me an invaluable credential as a writer. Without exception, those with whom we worked gave us an abundance of wise and friendly assistance and encouragement, and I wish that there were space here to mention each by name. Wilbur E. Garrett, Mary G. Smith, Robert C. Jordan, Neva Folk, Edwin W. Schneider, and Barry C. Bishop supervised and led us through the grant process and production of the article. They, along with those unnamed, have our highest regard and our heartfelt thanks.

The International Trust for Nature Conservation, Basel, in association with Tiger Tops/Tiger Mountain of Nepal, provided both financial and logistics assistance. Here, too, I wish that I could mention every person's name who had a role, both educationally and practically, in helping us adjust to living and working in Nepal. Management and staff alike were always knowledgeable, efficient, and unwaveringly friendly. John Edwards, Prem Rai, Chuck and Margie McDougal, and Lisa Van Gruisen Choegyal were those upon whom we regularly called for help and guidance.

The International Snow Leopard Trust came into being at about the same time as our project. Helen Freeman, the Trust's founder and President, is a warm friend as well as a leader in the preservation of snow leopards and their high mountain habitat. Her untiring dedication and that of her board and staff are exemplary models of human optimism and determination. The Trust's important work is described in the Appendix; I am particularly obliged to Helen for urging me to write and for publishing my notes from the field in the Trust's newsletter.

Other vital grants were provided by the New York Zoological Society's Wildlife Conservation International, the World Wildlife Fund—US, the King Mahendra Trust for Nature Conservation, the National Wildlife Federation, the Fauna and Flora Preservation Society, and the Mill Pond Press.

Frank Gress, President of the California Institute of Environmental Studies, and Jessica Brenner, C.P.A., provided administrative backup. John Garcia supported Rod during his leave of absence from BioSystems Analysis, Inc. The blessings and enthusiasm of these close and valued friends were equally important to the project's success.

Canadian artist Robert Bateman has long been dedicated to making a difference in the campaign for wildlife and habitat preservation. By creating the magnificent snow leopard painting "High Kingdom" and donating a portion of sales, he has given the world a wonderful work of art while reaffirming his commitment to conservation.

Dr. James Forster, Medical Director of the Children's Hospital Health Plan in San Francisco, provided advice and suggestions on how to put together a medical kit for nondoctors.

Many people in Nepal, besides those already mentioned, became our friends and benefactors. John Tyson, Headmaster of Bodhilnakantha School, and his energetic wife, Phebe, gave us unforgettable evenings of great Kanjiroba stories, wonderful meals, and opportunities to share our experiences through slide shows in Kathmandu and at the school.

Kazi Nepali, leading Nepalese bird expert, taught us how to distinguish the more difficult birds, including snow finches and rose finches, during many evenings in his home, where we feasted on delicious Newari food and rakshi.

Businessman, author, philanthropist, and true humanitarian, Karna Sakya is among Nepal's foremost Himalayan conservationists. Karna and all his staff at the Kathmandu Guest House made us feel at home, and Karna's candid counsel helped Rod through several difficult times.

Larry Asher, Director of the Jumla United Missions Project, and his wife, Phyl, as well as Frank and Anita Younkin, Buck and Gwen Deines, and Helen Matthews are among those not mentioned in the text to whom we are grateful for help and advice. Ruthie Overwold and Hazel Buckner, of the United Missions mailroom in Kathmandu, took care of our mail. The "two Nick's" and Raoul, working through various government aid organizations in Jumla, also were our friends.

On the home front, Mimi Conway and Dennis Houlihan have been instrumental from the start in reinforcing my belief in myself as a writer. Mimi's advice as an accomplished author and investigative reporter has been entertaining, enlightening, and enormously helpful.

Mardie Murie gave me both encouragement and inspiration, by her own exemplary life and through the words she wrote in my copy of *Two in the Far North*. The book is now wrinkled, tattered, and infinitely better for its journeys to Nepal. I hope the same can be said for me.

Arlene Blum, leader of the first women's ascent of 26,504-foot Annapurna I in central Nepal, is another writer/photographer whose encouragement was particularly valuable, coming from one who has faced great emotional and physical challenges in the Himalayas.

Hugh Swift, writer, photographer, and veteran perambulator, provided the wisdom of his vast experience of the Himalayas, his near-photographic memory, and his refreshing philosophy of life.

Ed Bernbaum provided advice on Tibetan definitions.

For Roxy Ahlborn, draftee into the Snow Leopard Project, there aren't words to say how much her contribution meant. Without her forthright acceptance of the hardships, risks, and lonely months—all of which we brought to bear upon her life and her marriage by removing Gary from it for so long—there is little doubt that the study would have fallen far short of its potential.

Janet Klein ignited my passion for birds, and Jackie Wilson introduced me to Georgia O'Keefe—two actions that certainly altered the path of my life.

Two people must share the "Best Correspondent" award for having a letter in every mailbag: Rod's mother, Margaret Jackson, and our friend Kim Schwarcz.

ACKNOWLEDGMENTS

I would like to mention each and every one of our families and friends, for they did more than words can say to help us, both with project work and specifically in my writing. That, however, would require another book. We turned repeatedly to core members of the Hillard clan: Terry, Sandy, and Molly; Kent, Grant, and Brett; Karen and Ron; Felicia and Dad (who died in 1986); Ginny and Van. Jeff Frankel was our housemate, and his parents, Peg and John, were the neighbors upstairs who became our "second family." Renee Lagloire and Susie Frankel typed, photocopied, and distributed the newsletters I had written with pen and ink and that they often received transformed for the worse by the journey to Jumla in Karma's pack. Anne Cervantes created our project letterhead. John and Ellen Sanger provided their house for my back-to-Nepal fundraiser, and John provided the computer on which this book was produced. All our friends gave us their unstinting support and encouragement: They came willingly to our "food packing parties"; they wrote us letters, knowing they might never reach us; and they dug into their pockets or wrote personal checks to help us keep the project going. Of all that life has given, this abundance of friends and family is our most treasured gift.

Those who read and commented on the draft manuscript—Tom and Mary Herrmann, Wayne Miller, the Clyde Hillards, Bob Holmes, Pam and Mark Stivers-Fritzler, Genie Murphy, Bruce Wolfe, and Helen Freeman—all improved the book in some way.

Kristin Throop enhanced the whole with her attractive and interesting maps.

Alan Rabinowitz, author of *Jaguar* (an Arbor House book about his radio-tracking study of jaguars in Central America), introduced me to his editor, James Raimes, an introduction that led to my publishing contract.

My agent, Carl Brandt, has provided a much-needed voice of experience and wise judgment throughout.

Jerry Gross, rich in editorial experience, was my writing guru, offering constructive and insightful direction, and later, Andy Dutter stepped in to see the manuscript through to publication. Being an enthusiastic, warm and kindred spirit, Andy and his participation have been one of the best things about the production of this book.

Finally, I want to emphasize again the role of our expedition team. Consistently true to his heart and his beliefs, Karan Shah weathered the hardships and conflicts without compromise in his own style. I hope that he, like Rod, Gary, and myself, feels richer for having known the Langu, and looks back on his experiences with the same good feelings about having known one another.

All the funding in the world would not have made the study possible without the Sherpas. We simply could not have lived in the Langu without their help. Working on the Snow Leopard Project was arguably the least desirable job any of them could have been offered, and yet having once made the commitment, they stuck to it—often going out of their way to see to our comfort, our safety, or, happily for us, to our entertainment when times were hard. To Lopsang, Nema Nurbu, and Kirken we extend our heartfelt gratitude. Karma, likely never to see or have this read to him, was to me like a younger brother. He might have been considered "gifted" in our society—exceptionally bright, motivated, and quick to learn. He is instead the proverbial opportunist, always alert for the soft scam. I doubt he'll ever change; I hope he lives a long, prosperous, and, above all, free life.

I haven't thanked Rod or Gary; I can only hope these pages say for me what ordinary words cannot.

Choosing a title was more difficult than one might think. *Vanishing Tracks* was suggested by Michelle Schirru while we were visiting her and Jim Sanderson in their New Mexico home.

Of our equipment sponsors, several have made especially significant contributions. Over the project's duration, Hain Pure Food Company provided hundreds of dollars' worth of lightweight, nutritious soups, seasonings, and fast-cooking prepared dinners. The North Face provided sleeping bags, clothing, and the bulk of our expedition tents, along with Sierra Designs and REI. REI also supplied the seat harnesses for our cable bridges and made a much-appreciated funding appeal for our project in their quarterly newsletter. Nikon, Inc., provided cameras, flashes, and lenses. Bushnell provided spotting scopes and binoculars. Cascade Designs of Seattle gave us our treasured Therm-a-Rest mattresses.

Other Equipment Sponsors
Autocad: Computer software
Eddie Bauer: Camping equipment
Black Ice: Camping equipment
Bristol Laboratories: Scientific equipment
Geyer Peak Wineries: Camping equipment
Karl Heitz, Inc.: Gitzo tripods
Human Systems Dynamics: Computer software
Mountain Safety Research: Camping equipment
Mountain West: Scientific equipment
Nike: Hiking boots and shoes
Nikon: Photographic equipment
Pelican Products: Photographic equipment
Polaroid: Photographic equipment
Precise International: Scientific equipment
Prisma Outdoor Products: Camping/scientific equipment
Quest Systems: Photographic equipment
Revue Thommen AG: Scientific equipment
Rollei: Photographic equipment
Swift Instruments: Scientific equipment
Telinject: Scientific equipment

Other Institutional Sponsors
BioSystems Analysis, Inc.
California Academy of Sciences
California Institute of Environmental Studies
Environmental Impact Planning Corporation
International Union for the Conservation of Nature (IUCN)
Smithsonian Institution
U.S. Fish and Wildlife Service
Woodlands Mountain Institute

CONTENTS

CONTENTS

LIST OF CHARACTERS

Central Characters

Gary Ahlborn—Western coinvestigator
Darla Hillard—Author
Rodney Jackson—Principal investigator
Karma—Local cook/*sirdar*
Kirken—Sherpa *sirdar*/cook
Lopsang—Sherpa *sirdar*/cook
Nema—Sherpa *sirdar*/cook
Karan B. Shah—Long-term Nepalese coinvestigator
Sonam—Guide and camp staff

Other Characters

Mr. Bogati—Health worker at Mangri
Wangri Cinon—Guru's son, occasional camp helper
"Crazy People"—Karma Chogyap, mentally ill villager
Wangri Guru—Energetic widow of Wangri village
Judy Henderson/Jenny Sutton—Doctor and nurse, respectively, who ran a health
    clinic in Jumla
Bob and Bobbie Holmes—Friends who visited our camp when we were away
Jamuna—Short-term co-investigator; resigned
Jickchor—Villager
Karma Lama—Villager (elected official)
Kartol—Karma's second wife
Lhakpa Norbu—Then-Warden of nearby Rara National Park
Lundup—Dolphu villager, carried a load for us when Rod got bitten
Pema—Owner of Jumla's "Tibetan" hotel
Kurt Stolzenberg—Short-term project volunteer
Tsang Tenzing—*Jhankri* (shaman) of Mangri
Tenzing Thakpa—Dolphu villager, our occasional guide and camp helper
Thondup—Sonam's father, hereditary headman
Tsewong—Villager who died
Wangchu—Karma Lama's father
Yangyap—Dolphu villager, first across the cable bridge without supervision.

17

PROLOGUE

The Himalayan Snow Leopard Project began as an idea in Rodney Jackson's mind in 1976. We did not know one another then. I was a secretary, thirty years old, working in an engineering firm in San Francisco. It never crossed my mind that I would meet an adventurer and come face to face with one of the earth's most endangered big cats.

The Snow Leopard Project became the world's first successful attempt to radio-collar and learn about the habits of this rare and elusive creature. But to me, the most amazing thing still is the turn of events that led me from the streets of San Francisco to walk almost a thousand miles with Rod through one of the earth's wildest and most remote mountain kingdoms.

Before our study, most of what was known about the snow leopard in its natural habitat was guesswork. Most of what little had been published consisted of hunters' descriptions of scenes that took place shortly before they dispatched their "trophies."

Beginning in 1969 and continuing into the 1970s, the renowned field biologist George B. Schaller had conducted a series of expeditions throughout the Himalayas.* Schaller wanted to know the status and

---

*Technically, "Himalaya" is plural, but since "Himalayas" seems to be more common, I use it throughout.

distribution of the mountain species, and he wanted particularly to study the fascinating and varied wild sheep and goats of the Himalayan chain. He later wrote, in *Stones of Silence:*

. . . I met many animals, marmots and wolves and high altitude birds. But none possessed me as did the snow leopard, a rare and elusive creature which lured me on, only seldom permitting a glimpse.

Schaller's first observation of a snow leopard in the wild happened in 1970 in the Chitral Gol (Valley) of Pakistan. The cat had a small cub, and by supplying the pair with a steady supply of meat, he was able to observe them for a week and to take the world's first photographs of a snow leopard in the wild. He devised a plan to study the cats while continuing his observations of the sheep and goats:

The old naturalistic techniques of following tracks, examining feces, and glimpsing an occasional animal were obviously not the best means of studying the habits of this cat. If I could place a radio transmitter mounted on a collar around the necks of several individuals, I would be able to locate them by picking up the signals on a receiving set.

But the study never took place. Seven snow leopards in and around the Chitral Valley were shot between 1971 and 1973. In four short years, the status of the snow leopard in Chitral had gone, in Schaller's words, "from tenuously secure to seriously threatened." The traps that were set to catch and radio-collar any survivors remained empty until at last Schaller gave up, expressing his bitter disappointment:

Markhor may still scamper over the precipices of the Chitral Gol and chukor may cackle among the sagebrush, but one of my dreams vanished with the last snow leopard.

The situation in Nepal wasn't much better. In 1973, Schaller visited Nepal's far western Dolpo District to record the rutting activities of the area's wild blue sheep, or *bharal* (a hoofed animal with characteristics of both sheep and goat). He invited Peter Matthiessen to join him. Naturally, they planned to look for signs of snow leopards. In the introduction to his book *The Snow Leopard,* Matthiessen wrote:

G.S. knew of only two Westerners—he was one—who had laid eyes on the Himalayan snow leopard in the last 25 years; the hope of glimpsing this near-mythic beast was reason enough for the entire journey.

But only when leaving the study area did Schaller briefly see a cat. In the time Peter Matthiessen spent in Dolpo, his hope to see one never materialized.

No one knows how many snow leopards may be left in the world. They are still being killed in retaliation for livestock raids, to supply the demands of wealthy Westerners for fur coats (despite fur-trade bans), or simply to prove the prowess of the hunter. But they also face an even more lethal threat, for the mountains themselves are at critical risk. The ecological balance of the Himalayas has been so altered by man that the children who play in the wheat fields today may be the last to till the land, for the soil will soon be gone and the plow's wooden blade will turn nothing but stone. The clearing of increasingly marginal land for agriculture, wood, and fodder, and the overgrazing of high-altitude pastures accelerate massive erosion. It is an inexorable, ongoing occurrence in the geologically young Himalayas.

Measures are desperately needed to reverse environmental trends that will, if allowed to continue, have a much farther-reaching effect than just the extinction of the snow leopard. Here the cats can play an unwitting but vital role. Within their ideal habitat they are at the top of the chain, living on the native ungulates (or hoofed mammals), as well as smaller mammals such as marmots and pikas (where they occur) and even game birds. Snow leopards are therefore dependent on a healthy population of prey, which in turn is dependent on a variety of plants. Where all of these interdependent species occur in numbers, you have a healthy mountain ecosystem. Thus the snow leopard's presence or absence in a given area helps to identify areas in need of protection or rehabilitation.

Compounding the environmental problems, many of Central Asia's high mountains lie in political border zones where relations among nations have been hostile throughout history: the Himalayas, much of which are in the tiny Kingdom of Nepal; the Altai Mountains, on the borders between China, Mongolia, and Russia; the Pamirs, surrounded by Russia, Afghanistan, Pakistan, and China; the Hindu Kush, between Afghanistan and Pakistan; and the Karakorum, shared by India, Pakistan, and China. All these are mountain ranges where snow leopards once did and still might survive, and they all form part of one or another of the world's most sensitive international boundaries.

Born in South Africa on January 19, 1944, Rod Jackson spent his childhood in the bush surrounding his home, searching for and finding pugmarks, or tracks, of leopard and antelope in the dusty yellow earth. As he grew up, he focused his studies on the animals, reading every account of early African exploration he could get his hands on, dreaming of the day he might fulfill his destiny as a wildlife researcher in the African forests and savannas.

Rod, then a Rhodesian resident, was attending the University of Rhodesia in 1965 when the country, led by Ian Smith, declared unilateral independence from Britain. It was to be a futile effort to stave off majority black rule. While at the university, Rhodesia's only multiracial institution, Rod and others were harassed by white racists whenever they were seen in the company of blacks, both on campus and on the streets. Facing imminent army induction, he decided his only option to avoid being forced to fight those whom he felt had legitimate rights was to leave the country.

He moved to Canada and then to California, completing his master's degree in zoology at the University of California at Berkeley, in 1971. He had been working for several years as a wildlife biologist when he attended a lecture that would change the course of his life. John Tyson, leader of 1961 and 1964 English mapping and mountaineering expeditions to Nepal's far West, came to Berkeley to talk about the Kanjiroba Himal region, showing slides and footage of the Langu Gorge, a northern tributary of the great Mugu Karnali. The gorge was too rugged for human habitation, and probably because of that, his expeditions had seen herds of bharal, a major item in the snow leopards' diet. Rod agreed with Tyson that the area seemed more than likely to support snow leopards. He decided to go to Nepal in 1976 to see if he could find and photograph the beautiful, haunting, and mysterious cat.

During the few weeks that Rod spent that fall and winter in the Langu, he had little trouble finding evidence of the big cats. Abundant tracks, scraped depressions in the soil, and numerous droppings were ample sign that several leopards lived in the gorge. He bought a goat and staked it out. In theory, the leopard would kill the goat under cover of darkness and still be there early in the morning when Rod would approach, cautiously, with his camera. The plan didn't work, though the goat was killed and partly eaten.

But Rod had found a pocket of prime mountain habitat, and he decided that what he ought to be doing, as a wildlife biologist, was a scientific study, not a photographic one. Was it a good opportunity for radiotelemetry? Given the right equipment and enough time, he was confident he could catch the leopards, give them radio collars, and release them unharmed. *If* he could keep the villagers from killing them all first.

Up and down the Langu, there was an active black market trade in snow leopard pelts. Poison-tipped bamboo spears set in the ground to impale bharal were also very effective at killing snow leopards. Up in the gorge beyond the village, Rod had found a skinned and rotting carcass hidden in some rocks. His Sherpa guides had helped him find the hunters and buy the pelt for the equivalent of about ten dollars. Rod turned it over to the Nepalese Department of National Parks and Wildlife Conservation (DNPWC), along with a report about hunting in the Langu. The area being so remote, however, it seemed unlikely that any official action could be taken against the hunters.

When he returned from Nepal in early 1977, Rod began to search for a source of funding for a radio-tracking study of snow leopards. With two friends, he formed a nonprofit institute, the California Institute of Environmental Studies (CIES), to serve as a sponsoring organization for their various environmental interests.

But Rod soon discovered that grants for snow leopard research were almost as elusive as the cats themselves. His proposals were rejected by every agency he approached. One reviewer put in writing the question that stood on everyone's lips: "What makes Rodney Jackson think he can do what George Schaller could not?" The message was, "You're asking to take on the impossible."

If they considered Rod to be too inexperienced, what would those reviewers have thought if they had known that the woman who would, for a time, become his chief assistant, one Darla Hillard, had no scientific background at all, and whose only credentials were a love of camping and the outdoors?

When I was small, my father used to take us to the mountains every summer, to the Sierra Nevada of northern California. We were a large family with only a small income, and a camping trip was our most affordable vacation. In the 1950s, before camping became popular, reservations were not required, and neighboring tents were few and far between. I remember those vacations as two weeks of heaven, playing cowboys and Indians, swimming in lakes and streams, sitting up late at night around the fire, and going to bed without taking a bath.

I grew up, moved to San Francisco, and took my first job, as a typist. A succession of secretarial jobs followed, including four years in a firm of architects in England. During one of those summers I hitchhiked around Europe. The highlight of the three-month trip was two weeks spent with a Greek family in a small village on Crete. With them, I realized how much more I enjoyed the rural life of the countries I visited than that of the cities.

By 1978, having been a secretary for thirteen years, I was growing intolerably dissatisfied. What could I do—without a degree or any special education—that was interesting and unusual? Each brief vacation, a few weeks spent in the mountains or desert, only made it harder to go back to the office. At thirty-two, I was reluctant to embark on a long, part-time journey through college.

It was then that I took a weekend backpacking trip, a course in natural history offered by CIES (the same California Institute of Environmental Studies that Rod and his friends had formed). I liked the friendly and

24

knowledgeable trip leaders, and the well-organized programs that CIES offered. I thought there might be a place for me.

I drove across town and knocked on the door of CIES's office. My knock was answered by a thin, medium tall man with a close-cropped beard and straight, light brown hair curving just below his ears: Rodney Jackson, codirector. He wore corduroy jeans and a plaid cotton shirt, and Famolare ripple-soled shoes. He gazed at me through large brown questioning eyes as he brought the downcurved stem of a pipe to his lips. A minor birth defect had given him narrow, rounded shoulders and a slightly hunched back, barely noticeable beneath his blue down vest. He did not appear to be either the brooding artist sort or the rugged outdoorsman that I had always been attracted to.

What Rod saw before him as he stood there in the doorway was a short woman with large round glasses and very frizzy, blond, permanented hair. He remembers the words that first went through his mind: "Of course it would have to be me who answered the door. Another volunteer. What in the hell am I going to do with this one?"

I grinned my best grin, and he invited me in.

As we talked about the institute and where I might fit in, I found myself liking this quiet, rather shy biologist. Rod recalls how we made our first date:

I invited Darla to a party at the flat I shared with a friend, to celebrate the completion of some home improvements. I remember going into the kitchen to get a beer, and hearing her exuberant laugh, certain in itself. "I like that," I told myself. She surely doesn't fit my stereotype of a secretary, timid creatures that keep in the background. Now she's in there explaining to a computer aficionado the wonders of Utah's Canyonlands and its birds. I like that, too—her being a person who prefers to camp than to stay in a hotel.

After ten years in California, this expatriate South African still said "torch" instead of "flashlight"; "adjustable spanner" instead of "monkey wrench". He pronounced "laugh" to rhyme with "cough." He had his own versions of our common expressions: "to hell in a hay basket"; "dead as a door post." Those were the "Rodney" things about him. But there was a "Rod" side, too. Maybe he couldn't recite the names of the day's celebrities, but he could show you where to look for great horned owls; he could spot a muskrat swimming in a stream; and in the hills he could find the tracks of a mountain lion. To me, those were magical abilities, and walks with Rod were always fun and packed with new experiences.

When two years had passed since Rod returned from the Langu, he began to despair of ever getting back. The barriers seemed too enormous, with conservation organizations unwilling to invest their limited funds in such a "high risk" project, with an unknown and unproven principal investigator. Then one day he saw an announcement in a magazine:

Is your work at the cutting edge of imagination? . . . Five Rolex Awards for Enterprise, in the sum of 50,000 Swiss francs each [$25,000], will be conferred to provide financial help for projects which seek to break new ground in their particular sphere. . . .

He asked if I would help him to type and edit his proposal—"A Radio-Tracking Study of Snow Leopards in Nepal"—to the 1981 Rolex Awards for Enterprise.

Using radiotelemetry and information from such signs as tracks and scrapes (deliberate scuff marks made by snow leopards using their hind paws), Rod proposed to find the answers to a list of questions, such as:

- Are wild snow leopards essentially solitary?
- Assuming "yes" to that first question, how do they communicate? How do they keep their distance from one another?
- What size and shape is their average home area?
- Do they share home areas, or maintain exclusive, defended, patrolled territories?
- What do they eat? How do they hunt? How often?
- How far do they travel in a twenty-four-hour period?
- Are they more active during the day, or at night?
- Do they have preferred travel lanes?

· Do they prefer one type of terrain over another, such as river bottoms, cliffs, or grassland?

A parallel study of bharal and Himalayan *tahr*, a wild goat found in the Langu, would supplement what was already known about the snow leopards' major prey. While neither have been fully studied, the tahr's taxonomy at least is clear. The bharal poses some questions. They exhibit goatlike behavior when rival males rear up on their hind legs and bash heads with a resounding clash of horns. Also like the goat, when in rut the gymnastic males take their penises into their mouths, stopping short, however, of the goat's determined attempt to lure a female by soaking itself with its own urine. In build, the bharal resembles a Rocky Mountain sheep or a desert bighorn sheep. Unlike goats, they have no knee calluses, or beards, and they lack the characteristically strong odor of a goat. Schaller concluded that the bharal is an aberrant goat with sheeplike affinities.

"Talk about taking on the impossible," Rod said as we put the proposal in the mail one day in March 1980, "I don't think I have a snowball's chance in hell of winning this." It would be eight months before the award was announced.

We continued to work on other institute projects, growing closer as we spent more time together.

We were stunned when a telegram came for Rod in November, announcing that he had been chosen as one of the five Rolex laureates. A letter followed, explaining that a week of celebration would be held in Geneva, Switzerland, in May 1981. The grand finale would be a presentation ceremony for which a half-hour film would be produced on the laureates and their work. The organizers wished to know who Rod might be bringing as his guest.

That the two of us would be going to Geneva was obvious. It wasn't so easy to see what was going to happen after that. With Rod planning to spend over a year in Nepal, some things had to be decided about *us*. Neither one of us had been married before, and neither was ready to be married now. But the sudden launching of the Snow Leopard Project made us realize that we must either part company or join forces for the expedition to Nepal.

I listened as he graphically described the Langu and the hardships and danger we would be facing: rockfalls, avalanches, exposed trails over high cliffs, isolation from other human beings, a monotonous diet of rice and potatoes, no hospitals, no doctors, no bathtub. Hoping I would want to come, he told me honestly that he wasn't even sure if *he* could handle the rigorous conditions under which we would have to live, in an unheated two-person tent that was a sixty-mile walk from anywhere.

I had longed for a chance to change my life, and here it was—beyond anything I could ever have dreamed up. I wanted to be with Rod, and I was confident of his judgment. The challenges did not seem overwhelming; I had read of other women traveling, alone, in much more difficult circumstances.

A hundred years ago, Isabella Bird, at age forty with a history of poor health, had wandered on horseback all through the Colorado Rocky Mountains and then gone on to western Tibet and Ladakh, Persia, and Kurdistan, traveling by horse, yak, mountain pony, junk, and sedan chair. When she was seventy, she climbed, with the help of a ladder, aboard a Moroccan black stallion and rode into the Atlas Mountains. She died at seventy-three, in bed, in Scotland.

Closer to home, I had a living role model, Margaret E. Murie, now in her eighties, who at twenty-two had married and joined her biologist husband, Olaus, on his surveys of the Alaskan interior in the 1920s, mushing huskies and either hanging on to or running behind a fourteen-foot sled over hundreds of miles of remotest Alaska. Less than a year after their first baby was born she was off again, traveling the Alaskan rivers for four months, in the height of the mosquito season, with Olaus and their son. She wouldn't have traded her experiences for the world. She never lost her love for the natural world and its inhabitants, and she remains active to this day in conservation and education.

Rod and I knew that for our task, new skills would be required. Some we could anticipate, such as photography. But others we would simply have to develop as we went along. We might have done some things differently if we had known that the study, intended to last fifteen months, would command the next four years of our lives.

Part

I

November 1981–September 1982

There can be few places on earth more savage and forbidding than the gorge of the Langu Khola.

JOHN TYSON
"RETURN TO KANJIROBA, 1969"
The Alpine Journal

Part

I

November 1981–September 1982

There can be few places on earth more savage and forbidding than the gorge of the Langu Khola.

JOHN TYSON
"RETURN TO KANJIROBA, 1969"
The Alpine Journal

CHAPTER

I

Threshold

I awoke on a mid-November morning in 1981 to the sound of jungle crows and myna birds chattering in the tops of golden-leafed poplar trees outside the window of our hotel room. For a moment, I didn't know where I was. Then I saw Rodney beside me and our twelve army duffel bags stacked in the corner, and I knew again the quickening excitement of a new day in a new land.

We had come to Kathmandu, capital of Nepal, heartbeat of the fifty-six-thousand-square-mile kingdom, a nation roughly the size and shape of Tennessee and lying between the northern border of India and the southern border of the Tibet Autonomous Region of the People's Republic of China. The sun was rising through silver mist to shine upon a bustling, exotic microcosm of East and West: a city with one foot in the 1980s and the other still back in the middle of the eighteenth century. Home to over three hundred thousand in a national population of more than sixteen million people, the city took its name (kath = wood, mon-do = house) from a temple that once stood on the valley floor and built entirely from the wood of a single tree. Now you can walk down the paved main street, past one or two minor *gagan chumbi ghar* (skyscrapers, or literally, "sky-kissing houses"), trip over a sacred cow, and nearly get run over by a bicycle rickshaw, which in turn might swerve into the path of a working elephant, causing a screeching of brakes as the sixty-thousand-dollar Mercedez-Benz behind it slams to a halt. You can sip French champagne in an air-conditioned room at the five-star Soaltee Oberoi Hotel, or you can choose a modest guesthouse room for under a hundred rupees, or about five dollars per night. You can wander through the bazaar's dirt alleyways and purchase your dinner—perhaps a pair of water buffalo hooves or a naked goat's head stained orange with turmeric—or you can step into a restaurant in Thamel, the tourist district, and eat spaghetti bolognese. If it is late summer, you might attend the Dasain day of sacrifice, where hundreds of animals are ritually decapitated, or, if you happen to have a toothache, you can visit the shrine of Vaisha Dev the toothache god and pound a nail in the wall to impale the source of your pain.

The back streets of Kathmandu are lined with tiny, open-fronted shops all specializing in a particular choice of goods: bolts of handloomed cloth; medicinal herbs; pots of beaten copper; fruits and vegetables; pungent spices in muslin sacks; or videotapes, television sets, and "ghetto blasters" imported from India and Japan. Mangy dogs growl and bare their teeth at passersby, but the barnyard animals pay little attention as they browse through organic garbage heaped on the street corners. Ripe smells of humanity mingle with the warm evening air. Just before dusk, waves of giant fruit bats wing their way over the city, heading for the verdant fields lying like patchwork over the land.

Kathmandu Valley, at just over 4,350 feet at the base of the high Himalayas, is still considered to *be* Nepal by the country's more remote and isolated inhabitants. The broad valley was a lake in prehistoric times. Later Kathmandu became a vital center of trade between India and Tibet. Now it is the international hub of one of the world's poorest developing countries, where the per-capita income is some $150 per year.

Kathmandu would supply a lifeline of communication and supplies without which we could not even think of entering the snow leopard's remote and inhospitable realm.

I threw off the warm cotton quilt and nudged Rod. "We'd better get moving." Much had happened in the week since we had arrived, but there was still a lot to be done before our expedition could begin. Today Kurt Stolzenberg, our associate, would arrive from the United States. We hoped things would be easier to accomplish with three of us working. We still had the grocery shopping to do—food for six people for six months. And somewhere in the bazaars of Kathmandu's old market, we had to find a dozen cotter pins, needed for Rod's traps but somehow forgotten in San Francisco. How do you describe a cotter pin to a storekeeper when you know about half a dozen words of Nepali?

Kurt, an avid mountaineer in his twenties, had approached Rod expressing a keen desire to come along. He would help set up Base Camp, learn radio-tracking, and generally serve as a project volunteer for the first few months of the study.

He was tall and strong and his mountaineering skills could prove extremely valuable. He had worked on a peregrine falcon recovery project in California, climbing to their cliffside nests and taking eggs to be hatched and raised in captivity, then released into the wild, but he had no direct scientific experience. Rod had weighed the pros and cons of accepting a second nonscientist into our group. Would his physical strength and abundant enthusiasm make up for his lack of training, our ten-year age difference, our untested ability to coexist, his never having traveled outside the United States, and particularly his lack of experience of Third World Nepal? In the end Rod decided that Kurt's assets outweighed his liabilities and accepted his offer.

When he and I had met for the first time in San Francisco, Kurt expressed his own reservations. "You know, Darla," he had said, "it isn't going to be easy out there. Are you sure you can handle it?"

As we stood at the window of Kathmandu's Tribhuvan International Airport later that afternoon, we looked down at all the passengers walking from Kurt's plane to the terminal. Over six feet tall, with blond hair and blue eyes, Kurt looked like a Viking among the small, dark-haired, brown-skinned Nepalese.

As he emerged from the Customs check weighted down with a full backpack and the additional two duffels of project gear with which he had been entrusted, Rod said: "Welcome to Kathmandu. Did you have a good trip?"

"Far out," replied Kurt. "Man, those peaks are a trip, they're gargantuan! What a mind-blower. I'm starved. What do the Nepalis eat?"

We took a taxi to our favorite restaurant, where Kurt ordered Nepali *dal-bhaat* and proceeded to eat the plateful of rice and vegetables with his fingers. He wanted to get right in touch with local customs.

There are over thirty tribes and ethnic groups throughout Nepal with as many different languages and dialects, scattered from the lowland jungles and plains, to the terraced foothills, to the high, frigid flanks of the towering Himalayas.

Outside Kathmandu, a few plains towns, some large enough to be called near-cities, support such one-factory industries as matchmaking, cement production, and textile and jute mills, but small farms provide the livelihood of the vast majority of the kingdom's population. Hindu or Buddhist or a mixture of the two, the Nepalese embrace a religious and cultural tradition that is hard for a Westerner to separate into its parts. Gods and goddesses define their existence, given substance in thousands of shrines and temples. The strong extended family provides social unity, and rituals, feasts, and festivals celebrate the deities around whom their lives, deaths, and destinies revolve.

While Kurt and I whittled away at the shopping lists, Rod would continue setting up the organizational framework for our joint study with the Nepalese government. We had intended to charter a plane and fly from Kathmandu to an airstrip within ten days' walk of the Langu. But no plane was available. The alternative was a two-day drive, then a 160-mile walk, south to north, across Nepal at its widest point. Rod was very concerned, knowing that the whole journey could take a month and put us seriously behind schedule. We would be racing the onset of winter to get to the study area, instead of having our base camp securely established and ready for the snows.

Kurt, fast emerging as even more outspoken than I and with fewer manners, voiced the opinion that Rod should have organized things better, but Kurt, too, was excited about the adventure ahead and quickly dropped the subject.

The motorable roads in Nepal add up to less than two thousand miles.

The East-West Highway was still under construction, but we were assured that we could get permission to use it and that the two hundred miles or so that we would have to travel on it could be navigated by Land-Rover.

Inside the two vehicles we had rented, our breath—hot with the effort of heaving trunks and duffel bags—made the early-morning air steamy. My feet rested on sixty pounds of red onions in a burlap bag; their odor mingled with the smell of dusty canvas duffels and motor fumes coming from beneath the Land-Rover's raised hood, where the driver assigned to our car was making his last-minute checks.

"My ears are cold," announced Rod. He began digging in the daypack. "Where's my hat?" He was always losing things. Or rather misplacing them, often finding them right under his nose. It was a holdover from the utter chaos of packing under which we had been living for the past few months. Really, it was surprising more things didn't get lost. He found his hat in his pocket.

Kurt and Jamuna, a Nepalese biologist in his thirties, rode in the white Land-Rover. Jamuna had been assigned to our project by the DNPWC as Rod's "counterpart" or coinvestigator. Jamuna's job was to study bharal, the snow leopard's major prey on the drier northern bank of the Langu, and Himalayan tahr, the wild goat that occurred in greater numbers on the moister southern bank. He would also act as liaison officer in our dealings with government officials.

With them was Kirken, a Sherpa, who at about twenty-two was undertaking his first job as an expedition *sirdar,* or foreman, responsible for managing porters and other logistics along the trail. Our Sherpa cook, Lopsang, rode in the green Land-Rover with Rod and me. A little older than Kirken, Lopsang lived near his close friend in the mountains of eastern Nepal.

Sherpas, ethnically Tibetan, have a reputation for strength, stamina, loyalty, and imaginative problem-solving, and they have a monopoly as mountaineering guides and high-altitude porters. Sherpas were instrumental in the British conquest of Everest (*Sagarmatha,* "Head of the Seas," in Nepali, or *Chomolungma,* "Goddess Mother of the Earth," in

Tibetan). The late Tenzing Norgay reached the summit in 1953 with Sir Edmund Hillary. Neither Kirken nor Lopsang had ever been in western Nepal, but they were energetically carrying on the tradition of indispensability started by the men of their grandfathers' generation. They were our guides and translators, introducing us to a new culture and teaching us to speak our first, tentative Nepali words.

Lopsang turned to me sitting on the seat behind him. "Is everything all right, *memsah'b*?" he asked.

"*Memsah'b?!*" I said. "Lopsang, my name is Darla. PLEASE—call me Darla. Don't call me *memsah'b*—it sounds awful, so imperialistic!" I couldn't suppress an ear-to-ear grin, though I tried my best to act grave and authoritative, the way I thought the memsahibs of the British Raj (or rule) of India (which gave rise to this honorific title for female foreigners) would have acted.

Perhaps being grave and authoritative was appropriate conduct in the "Wild West" of Nepal that we would soon be approaching, where the living conditions of the people were said to be very primitive. With poor, heavily eroded soils, no means for irrigation, and an utter dependence on the monsoon rains to nurture their crops, their lives were always balanced on the edge of famine. It was said that they were lawless, unpredictable, and highly intolerant of outsiders—except for the foreign outsider, wealthy beyond belief in their eyes and quite understandably fair game for whatever they could get in terms of jobs, wages, and fringe benefits. Teachers and government employees unfortunate enough to get assigned to Mugu District declared it to be the "Siberia of Nepal," and our traveling companions seemed glumly resigned to making the best of a bad situation.

Everyone we had talked to with any experience of western Nepal had spoken of endless problems with porters, such as daily strikes for higher wages, theft, and arguments over how much they were expected to carry. One anthropologist told of being abandoned by his porters at the top of a pass during a fierce blizzard; they had left him to die or live by his own wits in unfamiliar and frightening surroundings. Rod himself had experienced some difficulties during his visit in 1976, especially the strikes and arguments with porters, and the local villagers had been highly suspicious of the "Amrikan" who had come looking to photograph snow leopards.

We might have thought twice about returning to the Langu if we had known what kind of reception Rod was likely to get from the local people. His report to the government about their hunting activities, following his discovery of the snow leopard carcass in the gorge, had in fact resulted in several people being arrested and fined, including the headman and his son.

But as we found our seats in the Land Rovers and as I tried to control my excitement, we knew nothing of the trouble he had created. The driver turned the key, and the green Land-Rover jumped to life.

CHAPTER

2

Dirt Tracks and Footpaths

The road south from Kathmandu was well graded and reasonably smooth, even paved in places, and also very narrow and winding. Great numbers of large trucks traveled the road, transporting goods between India and the Nepalese capital. Their hood ornaments proclaimed "Tata-Mercedes-Benz" as their maker, but their owners and drivers had further adorned them with tassels, strings of colored baubles, and bright paint so that no two looked alike. Being on the road with them required nerves of steel. *Driving* on the same road required nerves of steel *and* sharp reflexes *and* a good eye for distances. Everyone drove as fast as they could, but the cars were at a disadvantage, being smaller and slower; slower because their drivers, saving gas, hated to shift out of fourth gear.

I stopped looking after we went around the first uphill curve and swerved off the road on the outside to avoid the oncoming Tata truck. All I remember of the journey is Rodney's repeated, "Oh, my God," and "Please won't you downshift?" and "We'll never get there at this rate" and "Darla, where's the aspirin?" Lopsang, draped over two duffels, slept the day away.

The East-West Highway runs roughly parallel to Nepal's border with India. Our goal, the town of Nepalganj, would put us about ninety miles south of Jumla, an administrative center where, had a plane been available, we would have landed.

We were near a town and it was almost dark when the white Land-Rover broke down. Jamuna spoke with the driver and reported the problem: The car would require a new clutch plate. We had planned to spend the night in the town, but it suddenly looked like we might be spending *several* nights there. Walking down the main street, we could see shops selling big cauliflowers, cabbages, apples and oranges, cloth, and pots and pans, but nowhere could we see any auto parts. We underestimated our drivers. By midmorning of the following day, the car was fixed and we were on our way. How they fixed it is a mystery to this day.

The pavement ended for the last time, and we bumped into a dry riverbed that would serve as a road until the surveyors finished their plotting. It was alive with foot traffic. Traders walked behind their laden ponies; bells tinkled and red tassels bobbed on the ponies' woven halters. Women wearing boldly colored saris and gold loops in their noses carried huge round clay pots, balanced with a ring of woven grass, on their heads. We splashed through a wide, shallow river, detoured around several incomplete bridges, and began climbing uphill on a narrow, dusty dirt track.

We passed road crews, whole families employed for as long as it takes to build the road by hand through terrain as steep and rugged as our Sierras. With hammer and chisel, chip by chip, a path was being cut through a wall of stone. Under the hot sun, groups of men broke boulders into gravel. Lines of men, women, and children, their brown arms streaked white with sweat and dust, took the gravel in wide, dish-shaped baskets to the road, where they dumped it in rows. These tiny little heaps would eventually cover the East-West Highway's more than six hundred miles.

Leaving the hills, we stopped for lunch beside the broad Rapti River. But when we were finished and returned to the vehicles, the white Land-Rover refused to start. This time it was the distributor cap, quickly replaced from the driver's cache of spare parts. As we started off a few yards behind, we saw its back door swing open and a large tin container bounce out on the road. We swerved, and our driver lay on his horn, trying to attract the others' attention, as the door flapped open again and a plastic twenty-liter jug of cooking oil hit the road in front of us with a splat. As the cars came to a dusty halt, a dozen oranges rolled beneath our wheels.

The cooking oil could be replaced in Nepalganj. We had squashed only a few of the oranges, and the dented container and its contents could still be used, but we knew that once we began walking, we would leave behind the possibility of replacing anything. Figuring out our food requirements had been a matter of planning six months' worth of menus in advance for six people. Were fifty pounds of egg noodles enough? Would we really go through eight hundred pounds of rice, along with 180 pounds of flour and eighty pounds of lentils? A few pounds of very expensive dried vegetables would be saved for special occasions. One hundred twenty pounds of powdered milk and three hundred pounds of sugar would mostly go into tea, of which we had twenty-five pounds. Five pounds of curry powder and twenty-five pounds of salt would join the onions to flavor our meals. There wasn't much room for luxuries like jam or hot chocolate mix. Two bars of bath soap each would have to last, and eight candles to light the tent at night. The only thing we could buy locally would be potatoes, and then only if the harvest had been good and the village had a surplus. If we had miscalculated our needs, then we would simply have to leave.

Without further troubles, we reached Nepalganj, a hot, flat, dusty, and lethargic border town and learned that there was another road under construction to the north. Driving it would save us several days of walking. Since footpaths seldom follow a straight line, the walk from Nepalganj to Jumla would be at least a hundred miles; from Jumla it would be another sixty miles or so to the Langu. By the time we reached our study area, we would know something of the lay of the land; our feet at least would be on intimate terms with the terrain of Nepal. We eagerly approached our Land-Rover drivers with the proposition that we might pay them an additional fee to take us a little farther. No amount of pleading would talk them into it. They were so relieved to have made it to Nepalganj that they had no intention of pushing their luck.

Jamuna asked around, and the following morning we found ourselves sitting on the top of our pile of gear in the back of a Tata truck grinding its way up into the hills. Darkness came and we were still toiling upward. Suddenly we shuddered to a halt halfway up a long grade. Up went the truck's hood as the driver and his assistant peered into the ancient, black engine. Out of the toolbox came a flashlight, pliers, a length of twisted wire, some nails, and a roll of tape. I waited, certain that a wad of bubble gum was coming next. Before an hour had passed we were on our way again, and soon the headlights revealed a small village: Chhinsu, the end of the road.

When the Nepalese villagers are working for themselves, hauling wood, grain, or perhaps a load of wool to or from the market, they will often carry as much as a hundred pounds, but when they are working as porters, their loads seldom exceed eighty pounds and usually are lighter. For our purposes, we would hire thirty people, each of whom would carry about sixty-five pounds of gear. Lightly loaded, we were hoping that we could make faster progress with fewer complaints.

Our ragtag group was made up of several subdivisions of friends, relatives, or fellow villagers, all teenage boys and men, except for one young woman. They dressed in clothing of cotton and polyester bought in the lowland bazaars, trousers baggy at the top with tapered, tight-fitting legs, or shorts and shirts that looked like pajama tops. On their heads were *topis* (snug-fitting caps) or cloths wrapped to form a turban. Some had jackets made in the fashion of sport coats, and others wore a sash with a wicked-looking curved daggerlike knife, or *kukri* sheathed and tucked into the fold. Each little clique banded together in all the activities of trail life, such as rest stops, lunch stops, decisions when there was a choice of trails, nighttime encampments, and wage strikes.

We made a long caravan of green canvas duffel bags, brightly colored nylon tents, mattresses and sleeping bags, orange plastic pans and jugs, big conical wicker baskets called *dokos* filled with sacks of rice and flour, and five shiny aluminum trunks containing the more delicate items of food and Rod's scientific gear. A rope and leather tumpline went from the

41

porter's forehead around his load, supporting the weight and spreading it between neck and back.

Kirken assigned Sharma, a particularly thin and ragged porter, to be "kitchen boy," in charge of carrying a doko with pots and pans and other cooking gear for the trail as well as each day's supply of food. Sharma was meant to go quickly, keeping up with Lopsang and helping with the cooking and kitchen chores, in exchange for his meals. Having such a kitchen boy was common trekking practice.

By now we had grown used to seeing the Sherpas eat enormous platefuls of food—quantities of rice that would have made us explode. They also worked hard and had not an ounce of spare flesh on their bones. By the end of the study we would find ourselves eating almost as much. But we had been unaware of this vast difference in stomach capacity when we had done our shopping, and even though the Sherpas had helped to make the calculations, we began to wonder if we were going to run out of food. After Sharma's first meal, running out seemed a certainty. Even the Sherpas were astounded by his appetite. He could inhale a mountain of rice and vegetables like a vacuum cleaner, eat another five-pound refill, and then finish off the leftovers, if there *were* any leftovers by the time the rest of us got something to eat. Rod became more and more dismayed as he did the daily figures in his blue spiral budget book.

"He's got to have a gutful of worms," said Rod one evening as he watched Sharma polish off his third helping. "Where else could all that food be going?"

Jamuna pointed out that this probably was the first time in his whole life when he could eat his fill without worrying about his family going hungry.

My favorite porter was a boy of about fifteen whose name meant "strong man" or "fighting man." He weighed about ninety pounds, and his load was one of the trunks weighing fifty-five pounds. Never once did he complain. Each evening he would come to our fire, his face lit by smiles, to be teased by the Sherpas and share a taste of our dinner.

The only woman porter, Devi, was young and pretty, and Lopsang did his best to win her heart, courting and flirting whenever he got a chance.

The only response I ever saw her give him was to carefully aim a rock at his head and throw it.

Each day took us higher up into the foothills, through forests of oak and rhododendron and out along the ridgelines to views of snowy peaks. Looking across the ranges we must yet cross, the greens and browns receding into hazy mauve, we could be fooled into thinking we were in the western United States, until we looked up at the white walls beyond. Other kinds of caravans passed us by—sheep and mules and men and women, all heading down.

We liked camping high. The whole land was a maze of hills and valleys and rushing water. At sunset and early morning, mist filled the lowlands and pastel light played with the shadows, softening the lines between earth and sky. Terraced fields hugged the hillsides, brushed yellow with mustard blossoms. Farmhouses of stone, plastered with mud and dung, dotted the landscape or clustered into whitewashed villages. In one of them we were treated to an evening folk dance. Beautiful black-haired women, young and vibrant with velvety, fawn-colored skin, danced as the other villagers sang, the fire crackled, and the sun set on the day's end.

Christmas arrived. It had been seven months since Rod had stood before an audience of three hundred people in a hotel in Geneva to receive his Rolex Award. Our pampered week in Switzerland seemed like ancient history when we emerged from our tent in the crisp December dawn, tied our bootlaces, and stood up somewhere in the middle of Nepal. I couldn't have said exactly where I was—only that we had been walking for a week. Lopsang cooked a Christmas chicken with spicy tomato sauce and fresh cauliflower.

The higher we got into the foothills, the colder it got. Our porters kept a fire burning all night, but still they shivered in their thin blankets, and by morning they would work themselves up into a revolt. Half would want to go home, all would want more money, and Kirken would have his hands full calming thirty yelling, gesticulating, ill-clothed porters. This was all the more worrying since between us and Jumla there still lay Houdi Lekh, a pass some 11,500 feet above sea level. Whether there was snow on the trail, or how long it took to get over the pass, were difficult questions to answer, and it didn't help to ask people we passed coming down. As Kirken commented, "Many people, many stories." One trader would say that there wasn't any snow; the next would chop at his neck with his hand, roll his eyes up into his head, and say, "It's up to here!" We learned not to rely on what anyone said, but our porters grew more and more leery of the pass as each day brought us closer to it. We had brought eight or ten pairs of Chinese-made sneakers as gifts for our local camp staff once we got to Base Camp. Kurt now insisted that these be distributed among the porters for the journey over Houdi Lekh. It took Kirken several hours to mollify those fifteen or so porters for whom we had no shoes.

Inevitably, on the morning in question, the threats of mutiny were louder than ever, but as we topped the pass, we found only small patches of snow here and there, and none at all on the trail. It was, however, wet and slick, and no one made it down the other side without at least one roll in the brown mud. Every porter who had wangled sneakers from Kurt went over barefooted with the shoes wrapped up clean and dry in his blanket on top of his load.

We were a tired and slightly battered group when we straggled into Jumla on January 6, 1982. The revolts and arguments were forgotten as the wages and customary bonuses were distributed and as our companions of the past weeks came, one by one, to say good-bye. Even the "fighting man" would not be going on to the Langu. Jumla's seven thousand feet of elevation were high enough for these people of the lowlands. From here on, we would have to find our porters from among those so-called primitive and unpredictable mountain people who lived in the clouds at the top of the world.

CHAPTER

3

Dolphu Jané

Jumla, apart from being the Karnali Zone headquarters, or "county seat," is also supposed to be the major trade center of western Nepal. We would never have guessed it, or that the town housed at least twenty-five hundred people as we walked down the two-block main street. Half the shops were shut, there wasn't a restaurant or hotel in evidence, and the place looked almost deserted. We knew that the Karnali Zone we were in was the only completely roadless zone in Nepal, but I guess we were still expecting a bustling bazaar, a last vestige of civilization before heading into the Great Himalayas.

A few men stood around, smoking *chillums,* cylindrical clay pipes held between their two palms. One sat cross-legged before a blanket on which he displayed his wares: a card of needles, a few dusty spools of thread, a bar of soap, some plastic combs, bundles of cheap hand-rolled leaf cigarettes or *bidis.* With a jingle of bells, a horse and rider trotted through the cobbled square. There was not a wheel in sight, even on a bicycle.

"In Jumla," said Rod, "more than any other part of Nepal, I get the feeling of stepping back in time. From now on we are really going to find out what it was like to be part of an eighteenth-century expedition."

Jamuna made friends among the Forestry Department officers stationed in town. They soon got up a game of cards and a jug of *rakshi* (home-distilled liquor), the makings of an evening's diversion and get-acquainted session. Jamuna soon learned more than he wanted to know about life in Jumla and the far-flung valleys of Mugu District.

Looking north along our route we could see Danphe Lekh, the first high mountain pass, nearly hidden by gray clouds. So far, the pass was clear of snow. If the clouds converged, tomorrow things could change.

We would store some of our rice and other staples in Jumla so we could reduce our enormous entourage and travel as quickly as possible. Kirken assembled a new crew of twenty-two porters, and it was immediately evident that they were different from Sharma and his friends. These were mountain people, used to the harsh conditions we were about to encounter, the narrow trails and high passes. They weren't deterred by the fact that we were going up at a time when anyone in his right mind would be coming down. Their houses were up there, in small villages perched on the mountainsides, and they were on their way home from last-minute trading trips before the first big storm.

Beyond the Himalayas, within a week's walk of their villages, stretches the vast, two-mile-high Tibetan Plateau, known as Bhot. Though our new porters were technically Nepalese, living just within the boundaries of Nepal, they were known as Bhotes, or Bhotia, and their Tibetan origins were dominant in their broad, Mongolian faces.

They had names like Tenzing, Tsewong, Dorje, and Guru. Their clothing was of wool, homespun and many-patched, but good enough protection against the uncertainties of prewinter on the summits. A few boasted the latest symbols of status, "Made in China" high-topped tennis shoes instead of their traditional and much more practical knee-high woolen boots. But all had handwoven blankets to wrap themselves up in warmly at night.

Men's and women's earlobes were stretched long and thin by enormous rings of turquoise-studded silver that swayed as they walked. Around their necks hung strings of orange coral and turquoise, lumps as big as walnuts. Some also carried several small cloth or leather bags on a thong around their necks. These amulets contained protective charms specially blessed by their high lama.

I would have hated to wear such a collection, the bundles thump-thump-thumping on my chest at every step. I wore no jewelry at all, which made them think Rodney was a poor provider.

Entire families joined our band, all but the toddlers carrying loads by a tumpline. When our porters added their own food, bedding, and goods purchased in the bazaars of Jumla and Nepalganj to the items they were carrying for us, they had loads of up to a hundred pounds each. For ten days' work they were earning three hundred rupees, or about twenty dollars, and they considered it a windfall, since there were few cash-paying jobs anywhere this side of India. They lived by a combination of subsistence farming and barter. The six months or so that they spent each year as "traveling salesmen" made them half nomadic and half tied to their little villages in the high valleys.

We would see, in our many journeys up and down the "Mugu Trail," that the incredible strength of their small, wiry bodies went far beyond the bulging muscles of their legs and necks. They would show us what it means to have nothing, to live without doctors and hospitals, without any medicine other than herbs and roots, without even a bar of soap in the house to clean an ax cut. They lived principally on potatoes, barley, and wheat flour. Dried wild nettles, large white radishes grown in small kitchen plots, and a few squash made up the vegetable menu. Meat was available whenever a cow or a yak met a fatal accident or illness; for special occasions a goat or a chicken might be sacrificed. They had eggs and, if the family could afford it, an occasional meal of rice.

It was hard to believe all that we'd heard about the dark side of these people in the face of their boisterous, joyful spirit, apparent every night around the campfire. Having just hauled a hundred pounds over a mountain pass, they would eat a meal of flat wheat bread *chapatis* dipped in thin potato soup, then stay awake till 4:00 A.M. joking about the day's events and singing every song they had ever learned. Then getting up with the dawn, they would do it all again.

The Mugu Trail led us out of the wide Jumla Valley, climbing four thousand feet up and over Danphe Lekh, the first of two major passes.

The pass, at eleven thousand feet, is not at all high by Nepalese standards, but the trail is steep, and it took half a day to reach the top.

There are no camping places once you begin the climb, and except for an occasional quick rest stop, the whole group must move steadily to reach the "hotel," Tharmare, nestled in a meadow at the summit. Storms strike the mountain with little warning, especially at the beginning and the end of winter—the times when people are most likely to take a chance and get caught in a blizzard. We saw a boy not yet in his teens who was crying, limping with an injured knee. None of his fellow travelers, including his parents, took any of his load, nor did they shout at him, or make him feel ashamed, as long as he didn't give up. The parents could not be considered cruel in a land where your life may depend on making it just one more mile.

We arrived at Tharmare—a filthy mud-and-stone hovel crowded with ragged travelers—in fine weather. While the twenty-two porters crowded into its two small smoky rooms, we pitched our tents on the roof.

"Now we're finally getting somewhere," Rod remarked as we un-rolled our mattresses for the umpteenth time.

I knew how frustrated he was that events had forced us to walk all this way. By now we should be in the study area, our tents pitched in the Langu's deep inner gorge, our base camp settled in for the winter. All along, he had been worried about our late start and our painfully slow progress. But I wished he could relax and enjoy himself more.

"We're so late now," he said, "if it snows we may have a hard time getting beyond Dolphu."

I tried to keep my own worries to myself. How was it going to be, living in a tent for six continuous months, through the winter, in some uninhabited canyon high in the mountains? For climbing expeditions, with all their support staff and specialized equipment, even three months is a long time. Rod had chosen the winter to begin because he thought the animals would stay at lower elevations and that snow would make leopard tracks easier to find. Once the cats were collared, we would have to stay with them. It wouldn't make sense to cut the field season any shorter than six months; if we could stretch it longer, we would. My mental image of the Himalayas was of nothing but snow and ice. Here on this low pass, the night air was already frigid. How could we survive in the real mountains?

I had believed Rod when he said, "I'm sure it can be done." He in turn had put a considerable amount of faith in me. We had known one another for nearly two years, but we had lived apart. Now we would be virtually stuck together twenty-four hours a day for the next year. So far everything was great, but we had yet to face any real tests. We could end up hating each other. I reached into my pack and found my copy of *Two in the Far North*. In it Margaret Murie wrote,

---

An ideal day to hit the trail; twelve below, just right for mushing. We were both running and I was soon too warm; I threw back the parka hood and pulled off the red toque; the crisp air felt good on my bared head. How light my moccasined feet felt, padding along on snow-sprinkled ice at a dog trot, exhilaration in every muscle responding to the joy of motion, running, running, without getting out of breath.

I closed the book and announced, "I'm getting cold feet, Rodney."

"My worrying's getting to you," he replied. "I'm sorry; don't pay any attention to me. It's just that I'm so anxious to get there and get started I can't help myself."

"I know that," I said. "I mean, my feet really *are* cold. Let me warm them on you!" He held me close beneath the thick mantle of our down sleeping bag, restoring my conviction that coming to Nepal was no mistake.

At our second-night camp, Rod and Jamuna decided to wake up early in the morning and go on ahead. Traveling light, they could get over Ghurchi Lekh, the second pass, to the town of Gumghari, an administrative center of Mugu District, where the local authorities would check our papers and possibly send telegraph messages to Kathmandu. Since Mugu District was normally off-limits to foreign travelers, it could take ages to get confirmation of our authority to enter it. But we could not avoid stopping; our group of twenty-seven people, with distinctive baggage, could not pass unobserved.

They left at dawn under a sky gray and thick with ominous clouds. Heavy snow began to fall before the rest of us were finished with breakfast, and our porters would not attempt the pass, saying we would all die if we tried. "Great," I thought. "What about Rodney?"

All day it snowed and all day we spent huddled in the shelter of a large overhanging rock. Kirken and Lopsang tried to put me at ease.

"Don't you worry, Didi," they said. "Everything will be okay. Ronney-Sah'b knows the trail."

"Sure," I said to myself, "Rodney was here six years ago. He probably remembers every stone in the path."

But at least they tried to cheer me up, and I liked it that they called me "Didi," the Nepali word for sister. It certainly beat "memsah'b."

The Bhote women, who I was certain looked at me with disapproval for my lightweight backpack and my men's trousers, sat down around our fire and stuck their tongues out. They weren't being rude. In the future I'd see them do it often, and I finally realized it was a warm greeting used among friends. They meant to show me that they understood and shared my concern. Even Kurt made an effort to be kind and polite.

We hadn't reached the Langu yet, and already I was getting acquainted with the sick, constricting feeling of anxiety. We had accepted the physical risks, knew that a minor injury or illness could be fatal so far from medical help, but now I could no longer bury thoughts of the hazards under the thrill of adventure. There was nothing to be gained by dwelling on the danger, but it would lurk there under the surface, and I would just have to get used to it. In practice that was very much easier said than done.

Evening brought clear skies; the morning, sun again. Our head porter, Karma, roused the group and helped Kirken convince them that we'd best get over the pass early while the snow was still firm. We crunched our way up and up until we gained the summit to find a mere six inches of snow. The howling wind had blown most of it off the top of the mountain. The descent was steep and icy. The porters slipped in their basketball shoes, and I slipped in my hiking boots as I kept looking off the trail, searching the depths below for signs of Rodney's crumpled body.

Down we went, through a forest of pine and bamboo. We stopped for tea at Pina, where the innkeeper told Kirken that Rod and Jamuna had passed by the previous morning, safe and sound.

We met up again that afternoon and learned that they had been to see the chief district officer. Jamuna explained the Snow Leopard Project, he and Rodney showed our official letters, and we were given authority to continue on, with an additional letter to Karma Lama, the elected representative of Dolphu, asking that we be given every possible assistance.

Now we could look forward to our walk along the Mugu Karnali. That river defines part of an ancient Nepalese trade route stretching from India in the South to Tibet in the North. We felt privileged to be among a handful of Westerners to know its well-worn path. Every traveler we met, trader and shepherd alike, wanted to know where we were from and where we were going.

"Kahan bata?" (Where [are you] from?)

"America bata." (From America.)

"Kahan jané ho?" (Where [are you] going?)

"Dolphu jané." (Dolphu going.)

Our reply was always met with utter disbelief, that we should actually be heading for Dolphu Village. What could possibly be of interest to the likes of us in such a place?

After Gumghari there are few suitable camping spots, and villages became our focus. We were entering the homeland of our porters; small communities of mud and stone perched tenuously on hillsides high above the river. Two things stood out as uniquely Tibetan about those villages. As we drew near, usually long before we could see any houses, we'd come upon Buddhist shrines, square columns of stone built alongside or sometimes right in the middle of the path. We were told that these *chortens* are often built to honor (or pacify) deceased loved ones. The other Tibetan feature was the cloth flags fluttering from long wooden poles on every rooftop. Each flag was printed with a prayer. It is important for Buddhists to say as many prayers as possible in a lifetime, and the flags helped: Every morning the wind would come up, and with every gust it would carry the prayer anew from the rooftop to the heavens. It was pleasing to imagine the thousands upon thousands of invisible prayers riding the airways of Tibet and its borderlands.

As they neared their homes, our porters shared in our excitement, putting aside some of their innate suspicion of strangers. Now they spoke at some length, answering Rod's questions about hunting methods, poison spears, and where the poison comes from. The poison was taken from a species of aconite or monkshood, a blue-flowered alpine plant of which there are many subspecies in Nepal. The most potent—known to hunters throughout the West—grew in several valleys downstream of Dolphu. This was good, accurate information, and Rod was surprised that it had been given so freely. The porters also told of giant white frogs with fangs. Tortoise-sized, they live up the Langu Gorge—good eating, but hard to catch!

We camped at the confluence of the Langu and Mugu rivers. The Langu runs thirty-five miles through a deep gorge, with headwaters in the northern highlands of Dolpo District. The canyon is so precipitous in its upper reaches that no human can travel along its banks. Jhobu La, a sixteen-thousand-foot pass at the end of the Langu Gorge, allows only late fall travel between the villages of Mugu District and those of Dolpo. Even then, the route is so difficult that perhaps only once every two years will anyone attempt it.

The trail climbed above the Langu, passing through Kimri, a village of about thirty-five houses, with such a grave water shortage that overnight visitors could not be welcomed. The spring has been dry for many years, and they must get their water from the Langu, two thousand feet below. It takes a villager half a day to fetch a five-gallon urnful of water that for six months of the year is so laden with silt that we refused to use it at our base camp. We had a choice. The Kimris didn't.

A new sound met our ears, the unique, high-pitched, chirping cries of the yellow-billed chough, as a flock of these cousins to the crow wheeled overhead. No other sound, even the ceaseless daily wind sighing through the junipers, so distinctively announces one's arrival in the Langu.

The final day's hike between the villages of Kartik and Dolphu was long, hard, and the most spectacular in the entire trek. Where we had previously walked on a road worn wide by centuries of foot traffic, we now threaded our way between boulders and cliffs, jumped over washouts where the path crossed eroded and unstable landslides, and climbed rock faces where flat stones were stacked to form steps rising and descending almost vertically. On our right was an abyss, the river a faint wind sound far below. Across the gorge, snowswept peaks rose thousands of feet, jagged pyramids of ice with hanging glaciers. Lower down were shaded forests of birch and conifer. On our side there was only rock, brush, and an occasional juniper. Few plants grew in the thin, exposed, sun-baked soil of the south-facing banks.

The path wound out onto a promontory overlooking five or six miles of the gorge. We could see the river snaking its course through a deep canyon. Rod, remembering this landscape from his 1976 visit, stood with his face to the wind, letting it whip his hair into strands of sun-bleached brown. Here at last was snow leopard country, the phantom of the snow mountains unseen, unheard, little disturbed by man in terrain too rough for ordinary travel. High above the ribbon of blue-green river, a pair of huge lammergeiers, golden-bellied vultures with black "beards" and an eight foot wingspan, turned on the wind, riding the spiral of a thermal updraft, mirroring Rod's high spirits—and in turn my own.

But gazing at the scenery could be dangerous, and we got to know our feet better than ever: How they can be aimed and placed with absolute accuracy and how easily they can wander without supervision. The trail had been "improved" with government development money. Rod had found no stepping-stones on his '76 trip, and he remembered places where a stumble would have meant certain death.

We crossed Bailung Stream and began the final climb, Murki La, steep and winding. Up we went, Rod's altimeter reading 11,500 feet at the crest. We stood in the blasting wind, paying tribute to the mountain gods for a safe journey by adding a small stone to the summit chorten. Would our stones, placed by foreign hands untaught in Buddhist ways and nestled there among the venerable ones, reach the gods with our messages of gratitude?

Ahead of us lay the fields of Dolphu, brown stubble after yielding a

November harvest of potatoes, wheat, and barley. Narrow pathways threaded through the stone-banked terraces. Hardly a tree broke the pattern; here and there an ancient juniper or a wild peach offered scant shade to the farmers. Weary and filthy from our long walk, that final mile seemed never-ending, our feet leaden, our backpacks full of rocks.

Then the children came. Attracted by the long line of porters, and the bright colors of our parkas and plastic kitchen wares, they abandoned their livestock-tending and wood-gathering duties to join the fun. Chattering and giggling among themselves, they danced along beside us. A few boldly pulled at our clothing or asked us questions, shouting at us as if that would break the language barrier.

The oldest looked about eight, the youngest four or five. Little girls with raveled braids, a hair halo of tangled, dusty, black wisps. Boys with homemade crew cuts just beginning to grow out for winter warmth. Their noses ran free in faces that had never known the touch of terry cloth. Their bare feet left tiny toeprints on the dusty trail. And their black hands, crusted with soot, looked like the bottoms of cooking pots used for years on a campfire. Pink skin showed in the cracks between their fingers. It's hard to say if brothers and sisters wore hand-me-downs. Their homespun pants and *chubas* (roomy, coatlike wraps) were more rag and patch than anything else. But not a soul among them was concerned with appearances. Like little brown buoys they hopped and bobbed, and they lightened our steps, magically, with joyful mischief in their round urchin faces and almond-wide, ebony eyes.

We couldn't even guess what they were trying so hard to tell us, or ask us, but it didn't matter; their smiles crossed the gulf between Bhote and Yankee with simple, welcome ease.

Up and over the final rise, we found ourselves in Dolphu, population two hundred, plus or minus a few—the closest thing to civilization we would know for the next five months.

Snowbound

People stopped their work and stared as we moved through the village. Calls rang out, greetings were shouted from the rooftops to our Dolphu porters, and we were shown to the village leader's house.

Four sprawling structures containing forty-four family units had been built into the steep hillside with stone, mud, pine beams, and sweat. Each three-story unit was connected to the next, like an apartment building, or the cliff dwellings of early American Indians. Entryways were along steep, stony pathways or shortcuts over the rooftops of friendly neighbors.

The ground level serves as the barn, where cows, yaks,* and goats are kept at night. The middle level is for indoor living. The largest extended family had nine members, including the oldest villager, a blind great-grandmother. It was one of the wealthier families, and they had two rooms. Many families did their cooking and sleeping—and in the coldest months of the winter, living—in just one room. For the sake of warmth,

*I have taken some liberties with the name "yak." In fact, most of the Dolphu "yaks," as well as those of other regions of Nepal, are actually yak-cattle crossbreeds. For example, there are naks and dzos, zums and zopkioks, each classed according to its sex, whether its mother was a cow or a crossbreed, and also what its father was. The system is quite complicated, so I have taken the easy way out and lumped them all under the name of "yak."

there are no windows, and smoke from the central hearth goes out (if at all) through a small vented hole in the roof. The ceilings are low, the doorways small so that the villagers themselves must bend to enter. Porches and terraces surround the middle level. Here, firewood is stacked for easy access, a pile of pumpkins might be stored, tools hung by wooden pegs, a plow leaned against the wall, skins or rugs folded into a corner.

The third level is a rooftop terrace of hard-packed earth over flat slate stones. Here the women work at winnowing and pounding wheat and barley; grinding and kneading mustard seed for oil; weaving rugs, blankets, and clothes. A man may spread a rug in the weak winter sun, to sit with needle and yarn and sew a new pair of woolen boots for his wife or child, or to carve intricate Tibetan letters, delicate birds, animals, and deities into a block of birchwood for printing the prayer flags that fly over every house. Late in the evening a young son or daughter may climb the notched ladder to add a load of cut grass to the fodder stored in a shed at the back of the roof.

The time would come when, with the help of one of the villagers, I could do an informal survey of the village population. I would be told that there were seven babies under six months old in the village. Eight had been born that year, but one died after living for only about a month.

Nepal's infant mortality rate is high. One of every five babies dies in its first few weeks. Malnutrition and disease take their toll, but dehydration caused by common diarrhea also is a major killer of infants and children. Dehydration can easily be avoided with a simple combination of salt, sugar, and clean water. Even mixed with dirty water, it can save a child's life. Ready-made packages of powdered formula are being distributed in less remote areas, and habitbound mothers are being convinced by example that it works. Sadly, it had yet to come to Dolphu. Many of the high mountain villages, in marked contrast to the rest of the country, seem to have a low fertility rate, and their populations seem to remain fairly constant. We heard no evidence of contraception being practiced.

In 1985 Dolphu had 212 people living in its forty-four houses, with households made up as follows:

Number of Persons in Household	Number of Households
1	1
2	3
3	8
4	9
5	8
6	9
7	0
8	3
9	3

One orphan boy was shared among several families. One man in Dolphu had two wives, the elder of whom had no children. As elsewhere in Nepal, wives commonly join the household of the husband, and up to four generations will live together under the same roof.

Names were given by the high lama and often were taken from nature—for example, Nema, meaning sun, and Karma, meaning star in Tibetan. Many of the older women, however, seemed to be referred to simply as so-and-so's wife. I wondered if the married women followed a similar custom to that of my Hindu friend who referred to her husband (at least outside the home) as *Raja* (ruler or chief), hardly ever using his actual name.

We were shown to the house of Karma Lama, the *pradan panch* (an officer similar to our mayor), where the loads of the twenty-two porters were finally laid to rest in a huge pile on his flat rooftop. Tents were pitched in a corner beside a four-foot-high wall made of stacked stones.

While Rod and Kirken paid the porters, I got a bowl of water to wash off some of the trail dust, taking a towel, a bar of soap, and a small nail brush out of our duffel. My every movement was followed by several dozen pairs of children's eyes, fascinated and incredulous as I scrubbed my hands and washed my face. I ducked inside the tent to find some relatively clean clothes. The doorway of the tent was filled with little faces. I zipped it halfway up, and all the faces consolidated in the opening. I zipped it three-quarters up and cheeks and eyes still filled the space, children shrieking and jabbering, pushing and pulling at each other to get a peek. "God help me when I have to pee," I thought.

With the porter business concluded, black yak-hair blankets were spread on the packed mud of the terrace, the village dignitaries were summoned, and we were invited to sit.

Plates of boiled potatoes were produced by Karma Lama's elderly mother. Following Karma Lama's example, we peeled off the skins, dipped the small white potatoes into a fiery sauce made from dried peppers, and popped them hungrily into our mouths.

On a corner of the terrace several men were working with jugs of water and pots of fermented barley. They were preparing *chang* (Bhote beer), to be offered to the guests. I watched out of the corner of my eye as a heap of fermented grain was placed into a bowl and water (unfiltered and unboiled) was added. Several pairs of hands that may or may not have been washed (without soap) then proceed to knead the mixture until it was well mixed. Then someone held a woven basket strainer while the others poured the brew into a copper serving jug.

Karma Lama's mother sat before a stack of silver-lined wooden bowls, wiping the inside of each one with a rag so blackened with use that I dared not look too closely. Then she filled and passed a bowl to each of us, and with a nod and a toothy grin signified that we should take a drink. Rod stoically avoided looking into the murky chang, tipped it up, and sipped. His bowl was immediately refilled. This was the chang ceremony, the welcoming touch of hospitality extended to all visitors. And as in most special rituals, one never refuses what one is offered, no matter how many little black things may be floating in it, or how strange it may look or smell. Actually, the taste of chang can be quite nice, a little like yogurt with a punch.

Jamuna was again our spokesman, and he formally presented the Snow Leopard Project to the assembly—our intentions; our needs and desires; our wish to avoid disrupting the villagers; our wish ultimately to carry out the study in the inner, uninhabited portion of the gorge, several days' walk from Dolphu. We would need a great deal of help from the village, he explained, and we hoped to work to mutual advantage.

That's when we found out about the hunting arrests, the march to Jumla, the fines, and the sworn statements. Jamuna kept a bland expression as he translated the Dolphu men's angry assertions of deception by Rod and the Sherpas who had come with him in 1976. Voices were raised as slender brown fingers punctuated staccato speeches, black Bhote eyes flashed at Jamuna and Rodney, and clenched fists passionately reinforced the points being made.

Rod, his face drained of color, began to explain his side of the story, and as he spoke he recovered his composure and also some of the anger he felt when he had held the rotting carcass of the snow leopard in his hands. His calm, steady flow of words belied the agitation he felt.

"Why were they killing snow leopards in the first place?" he asked, directing the words to Jamuna. "For a profit of less than ten dollars it doesn't make sense, but even if it did, I thought that as Buddhists they were prohibited from killing any creature. It is true I purchased that skin under false premises. I knew that if I bought it the hunter probably would go out and kill another, for someone else to buy, but it was a chance I had to take. The cat was already dead, and there was only one way to see that it did not die in vain: Use it as evidence that despite the laws, poaching still goes on. I had nothing personal against anyone in Dolphu. Frankly, I am surprised that my deeds resulted in police action—but I'm not sorry."

Jamuna, in an impressive display of diplomacy, took the facts of Rodney's case and translated them into a short discourse on "man's duty to his god and to his conscience." Rodney, he submitted, had no choice but to do what he felt compelled to do. He asked the Dolphu men if they knew that hunting was against the law. They did. He asked if the villagers or their livestock suffered regular attacks by snow leopards. They didn't. He asked them what they would have done if the tables had been turned. On that he got less agreement, but slowly, as the chang cups were refilled and bare-bottomed children climbed onto their fathers' laps, the hot fires of anger turned to embers.

For the time being, the village would accommodate the strangers in their midst. They would obey the chief district officer in Gumghari. They would do what was asked of them, but they wouldn't easily forget what had been done to them. It would be up to us to win them over, and obviously it was not going to be easy.

The two Sherpas had joined in the conversation, speaking in Tibetan rather than the Nepali used by Jamuna. Jamuna said later that all but the oldest people had learned to speak Nepali, the "official language," but the villagers had a dialect he'd never heard before, and it was difficult to understand. Even their native Tibetan was peculiar and difficult for the Sherpas to understand. This trouble with the language did nothing to ease the conflict over hunting, and communication problems were to linger throughout the study. Though Rod and I learned to speak a little of the Dolphu version of Nepali—somewhat easier than the tongue-defying Tibetan—we never became very fluent, surrounded as we were by English-speaking Nepalese team members.

By the sixth round or so of chang, the general mood was much improved. It was arranged that we would stay temporarily in a house that wasn't being used about an hour's walk above the village. It would take some time to sort and organize our gear and supplies, explore the possibilities for a permanent base camp, scout the gorge, and get everything moved.

The house, known as Thangdum Gomba, was owned by an aging lama, Jabyam, who spent much of each winter with his sister in another village. According to Rod's altimeter, it lay at nearly 12,500 feet, a thousand feet above Dolphu.

Just as we had experienced on the high passes, we found that we became easily winded with any kind of exertion. Remaining now at high altitude, it would take a month for our bodies to adjust; our red blood cells would increase and other physiological changes would take place, resulting in more oxygen reaching our tissues. Until then we could come down at any time with serious altitude sickness. It could take several forms, showing up in the lungs or in the head, and the symptoms might mimic pneumonia, with coughing, headache, and vomiting. We knew that previous experience is no guarantee of one's ability to acclimatize and that a person could die within twenty-four hours if not taken directly to lower elevation. Working in our favor, the ascent to Dolphu had been gradual, and we would follow other suggestions offered by doctors who had studied the problem—drinking lots of liquids, eating lots of high-carbohydrate potatoes, and taking frequent rests. Fortunately, all of us adjusted well.

Though the house was far from perfect, it would suit our immediate needs. Only later would we discover that Karma Lama had rented it to us without permission from Jabyam Lama, that he had spent the rent, and that it would be very tricky to find a solution that made Jabyam Lama happy and saved face for Karma Lama among the villagers.

Though it was called a *gomba,* or Buddhist temple, our borrowed home had no altar or other fittings that would identify it with those we had seen along the trail. Dolphu's community gomba was a big building, newly constructed near the village center with government financial aid. Thangdum Gomba consisted of an entry hall and two virtually empty rooms about ten feet square. It was dark, with one small wood-shuttered window in each room; and smoky, with a typical hearth in the middle of one room and a little hole in the roof for the smoke to escape.

"Just as well I didn't bring any curtains," I said to Rod as we surveyed the place. His smile lightened the gloom.

"Let's pitch a tent in the field," he suggested, indicating the terrace beside the house. "We'll have to level it out to keep from sliding back down to Dolphu, but it will be nice to wake up to a view of the mountains across the gorge rather than the smoke-black ceiling of Thangdum Gomba."

We celebrated Rod's thirty-eighth birthday on January 19 in our "tent annex," the first time in weeks that we could pitch it and unpack all our things knowing that we wouldn't have to pack it all up again tomorrow. Eventually everyone took our cue, even the Sherpas preferring to sleep in a tent.

A week after our arrival, a storm that had been brewing for several days finally broke in a raging blizzard. The first time Lopsang lit a fire, we were driven out of the gomba by smoke onto the roof where a storage shelter was converted for cooking. Sometimes we ate in our tents, sometimes we all huddled together with our plates in the cold, dark house, among the piles of food and equipment stored there.

After four days the sun reappeared, hot and welcome. We unbent our stiff limbs and dug ourselves out, uncovered the tents and the latrine (an open pit the Sherpas had dug at the edge of one of the fields, sheltered and given a bit of privacy by the stone terrace wall). On a short walk to the spring, we saw the world's most beautiful winter bird, Stoliczka's tit warbler, four inches of rust, blue, and lilac-colored energy flitting at the base of the bushes. We saw spot-winged grosbeaks, striated and red-throated thrushes, choughs circling. Then we saw monkeys on the hill opposite the spring—two gray langurs, trim, long-tailed creatures, with a white disk of hair surrounding black faces! They were using the longer branches of handy bushes for snowshoes, bending them down and walking on the ends as they made their way across and down the slope. But it was a short, one-day respite before the clouds again converged and heavy snow returned. The intensity and duration of that first storm, followed so closely by another, equally severe, were both depressing and worrying. All reports and indications had led Rod to believe that the Langu lay in a rain shadow (the leeward side of a mountain), sheltered from the weather's brunt; that storms were blocked by the Himalayas' massive range of peaks of over twenty-thousand feet. Even in the height of winter there should be relatively little snow. But our tents were sagging and our rooftop kitchen was a leaking mess of mud and clutter. If this was a rain shadow, what was happening in the rest of Nepal?

"This place is like Siberia," said Lopsang. "I am sure I cannot live here. We must all go back to Kathmandu; try some other area. You can find the snow leopard near my home in Solu Khumbu." His sentiments were shared by Kirken and Jamuna, but Rodney knew that there had been no confirmed snow leopard sightings from Solu Khumbu for many years.

As for Kurt, things had so completely deteriorated that we were speaking only in "yes's" and "no's." In his opinion, Rod really didn't know what he was doing. He felt everything that had gone wrong was a result of Rod's misjudgment or ignorance, that he was out of his depth and doomed to failure.

Interpersonal conflicts are not uncommon on mountaineering expeditions, with their prolonged physical and mental stresses. Perhaps it's fair to compare the three of us to a group of ill-matched mountain climbers. We all let the minor irritations grow into a situation that could have only one end result. And we all behaved in ways that none of us could be proud of.

Kurt decided that he had made a huge mistake in leaving Kathmandu with us and that if he stayed in Dolphu he would suffer from starvation. He and I had long since declared war; one evening he had overheard me in a conversation with Rod referring to him as "that jerk."

To Rod's and my great relief, he announced his intention to quit the project. What he actually said, to Rod, was, "We have big appetites, man, not little-bird appetites." To which Rod replied, "There's plenty of rice and potatoes to fill you up." To which Kurt replied, "Yeah, and get sick on that shit. You and your little playmate can stay here and freeze your butts off if you want to, but we need decent food to keep us alive in this weather."

Herewith a passage from Rod's diary: "For a person of twenty-eight, Kurt has the maturity of an adolescent teenager, adrift in insecurity. His need to draw attention to himself leads him like a blind man to giggle, fart, and belch aloud. Somehow he has got the idea that loud belching during meals is a compliment to the cook, though the Nepalis—if they have to belch—do it quietly. As for the farting, he says it's the crummy food that makes him do it."

Unfortunately, Kurt and Jamuna had become friends during the trek in, and once things began to go sour, Kurt had sewed seeds of discontent in Jamuna that would flower into the project's first major setback.

Jamuna had just two weeks before leaving for Kathmandu. His two younger sisters were having a double wedding, and he was obliged to attend. He had done his first duty, of seeing us safely to Dolphu. Leaving with Kurt (whom we have not seen again to this day) and Lopsang, he promised to return in about six weeks to begin his fieldwork, though he confessed to Rodney that his heart had sunk when he saw the place where he would be expected to live and collect data on bharal. He was not looking forward to the job.

If we had known that we were about to experience Dolphu's heaviest winter in decades, we might all have opted to leave—to wait it out in the comfort of Kathmandu.

All of February and most of March followed a similar pattern: never more than four clear days between storms lasting up to four continuous days and nights. The temperature dropped to five degrees Fahrenheit. Some mornings dawned bright blue, but lunchtime would find us seeking shelter and diversion while more and more snow fell.

Five miles of wild river gorge lay between Dolphu and the closest of our prospective base camps. The gorge was hardly passable when the weather was good; it was out of the question with so much snow.

The paths around camp became too deep to shovel, so we floundered to the spring, slipped and slid to the latrine, and wondered how on earth the wild animals were managing high on the slopes and deep in the Langu Gorge. Had we been snowbound in there and one of us injured or taken ill, there would have been no hope of rescue. As it was, the nearest radio contact was at Gumghari, where the radio sometimes worked and sometimes didn't, or at Jumla. The village cattle, yaks, and goats grew gaunt and ribbed, feeding on meager stocks of grass that had been cut in the fall as emergency fodder for the few bad days of a normal winter. During the brief moments of sun we dug out or washed clothes, hoping that the good weather would hold. We even braved a "shower" with the blue plastic bucketful of precious warm water, in spite of a shortage of wood to heat it. Our wet hair became icy spikes, and our clothes hung frozen stiff on the line.

During storms, we stayed in the tent. The house was cold and too dark to read or write. The others might go down to the village and spend the day visiting with friends, going from house to house remarking on the terrible weather, sharing a bowl or two of chang around the hearth fire. But we felt unwelcome in the village, though with hindsight I'm sure many of the villagers would have been pleased to have us in, to offer us something to eat or drink, and to have the novelty of our presence. Our stomachs couldn't handle the chang, or the special guest offerings of meat, often green; our eyes couldn't take the thick pine and juniper smoke hovering like tule fog in every windowless house. Neither the Sherpas nor Jamuna could adequately translate the rambling tales the elders spun to wile away a long day, so culturally there was not much we could get out of a visit. And I couldn't forget the body lice we had found in our clothes after the first chang ceremony at Karma Lama's.

It occurred to us that our lethargy could be caused in part by the altitude, but whatever the cause, we simply hadn't the energy or the interest to participate with the villagers in making the best of the worst winter anyone could remember.

We had a small shortwave radio that we allowed ourselves to turn on for an hour or so each day. A few sets of AA batteries had to last the field season; the snow leopard receivers also used AA's, and they took priority over the "luxury" of the shortwave.

Without the radio, we might have lost our sense of humor altogether. We listened to the morning magazine show, to radio plays, and to the world news on the BBC. To Rod, the news was like food—necessary to sustain life, and he hungered for it, craved information, and savored it almost as much as he did his weekly ration of chocolate.

We sat or lay in our North Face two-person expedition tent, wrapped in down as the snow swirled outside. It was not unusual to spend twelve hours at a stretch in our sleeping bags. We wrote in our diaries and talked for long hours. Rod, so recently eager and happy to arrive in the Langu, seemed now at the point of defeat. We were accomplishing nothing except depleting our stocks of food. Now he began to wonder if after all he had been wrong about winter in the valley.

"It *is* a rain shadow," he told me. "The vegetation proves it. Caragana, ephedra, berberis, sage, juniper. These are high-desert plants. If the Langu was exposed to normal rain and snowfall, we would find moisture-loving plants instead of these that thrive in dry conditions."

But despite this confirmation, his confidence had been seriously eroded by the delays, by deep snows, by the dismay of the Sherpas and Jamuna over the study area and living conditions. And then there was the matter of what had happened with Kurt.

"If I fail at this," he said, "I'll never get another chance; my reputation will be down the drain. I can forget about being a field biologist."

"You haven't failed," I said. "You haven't even tried yet. The winter can't last forever. All we have to do right now is get through it, hold out long enough to *get* a chance. Then you can worry about the next step. Don't let the others make you stop just because they want to go home. Now, please, let's try to forget all our troubles. Let's play Scrabble."

"I'm tired of Scrabble."

"Okay, then let's play something new. Guess how many moles I've got on my left leg and I'll give you my whole week's chocolate ration."

The thing that kept us sane, I think, was not knowing. As long as we could think that each storm might be the last, we could face another three days, or whatever, in the tent. Being snowbound would have been a lot harder to take if we had known that it was going to go on for more than six weeks.

In addition to the Sherpas, we hired two camp assistants. Sonam, son of Thondup, Dolphu's traditional headman, or *mukyia,* would help with such chores as wood-gathering and clothes-washing, and later when the snow melted he would guide us throughout the study area.

He was the oldest of four children born to Thondup and his wife over a period of some twenty years. His sister, at about ten, was the youngest; one of the three boys had died. Sonam was in his late twenties, married, with one son about three years old. He was a gentle man who seemed to yield entirely, and happily, to the gods and spirits of the mountains, to the beliefs and superstitions that had guided his ancestors through their lives. He was shy and soft-spoken and I liked him at once.

Karma, our head porter from Jumla, stayed on primarily as mail runner, after Jamuna had found letters waiting at the Forestry Office for us. Karma was a few years younger than Sonam and also married with a young son. His family now lived near Jumla but had migrated there, he said, from Mugu, once a large thriving Bhote village on the Mugu Karnali three days' walk from Dolphu.

Karma was small like most of the Bhotes; he could fit easily into most of my clothes, but he was also amazingly strong, and as outspoken as Sonam was shy. Karma arrived unexpectedly out of a snowstorm, thrusting his head through the crack at the top of the tent door. I looked up from my diary to see a cascade of grubby envelopes landing on the sleeping bag. Karma had walked ten days, through snow waist-deep on the passes, arriving at our camp with a mantle of snow from head to toe to bring our mail and a pocketful of apples. It was the first mail we had had for two and a half months, and the last we would get for the coming three.

During February, there was a death in Dolphu, and two across the river in Wangri. Perhaps three people isn't a lot in a combined population of about 350, especially in the coldest month of the year, but the smoke from their funeral pyres emphasized the difficult living, especially in Wangri, where the sun breaks the ridges for only a few hours each day, melting the snow long after Dolphu's ground is bare. About the man who died in Dolphu, I could get no better explanation of his passing but that "He was bored to death by Dolphu life," from Kirken, who was beginning to get a reputation for his sarcasm.

"Seriously," I said, "was he sick?"

"He was seriously bored."

All three were cremated at night, the big fires glowing against the stone-banked terraces. We trained the scope on Wangri, less than two miles away as the crow flies but half a day away by foot; more with deep snow on the trail. Shadow figures huddled against the backdrop of tall flames, and a line of pine-pitch torches moved slowly down from the village.

People are seldom buried, but neither are they always cremated. Instead of building a funeral pyre, sometimes an ax is sharpened and the body is chopped into bite-size chunks and placed on a prominent ridge or rock. The pieces are carried off by the hungry vultures, ensuring that the spirit of the dead is released from the corpse, where it might cause trouble for the living.

According to Sonam, there was one person in Dolphu for whom the villagers would like to arrange a funeral; it was alleged that someone had even tried, but the poison didn't work. The intended victim was Karma Chogyap, the village mental case. We were simply told to watch out for the "madman" without being given any details, and when inevitably he paid us a visit, we were wary and just a little frightened. He came up shouting that he was bringing wood, and he proceeded to forage the nearby wild rosebushes, gathering a fistful of thorny twigs as admission to our camp.

We didn't dare interfere as he grabbed at everything in sight with unbelievably filthy hands. Kirken turned his back for a minute and found his lunch finished off. Wild-eyed, his tattered chuba flapping in the breeze, Chogyap poked in the garbage for prizes of soup wrappers and hard bits of stale cheese. His exclamations of delight alternated with bursts of angry garble.

We tried to distract him without getting in his way. For a while he was content to sit with a pencil and paper. His tousled black head moved gracefully to music that only he could hear. He wouldn't give the pencil back, and we were afraid to take it away from him. Thoroughly terror- ized, we did our best to keep him in sight and away from the kitchen. He finally left, promising to return the next day. And the next. And the next.

What to do? Each day he came a little earlier and stayed a little longer, refusing to go home until the trail was in darkness and our nerves frayed. One snowy day, Karma Lama paid us a visit to ask for eye medicine, and he told us the only way to deal with Chogyap was to beat him and chase him and be mean and horrible.

He appeared that day in late afternoon, half dressed in the blowing cold. Kirken chased him halfway to Dolphu, shouting abuse. It worked for as long as it took Chogyap to come slinking back, again bringing "wood," if you can call rose twigs wood.

Again Kirken chased him, brandishing the ice ax and threatening to use it on Chogyap's head. Soon we heard his voice, and saw him standing by the "first chorten" at our terrace gate. He stayed for several hours, shouting his intention to kill "Sherpa" and to come in the night and steal all our food.

A ruckus in the night woke Rod and me up. "What is it?" called Rod. "It Crazy People" came the reply from Kirken, who had heard him singing to himself as he climbed the ladder to raid our kitchen. He had managed to open, and eat, most of a can of snowseal, a waterproofing preparation for hiking boots. Whether or not the village would thank us, we did not want him to die on our account.

Cowards, both of us, Rod and I could not bring ourselves to violence, but Kirken had a slingshot for the potential partridge dinner. He and our Karma loaded the slingshot and their pockets with small stones. That day "Crazy People," seemingly none the worse for a bellyful of boot polish, was greeted by an equally crazed duo of stone-slinging, yelling Nepalis, relentlessly pursuing him all the way down the hill.

"Don't hurt me! Don't hurt me!" he hollered at the top of his lungs as pebbles zinged past his ears and he somersaulted over bushes and boulders. Still, it took one more attack with the slingshot before the visits stopped.

When Kirken was next in Dolphu, Chogyap's father asked for payment for the "wood" his son had gathered for us.

As February drew to a close, we had a spate of good weather—five whole days without snow—and Rod called everyone together to organize an expedition into the gorge. It was an expedition no one would forget.

5

Attack

Rod and Kirken filled their backpacks with food, sleeping bags, spotting scope, notebooks, and plastic Ziploc bags to collect leopard droppings, and set off with Sonam in an attempt to reach Dhukyel, a deep side canyon up the gorge that could normally be reached in a day's walk. They hoped to find leopard sign and a good place to make a base camp. The going would be rough and dangerous, and I was happy to stay behind with Karma.

Not long after they disappeared down the hill, Karma Lama appeared with a message from Rod. As he intended to leave next day for Kathmandu, Karma Lama wanted some Polaroid pictures of himself and all the other Lamas to take with him, and would I please get the camera and go down to the village and be photographer? "Me? All alone—on my first *day* alone? How can I communicate? What'll I do if they offer me a bowlful of rotten meat?" I got the camera and ran down the trail after Karma Lama. Our Karma ran after us, inquiring what time I'd be back. "Four hours," said Karma Lama, and I knew I was in for the whole hog Dolphu treatment—oh, Lord. We made short work of the nearly vertical trail, and reaching the village, stopped at each of the dozen or so lamas' houses, calling to them from the path below. One by one they emerged, tousled and sleepy, scratching their ashy heads as though they, like us, had been hibernating.

At Karma Lama's house, I was seated by the fire in the dark main room; potatoes and chang were produced while I waited for preparations to be completed on the rooftop above. So far, so good. The chang was tasty, as long as I didn't see it being prepared. Karma Lama's wife and tiny daughter kept me company, laughing at me, sticking their tongues out, and pushing more potatoes and more chang until finally everyone was ready and my presence was required on the roof.

Fitting twelve lamas into the limited frame of the Polaroid wasn't easy, especially as they were in full red dress with masks, peaked hats, and instruments, but I was fortified by the chang and I needn't have been nervous. Karma Lama stood in the foreground, his long hair drawn back in a ponytail, his delicate features contrasting with those of the garishly painted spirit masks worn by some of the others. The first picture was quite reasonable, and of course they wanted more. They traded their blue and red painted wooden masks, human legbone and brass horns, and skin drums for their regular attire, and posed, somber as condemned murder-ers, and *loved* the results. Hard as I tried to make them smile, aping their expressions or frowning in gross exaggeration, they always stopped laughing just before the camera swooshed out the picture.

But the job was definitely a success; the photos were passed around and around. Now they were really laughing, and they happily pointed out each others' faults with fire-black fingers, smudging the glossy snapshots.

I was then escorted back downstairs for lunch. We ate *roti* squares, deep-fried wheat flour "chips"—a treat, since oil is so hard to get—with chili-potato sauce for dipping, and rakshi to drink—also a treat, since the rice they had used to make it is so expensive. There was enough to send me rolling back home, led by Chanjor, a young *chumba* (novitiate lama). He had no appreciation for the difficulties of running uphill at twelve thousand feet experienced by those of us who live at sea level, rakshi or not! I arrived at Thangdum Gomba an hour late, to be revived by a cup of Karma's sweet tea.

* * *

While I was photographing the lamas, Rod, Kirken, and Sonam were making their way to the eastern ridge beyond Dolphu. They found leopard sign: two sets of tracks, a scrape, and fresh cat urine. Rod was determined to follow the tracks as far as possible, even though they led along icy and dangerous places. Sonam refused to venture upon the lower trail, and waited while Rod took up the challenge. Kirken, with ice ax, took on the upper tracks, working his way slowly along a snow-covered outcrop of rock.

Suddenly a deep, rumbling roar split the air, and Kirken Sherpa, looking up, found himself face to face with a big, male, black and yellow forest leopard, his teeth bared in astonishment to see a human invading his rocky shelter. Kirken was on a narrow ledge just below the entrance to the leopard's daytime lair and smack in the middle of its only avenue of escape. The cat glanced down at Kirken in momentary hesitation, and then it sprang toward him in one great leap.

Kirken flattened himself against the uphill side and thrust the ice ax at 150 pounds of fast-moving leopard. A paw swept his thigh, and the cat loped out of sight over the ridge.

They stood rooted and silent for a long minute. Sonam found his tongue first, whispering, "Oh, my Father." Rod came next with, "What in the hell is a *forest* leopard doing here?" And then Kirken said, moaning, "Why did I leave my cigarettes behind?" When their knees stopped knocking, they continued on to Shimbu Khola, a deep gully with a rushing stream at the bottom. They found more tracks, none fresh, and now the big question was, "Which leopard are they?" Rod recalled the locals saying in '76 that they found forest leopards only in the *forests* downstream toward Jumla, and that in years of hunting, no forest leopard had been seen, or killed, on this side of the Langu, near Dolphu. Put this beside Sonam's insistence that what he saw lunging at Kirken was a *snow* leopard, and you have the essence of "many people, many stories."

The eastern ridge of the Shimbu, notorious for literally being the downfall and death of Bhotes like Sonam, looked particularly evil with a veil of ice and snow and a sheer drop of five hundred feet. They turned back and spent a snowy night in a small hunters' hideout that Sonam revealed only under pressure.

72

They sat by a warm fire, reliving the excitement of the day. Rod asked Kirken what stood out in his memory. ". . . its large mouth, long canines, and sleek, close fur, its odor and enormous strength imparted by the paw hitting my thigh, its pads taut as the cat tried to grip the sloping rock and pass me as soon as possible." Kirken's English was perhaps not as fluent as Rod's diary entry of the account, but the impression was vivid.

"I wish I'd noticed its eyes," he finished. "I don't remember what color they were—but I wasn't really in the mood to look around!"

They all returned to Thangdum Gomba, and Rod and Kirken went back to the scene of the encounter and set three traps on the ridge above the leopard cave. Rod felt sure the leopard was hungry and ready to make a livestock kill. For five days and nights the traps were set, but no cat was evident, and Rod's theory was falling apart.

Then, early on the morning of Tibetan New Year, nearly a week after Kirken's encounter, a villager reported that a yak had been freshly killed by a leopard. It was on the low trail, not far from the traps.

Off went the men, dashing down the hill. The leopard had hardly eaten any of the yak; perhaps it had been disturbed by an early-rising villager. Tiny punctures on its throat were the only marks of death. A small portion of its rump had been eaten.

Tibetan New Year is the biggest holiday of all, and the whole village was celebrating. The owner of the yak was too full of chang to be bothered with salvaging the meat that day and had simply covered it up to await a more sober moment. Rod hoped the leopard would return for its missed meal, and he set the last three traps in its path to dinner. He didn't sleep too much that night, and neither did I.

"Where's my watch?" he asked in the dark. "What time is it?"

"Twenty minutes past the last time you asked," I replied.

"Sorry if I'm keeping you awake," he offered, rolling over for the hundredth time. "I can't stop thinking about that cat. It would make the study very interesting if we collared a forest leopard along with several snow leopards. But what am I going to do if we *do* catch one? Forest leopards are bigger and more aggressive than snow leopards, and tranquilizing one may not be easy. Why isn't it light yet? It must be six o'clock."

During the night the leopard returned but never came closer than ten feet to the hidden and altered yak carcass, now saturated with the scent of man. The traps had been set close around the carcass and the cover left in place, as to have removed it without lengthy negotiations with the tipsy owner would have been asking for trouble. To make matters worse, one of the traps had been tripped by a live yak going to pasture in the early morning, but it had not been caught. If the traps don't catch a slow-moving yak, how could they catch the quick and wary leopard? A close examination revealed that the covering of moist earth used to hide the traps had frozen at night—and the spring mechanism probably had as well. The whole trap was just too slow.

We decided to buy a *bhakara*—a domestic goat. This was no easy task, as every villager knew how badly Rod wanted to lure the big cat, and the price was suddenly doubled. They couldn't understand at all what we were up to with those radio collars. If we were lucky enough to catch a leopard, they reckoned, we ought to kill it before it ate any more of their livestock. It was no consolation that if we radio-collared it, we'd always know where it was, that we could sound a warning when it came near the village.

The goat Kirken bought was pregnant. Two for the price of two. The villagers let us know what they thought about staking out a goat "in the family way" to be leopard bait. Such a waste. We felt like real villains. This time very near the leopard cave they created a little scene calculated to make the hungry cat's mouth water. At the edge of the cliff they tied the goat, just next to a small bed of juniper boughs and freshly cut grass to eat. All around her, keeping her just out of leopard paw's reach, they set the traps, this time with dry earth to conceal them. Bushes were cut and placed to influence the cat's path in stalking the helpless bhakra.

If the leopard eluded the traps and killed her, he still had to find his way out—so there were two chances to catch him. But would he return to the scene of his fright, and if he did, would he conveniently place his foot directly in the hidden noose?

They activated a collar and took it with them so we could carry out a test of the equipment, and I could practice the subtle techniques of radio-tracking.

They placed goat and traps where we could see them from our camp with the scope, though it was an hour's journey away, and they returned well after dark. The possibility of Mrs. Bhakra's early demise due to heart failure was not lost upon us. She was a goat of some character, but she did not at all like being left alone in the dark and cold at the brink of a cliff.

That night Rod's tossing and turning were only moderate. A week could easily pass before anything happened. In the meantime, someone would have to take food and water to the goat each day. Next morning, I went along to feed Mrs. B and help Rod set two more traps for added insurance.

After a week of sun, the weather once more turned ugly. By the time we returned to camp, it was snowing again. The ground soon would be frozen, the traps useless until the snow melted. Mrs. B could not survive the storm while tied on the exposed cliffside. It was Rodney's last straw.

"I can't stand it," he said with a moan. "It took us hours to get everything set up right. I can't get down there and back with two hours of daylight left. Kirken will have to find someone to help him get the goat and take her to the village."

Something snapped in Kirken, too, and he angrily refused: "I'm not walking up and down any more hills for the money you're paying me. This Dolphu is no good."

He hated western Nepal, its poverty and isolation and the people he considered so backward. Also, he may have been too young and inexperienced to be in the position of sirdar under such difficult conditions. He was used to leading tourists on two- or three-week vacations in eastern Nepal, where the sophisticated Sherpa villages of his friends and family dotted the pathways and where at the end of the trek he was always given a good bonus and gifts of valuable clothing and equipment no longer needed by the trekkers. But he had agreed to work with us, and nothing could be done about it short of his quitting. It was too much: no trapping for *another* two weeks, a dead pregnant goat, and a Sherpa at the end of his rope. What more awful things could happen, and when would the damn snow ever *quit*?

Kirken appeared at the tent, announcing curtly that we should get our own dinner—he and Karma would get the goat after all. The snow was falling heavily, but those two with their sure feet and big lungs made the return trip in record time, boarding Mrs. B in her former home. Rod and I had kept busy, stoking the fire, finishing the dinner preparations, consoling each other—and waiting. They steamed in out of the darkness and we ate in silence, everyone frustrated and unhappy.

The ferocious storm continued as February ended. Three days of howling wind threatened to pull our tent apart, and a foot of new snow removed all possibility of trapping. Where once our hearts had soared just to reach the Langu and to be among mountains that some have called "the roof of the world," now our spirits plunged as if to the bottom of the world's deepest canyon.

CHAPTER

6

Capture!—"Ek"

It snowed on eleven of the next fourteen days, but the flakes were different; wet and heavy, a sign of hope that winter might at last release its grip.

We were surprised when Jamuna arrived toward the end of March. We thought for certain that the storms would delay scheduled flights. But there had been a few clear days on which planes could fly into Jumla. He had managed to get a ticket, but with the baggage limit of thirty pounds and all the seats filled, he was unable to bring any supplies with him.

We were running out of food. The lentils and dried vegetables were gone, and we were down to rice, chapatis, and potato curry. We bought a yak on the hoof from Wangri, as no one in Dolphu had one to sell. Someone slaughtered it at Dolphu—tied its nose and mouth and suffocated it—since Thangdum Gomba was a sanctuary where the taking of all life, even that of flies and plants, was forbidden. Four young teenagers brought it up to us, a large bloody hunk in each doko—a far cry from shopping at the Safeway Meat Department! Cooked up with curry spices and red chili pepper, like most everything else we ate, the meat tasted like the finest grade of beef.

As a friend later pointed out, we had a yak-in-the-box, but still our group complained at the poor quality of our diet. It was obvious that we would have to make another attempt to charter a plane if we hoped to stay in the Langu through the summer.

Our status as a joint project with the Nepalese government entitled us to charter a Sky Van, an Irish-made transport plane, if one of the army's three was available. Last December they had all been reserved for other uses. There are no private planes in Nepal. We could have chartered an RNAC (Royal Nepal Airlines Corporation) Twin Otter, but they were twice the price of the Sky Van, and we hadn't the money.

Assuming we could get a Sky Van this time, we'd have to arrange the charter before the end of May, as air service to Jumla was highly sporadic during the June-September monsoon season. To walk to Jumla, fly to Kathmandu, charter the Sky Van, complete the paperwork, buy the supplies, fly back to Jumla, and walk to Dolphu could take two months.

That plan left Rod with only one month to find, trap, and radio-collar a snow leopard. If he went back to Kathmandu having failed to do so, the DNPWC would be unlikely to authorize the charter or renew the project. Jamuna couldn't go; the wild sheep and goats were due to begin giving birth in late May. If he left, he would miss a critical chance to gather information on reproduction and survival among the bharal.

Jamuna brought an urgent letter for Kirken, calling him home on family business. We wouldn't have been surprised if he never returned, but he did, six weeks later.

Rod was both encouraged and worried that snow leopards had not been seen around the village—even in such a heavy winter.

"Why haven't the cats tried to raid the livestock, like the forest leopard did?" he mused one morning. "Is there enough wild meat for them to eat in the gorge? Or are there just no cats left? If the Dolphas have hunted them out, then we're in serious trouble."

The only way to find out was to get into the inner gorge. Again Rod made a plan to try. This time he, Jamuna, Lopsang, and Sonam would attempt to get at least as far as Dhukyel and spend a week of concentrated effort exploring for leopards and for a place to make a camp. Still another

snowstorm delayed the expedition for a week, but it was the last and the snow melted quickly, even off shaded, icy Shimbu Cliff.

The less food and gear they had to take, the easier the going would be, so I stayed behind again, though this time I half wanted to go. The suspense of not knowing what was happening was almost worse than seeing for myself how bad the trail really was. If the reconnaissance worked out, we would all move in and mount an intensive trapping effort.

They returned to Dolphu after three days. Rod was elated, having found ample fresh sign of leopard. Five porters were hired from Dolphu to carry food and equipment, as well as a goat man to lead Mrs. B and another we had bought to increase our chances of catching a cat in the two weeks we would have to try.

We set off on April Fools' Day with our entourage of Dolphas and two reluctant goats. Jamuna stayed behind, too afraid to venture a second time into the Gorge's trailless wilderness. But there *were* trails—faint paths used by wildlife and once or twice a year by small village groups hunting or harvesting wild plants.

I remembered what our friend Hugh Swift had said about the inner Langu. Author of *The Trekker's Guide to the Himalaya and Karakoram*, Hugh has probably traveled through more of the Himalayas by foot than any other living person. Visiting Wangri in 1976, he paused on the hillside, where he could see into the gorge along much of our trail, and he had described it as being "the most precipitous and forbidding valley I have ever seen."

Beyond the village we walked across dusty slopes dotted with dry bushes, emaciated goats, and crossbred cattle. The day turned hot, with summerlike smells of sage and juniper on the warm breeze. We scrambled quickly through Pamalang and Shimbu, deep, eroding gulches plunging down from the snow-covered peak above.

"Goat man," wearing pre-Second World War expedition goggles held on by string, somehow pushed, pulled, carried, and otherwise coaxed his charges over teetering rockfalls and towering Shimbu Cliff without crashing to *his* doom in the Langu far below. He and two of the other porters had long been senior citizens of Dolphu, and they put me to shame as they fearlessly and nimbly balanced themselves, and their awkward dokos, hundreds of feet above the river.

"Don't look down," I told myself as we climbed ever higher. Rod called back hints and advice: "Be careful, Darla. Here, hold this juniper stump. Now, put your left foot here, your right on this little bump, and take my hand."

"If I make it out of this alive," I said, "they'll have to tie me up as a porter load for the way back."

"I hate it, too," he agreed, "I wish we'd had some climbing lessons."

Mercifully, the other side was a gradual descent down a long slope, and Dhukyel Camp was well worth the dose of fear. Our tent was pitched under blue pines and poplar just in bud on a broad sandbar beside the Langu. Flat ground sandy and soft with shed needles and last year's leaves, plenty of water, and driftwood for big smokeless fires. Butterflies, birds, lizards, yellow-throated martens, various creepy crawlies, langurs, bharal, tahr—and leopard—they were all welcome visitors. So were the silence and solitude, far away from the chatter and insatiable curiosity of our Dolphu neighbors. Only the river roared on its never-ending southern journey close outside our tent door.

We had a joke about what happened to things that fell in the river. "Gone to India," one of the Sherpas would say. Water from the Langu, joining the Mugu Karnali, flows all the way to the Ganges Delta. Most of us had had at least one hat blown off our heads by the wind.

We walked down to the Langu's edge, where Rod pointed to the sand at the side. "See those shallow depressions?" he asked.

"Yes," I replied. "They look like tracks."

"They are," he said, beaming. "Snow leopard tracks. And see that scrape—the scuffed place where the cat stopped and scraped the sand with its back feet? It came along and did that while I was sleeping. I could have seen it from sixty feet away if I'd woken up and shone the flashlight."

"Weren't you scared when you found the tracks?" I asked. "Couldn't it have attacked you?"

"If I had somehow cornered a mother with cubs, maybe," he replied, "but this one was by itself; I'm sure it would have run away if I had disturbed it. I hope like anything we can catch it."

We set traps on April 2 with the goats, both upstream and down. Lopsang shaved a tall, straight pine bough of all but its topmost branches. In the morning he would stand it in the ground by the river with a flag flying below the green topknot—a prayer for our camp and its isolated inhabitants. That evening, with our dinner still warming our insides, we sat around the fire, utterly contented.

"At last," said Rod, "we have a real base camp, and we've got some traps out there that I feel confident about. Now all we need is a cat to walk through. It has to happen soon, though. We need a miracle. Two weeks is nothing—it could easily be a month or six weeks before any cat comes back this way."

April 3 dawned blue and gold, and Rod rose before the sun topped the ridge. He took his binoculars and climbed a nearby boulder to view the upstream traps. "Funny how your eyes can play tricks," he said to himself as he focused on a rock at the trap site—a rock shaped just like the head of a big cat. Did it move?

"Lopsang, would you bring the scope over here?" drifted through the morning to my sleepy ears.

Rod's excited "Holy God! We've got a snow leopard!" brought me to the boulder, dressed and out the door in one motion. I looked into the scope, and there—astonishingly close through the lens—was the animal that had become the object of all our thoughts and actions, virtually the sole purpose of our existence. It lay beside the trap, moving just its head now and then as it looked around.

"Jesus," he said. "We did it. The first bloody night. I must have done *something* right."

All through the winter, as storm after storm battered his dream, Rod had clung to the thought of this day, positive that if he could just get the chance, he could catch a cat. In California he had taken a course in wild-animal handling and tranquilization procedures—practiced on a live coyote, injecting it through the wire mesh of its cage with a syringe on the end of a four-foot-long jabstick. It had been simple. But this was the real thing, a rare, endangered snow leopard to sedate, radio-collar, and return to freedom uninjured. No one could tell him precisely how—it had never been done before. Here, there was no wire cage—just one forepaw held by a three-foot length of aircraft cable. He had sought the advice of experienced zoo vets, but they disagreed on what sedative combination and dosages should be injected in the wild. No one knew what the animal's reaction might be to any of them. Now Rod's head was swimming with all the instructions he had been given, all the possible trouble signs, and what to do in a crisis. We gathered up the drug box, radio receiver, and other things we would need.

"I can't believe this is really happening," I said. "It's too sudden. I'm not ready. I don't know what to do."

"Neither do I, exactly," he agreed, as he put the adjustable radio collar into his pack. "My heart's pounding so hard, it hurts. At least we know the trap works. But now that I've got my chance, I'm scared to death of blowing it. Let's get going; we've got to get up there and deal with it, no matter what happens."

Lopsang and Karma followed with guarded excitement, their hunting instincts kindled. But just *how* did "Ronney-Sah'b" plan to make this leopard "sleep"?

It was up to me to capture the moment in photographs. And I had never taken a serious picture in my life.

We made our way along the sandy, boulder-strewn bank half a mile upstream to the mouth of Dhukyel Canyon. From there the path went up the bank through thorny brush to a series of natural terraces.

We stopped below the second terrace. Eighty feet above, hidden by the bluff edge, lay the cat. It had seen us coming and hadn't moved a muscle as we approached, melting like a chameleon into the dun and shadow of its surroundings. No wonder the snow leopard is a near-myth.

Now its ears and nose would be telling it that we were very close. Had this leopard known the smell of man before, or were we something entirely new?

"Determine the dosage of tranquilizer according to the weight of the animal," Rod recited his instructions. "It's full-grown," he whispered. "Must be a male, from the size of it."

He decided against using the blowpipe. It had a special syringe and he thought the jabstick would be easier to load, even though he'd have to get much closer to the cat. Nervous, he found it difficult to draw up the drug without getting air bubbles in it. Finally he was satisfied all was correct and gave me the nod to accompany him, with the camera.

We scrambled over the blufftop and quickly covered the short distance to the trap site. The leopard's eyes, narrow slits of icy green flecked with amber, flashed in the morning sun. Spots of black and smoky gray blotched the dense fur of his off-white body. His thick, yard-long tail whipped the dust stirred by a desperate leap away from the trap and the man drawing near. One huge forepaw, its claws extended, knew the limits of the snare that held him captive.

Rod approached quickly. He wanted to get it over with, to frighten the cat, and himself, as little as possible. He stepped up and pushed the stick toward the cat's flank. The leopard flattened himself to the ground, ears laid tight against his head, jaws stretched wide showing two saber teeth, hissing and snarling. Suddenly he lunged sideways as Rod jabbed, deflecting the needle with his free forepaw and spilling the liquid tranquilizer into the dust.

"Damn," he said. "I should have got closer."

We backed off down the bluff, out of sight again, and Rod took the blowpipe from the backpack. Sweat glazed his temples and darkened patches of his plaid cotton shirt. He dissolved a vial of the powdered ketamine hydrochloride, twice as potent as the liquid, and filled and assembled the blowpipe syringe for a second attempt and a different tactic. Again we approached, and again the cat began to lunge away. Rod stood a few feet from the leopard, aimed the pipe, took a deep breath and blew. Out flew the syringe. It bounced off the cat's thick coat and landed at the base of a cotoneaster bush.

"Shit! Not again," he said with a groan, sucking his breath between clenched teeth. He went back to the jabstick. "I wish it didn't take so long to mix the drug and load it," he said to me, his eyes clouded with worry. For the third try Lopsang went along, somewhat reluctantly, his courage fortified with the ice ax, to distract the leopard from the opposite side while Rod moved in. "Just please cooperate for half a minute," he pleaded with the cat as we approached.

"It *has* to work this time," he said. He forced himself to take his time, crouching low to make himself less threatening, waiting until the cat faltered, fooled for an instant by Lopsang's mock attack, turning away from Rodney. At last the needle made its mark. A strong jab in the left flank, and the ketamine began its work.

The tan reappeared on Rod's face, the muscles in his jaw relaxed as his teeth unclenched. His chest heaved with relief. We organized the implements to fasten the collar and examine the cat, waiting for the drug to take effect, waiting for our own trembling to subside. It was forty-five minutes since the first attempt.

When the cat lay sedated, Rod and Lopsang, who was not entirely convinced that this wide-eyed creature was really "asleep," moved him to a relatively flatter spot. They covered his eyes against the glare of the sun and placed the collar around his neck. The band, made of industrial-grade rubber belting, was attached with two locking nuts and bolts. The transmitter unit, rated for a battery life of two years, measured 3" x 1 3/4" x 1 1/2" thick, including a protective coating of hard resin. Similar collars had been developed for use on mountain lions and common leopards.

"Ek," the Nepali word for the number one, strained against the human hands, and Rod knew the dose of ketamine could have been stronger.

"We'll have to work quickly," he said. "The drug dose I gave him may be enough for zoo cats, but not for wild ones. He's just too rigid and aware of his surroundings." We removed the snare. It had caught only three toes, but there were no cuts or broken bones where the looped cable had caught. Rod injected him with an antibiotic as a general precaution. We collected ticks and fur samples, tucking them into small plastic bags to be dealt with later. Since the ear-tattoo kit had not arrived from the United States before we left Kathmandu, we made a small nick in one ear to identify him in case his skin turned up one day among some villager's hunting booty. We stroked his luxurious coat for an instant, burying our fingers in the dense hair, knowing we could not waste another moment in idle admiration.

We had ten minutes before "Ek" recovered enough to get to his feet. There wasn't time to weigh or measure him, but he must have been nearly one hundred pounds, and his tail, at some three feet, was as long as his body. He escaped but his muscles failed, and he rolled down the dirt slope. He did not go far but lay in the hot sun beside a bush, keeping *us* in sight. The rectal thermometer had indicated a somewhat high temperature. Now Rod became concerned that the cat did not seek shade and went to cool him with a spray of water, or make him move to a better spot. He was quite mobile and quickly crawled away, sliding down the steep bluff to the river, where he disappeared.

"Damn," Rod said. "I wanted to watch him recover. God, that's a long way down. I hope he's all right." We quickly repacked the gear and retraced our path to Dhukyel Stream. Using radiotelemetry, Rod followed "Ek" up the Langu. The signal was strong, but nowhere could he see the cat, surely only yards away, camouflaged so perfectly with the sandy soil and stone that he only *seemed* invisible.

We returned to camp for lunch, and our vigil began. We could not tell if our leopard rested safely in the shade or was in trouble in the hot sun, having only the receiver's fast or slow pulse rates to indicate movement or a still cat. The jubilation so long anticipated was overpowered by fears for "Ek."

Rod was hardly satisfied with the way things had gone: his overwhelming anxiety, the failure of the blowpipe, the too-short sedation period, the lack of time to do a calm and orderly job while the cat was down, and then the loss of visual contact when the cat went over the bluff, dropping ten or fifteen yards down into a pile of rocks. The collar was transmitting the slow, "inactive" pulse, meaning the cat was not moving. Was it injured? Under the circumstances, he was glad the drug dose was light.

After lunch, which no one ate, Rod and Lopsang returned to the site. They traced the signal to an inaccessible gully some distance upriver. Enough time had passed for the drug to wear off, and he *should* want to get far away from Dhukyel Khola.

From 6:00 P.M. to 9:30 P.M. we monitored a nearly constant slow, inactive signal. A few short speed-ups meant small movements—stretching or looking around. Dark came, with a bright half moon, but still the leopard did not get up. Then, at nine-thirty, everything changed. A full minute of active, fast blips came through the headphones. Then two minutes; then ten. They slowed again for four minutes, then half an hour of constant motion. Our leopard was on the move!

For another hour, Rod was glued to the antenna and receiver as the signal, still active, became fainter and finally was lost as the leopard moved up into the canyon out of range from camp.

From out of its hiding place came a small flask that we had been saving for just such an occasion. Sipping sweet Kukri Rum, a product of Nepal's then-fledgling distillery, we wondered what Lopsang and Karma were thinking. Their big smiles were matched by wide-eyed side glances at Rodney draped in metal and wires. Rod, with the acquired caution of his profession, would not be entirely content until the next day's tracking proved the leopard was still on the move. By now I knew that Rod would almost never leap and shout; he would leave that up to me, and show his own emotions in more subtle ways. Still, his happiness was evident; his brown eyes were shining as we moved out of the firelight and held each other in a close embrace. I could feel the wild pumping of his heart, a declaration no less intense than if he'd sent his triumph echoing down the canyon with a resounding yell.

What about Mrs. B? We all assumed, when we discovered the leopard through the eye of the scope, that he had gotten her, since we couldn't see her from camp. But when we reached Dhukyel Khola, there she was, near the water, chewing leaves. Lopsang said he had tied her well; a huge surge of goat adrenaline must have set her free.

CHAPTER

7

Kathmandu

While Karma and the Sherpas made preparations for leaving Dhukyel Camp, Rod and I made several forays high above the swelling river searching for "Ek's" signal. We crossed to the southern side on a log bridge just beyond the Dhukyel confluence. The Sherpas, with help from the villagers, had cut two sets of poplar trees, placing one set from the bank to a large boulder midstream, the other set from boulder to bank. The logs wobbled perilously as we sidestepped across, and water from snow melting on the high peaks lapped at their edges. We knew that any day our bridge would be washed away. When it went, we would be confined to the Langu's northern banks and be unable to travel upstream beyond the confluence. There was no upstream path on our side; the way was blocked by a slick slab of tilted rock several hundred yards wide.

We made our way along the southern bank, climbing toward a high cliff where finally the trail faded into the rocks. Eight hundred feet of dark stone rose from the water straight into the sky. Dwarf junipers and tufts of grass found a footing in small ledges that ran along its otherwise smooth face. Small piles of pellet feces told of tahr and bharal bounding from ledge to ledge. A log ladder, worn and weathered, propped against the stone stood in evidence that people, too, had found footing in those narrow clefts of limestone.

In his accounts of the English mapping and mountaineering expeditions through the Langu, John Tyson had written of crossing a particularly awesome cliff. Guided by Dolphu porters, they came to a place along the gorge's summer high route where they had to climb "roped and barefoot on small holds." We took this to be the place, and from then on we referred to it as "Tyson's Cliff."

We had insufficient climbing gear, so we returned to camp and added another item to our Kathmandu shopping list. As we packed to go, our thoughts turned to the big-city luxuries awaiting us at the end of the week-long trek and ninety-minute flight.

"I'm going straight to the hotel for a hot shower, if I can make it past all the 'cold beer' signs," Rod said as he stuffed a shirt into the duffel.

"Just the *thought* of a hot shower after five months with the blue bucket makes me weak," I agreed. "Best not to think about such things: juicy ripe tomatoes, lettuce and cucumbers in the bazaar; chicken you can chew; a real bed with sheets; dark chocolate—"

"Stop!!" he cried, grabbing my arms and clamping a suntanned hand over my mouth—a hand soon replaced by his soft lips and the brush of his beard against my cheek.

For a few moments Rod and the Langu evening crowded out my longing to be somewhere else. He had shed much of his anxiety since the Thangdum tent days. A smile hovered at the edges of his mustache. There were still problems to be solved, logistics to work out, and he was torn between staying and going. But at least we would be carrying good news to send home via telegram of "Ek's" capture. We sat watching as the last light of the setting sun turned the needles of wind-stirred pines to shimmering tinsel. A pair of courting whistling thrushes skipped their flute notes like small stones across the surface of the river in tinkling counterpoint to its liquid melody.

"I hate to think where I'd be now if it weren't for you," said Rod. "Your trust and support have meant a great deal to me personally, and to the success of this project. During the winter, with everyone pressing me to give it up and go back to Kathmandu, I'm almost sure I would have given in and never have made it into the gorge. I'd never have caught 'Ek.' I'd have gone home with all the feelings of failure."

"Maybe," I replied. "But right now I feel like it was all worth it—like we both got a reward for sticking it out."

"I've been thinking about Kurt," he continued. "I should have dismissed him the first time he mouthed off, and because I didn't, the others must have lost a good deal of respect for and confidence in me. I must see that it doesn't ever happen again, somehow, without looking like a tyrant."

"Don't be too hard on yourself," I said. "You had to bear all the responsibility for this expedition, and I think you've done a good job under the circumstances. But if there's one thing we've learned, it's to be extremely careful about choosing teammates."

"Some teammates," Rod said. "A lot of people thought you'd be the one most likely to fall apart. Yet in many ways you've been the strongest; you have certainly been the chief optimist among us. I may have misjudged some things, but I was certainly right about you."

We had both been right. We had helped one another to endure the most difficult conditions we had ever encountered. We had faced the possibility of failure and emerged with growing love, a great sense of accomplishment, and shared excitement about our future. Glowing with such newfound confidence, I never would have guessed that upon reaching Jumla the lure of sudden luxury would lead this hardy traveler to make a grand fool of herself.

I was determined to get back down the Dhukyel cliff on my own two feet. I must, I told myself, have acquired enough surefootedness that I needn't suffer the embarrassment of becoming a porter load. But I managed to rip a long tear in the seat of my pants, so it was pretty obvious that my feet weren't all I'd used.

We stored most of our camp gear at Thangdum Gomba. Kirken, back from his journey home, would accompany us to Jumla and then return to Dolphu to keep an eye on our things. Jamuna also decided to come with us after all, an ominous change of plan that Rodney correctly interpreted as his impending resignation, though nothing was said until we got to Kathmandu.

It was now the middle of April, and the sun was setting later and later. Once we left the Langu and the trails opened out, we would be able to cover many miles each day. Rod suggested that we try to make Jumla in four days from Dolphu.

"Four *days*?" I replied. "We'll have to run all the way. You and I may be in a hurry to get to Kathmandu, but I can't imagine you'd ever get the porters to move that fast."

The spring planting was in full swing, and our three Dolphu porters were quite agreeable to a quick pace. But they would take us only to Mangri, two days away. We thought that Mangri, nearly four thousand feet lower in elevation than Dolphu, would have finished its plowing and planting, or at least that such a big village could spare a few people who wanted to make some money. But we were wrong. Three people finally offered to carry to Chaila, half a day away, for three times the normal day rate.

The Sherpas argued, got nowhere, and were ready to give up. But if we gave in to the Mangris' demands, it would only set the stage for future wage strikes. Rod was getting angrier by the minute.

"You know, our budget isn't just a bottomless pit," he said to Kirken between clinched teeth. "We may look like millionaires to everyone around here, but we are extremely short of cash. We may, if we're lucky, have *just* enough money to get us to Jumla. I don't *know* how we're going to buy the plane tickets. So you'd better just divide up those three loads, and we'll carry the bloody things ourselves!"

We filled our packs with sleeping bags, tents, sacks of rice, and extra clothes and set off, muttering and grumpy, for Chaila. My boots—more suitable for glaciers than stony trails—were too heavy, and they pinched my toes. My neck ached from the strain of extra weight in my pack. I had walked behind enough Bhote women no bigger than myself to know it probably wouldn't kill me to carry forty-five pounds for a few days, but still I complained loudly, as if the others were not carrying loads that were far heavier than mine. We staggered into Chaila, hot, dusty, and sweaty, and Kirken produced a miracle in the form of three porters ready and willing to walk to Jumla at the normal day rate of thirty-five rupees. "You are a spoiled rotten memsah'b," I said to myself as I happily unloaded my pack.

All along the Langu and the Mugu we walked beneath trees and bushes newly leafed and shining with every shade of green. Our quick pace meant no lingering over fragrant blooms or unfamiliar calls of birds hidden in the foliage. We walked steadily from sunup to sundown with a two-hour break for lunch, a rest period long forgotten by the time we reached our night's destination.

I walked alone a lot, slowly and at the back of the line. It made me uncomfortable to have people behind me. I always felt pressed to walk faster, so I'd be constantly stumbling over rocks in my heavy, clumsy boots, trying to see some of the scenery. Rod found it hard to be last, and though he'd occasionally join me for a mile or two, he usually was out of sight ahead.

We got to Jumla at the end of the fifth day, cutting the normal time for the journey in half. I was never so glad to get somewhere in my life. Standing at the top of Danphe Lekh, with Jumla Valley spread out below, I wondered if even a cold beer and a hot shower were worth it. "Yes," said Rodney, "just you wait." He was hell-bent on making it to the airplane ticket office before it closed, and he dashed down the steep mountainside, leaving me stumbling in the dust. He knew the planes would be heavily booked and the schedule uncertain. To delay until tomorrow morning could result in a week's wait for a ticket. Tired, blistered, and dejected, I trudged down the trail, wishing I could magically transport us all to Kathmandu—better yet, home. I could be lying in a hot bathtub in northern California with a glass of wine in my hand listening to an Emmylou Harris record. But then I remembered we didn't have a home to take a bath *in*. It was the excitement of the unknown, good and bad, I reminded myself, that I had been looking forward to as we had packed the dishes and loaded the truck with the furniture and boxes we would store in a friend's garage.

Several Westerners lived in Jumla, working on aid projects through the American Peace Corps or the European Volunteer Service Overseas or the United Missions, but we weren't yet well acquainted. There was a hotel in the "New Bazaar" section of town, where the Tibetan traders stayed. The owner, Pema, had supplied Rod's 1976 trip, and since those days, when his store was a small hole in the wall, he had become a wealthy man by Jumla standards. He also had brought Karma to us, and so we went to Pema's hotel in the early days of the project.

For about a dollar a day, Pema supplied a wooden bed and two meals cooked by his wife. There was no bathroom or toilet in the building, nor anywhere nearby. The few government-built outhouses had been put to what the townsfolk considered a much more practical use than the one intended: They were fine for storing potatoes. It was therefore a long walk to find a bush offering any degree of privacy, but invariably privacy gave way to urgency after a day or two of Pema's wife's cooking. But the worst things about Pema's hotel, worse even than the fleas and lice and rats, were the bedbugs. They tend to lie low during the cold months of winter, but let a few sunny days warm up the atmosphere and they come crawling, literally, out of the woodwork. You can't see them until they're already swollen with your blood. I swear I could hear their high-pitched laughter as they lapped up the insect repellent and punctured another hole in my tender skin. The bites turned into big patches of watery, itchy blisters; then the blisters turned into scabs and *still* they itched. Months ago, hearing of my plan to join the Snow Leopard Project, many of my friends and family had asked, "How can you just give up everything and go off to God-knows-where, for God-knows-how-long?"

"It's going to be a wonderful adventure," I had replied.

So why was I mad at Rodney for rushing to the ticket office to try to get us out of there on the next morning's plane?

There was mail for us at the Forestry Department office. The letters, a rest, and several cups of steaming tea brought back my good spirits—for about an hour. The next day's flight was fully booked. Still Jamuna managed to secure two "government" tickets: one for him and one for Rod. One seat on every flight is reserved for use, even at the last minute, by government officials, so he had done well to get the two. It was a particularly busy time, and I might have to wait a week until a regular seat became available. It didn't make good sense for Rod to stay behind, with all that was waiting to be done in Kathmandu, but still he was kind enough to offer. We could try for a last-minute cancellation in the morning.

The airstrip is Jumla's entertainment center—twenty or thirty onlookers to every passenger. Shortly after dawn we pushed through the crowds and made our way into the small ticketholders' waiting area. I waited with the baggage while Rod and Jamuna went to consult with the ticket agent. Rod soon returned.

"The ticket office is in chaos," he said. "Absolutely hordes of locals are in there badgering the agent for a seat. You might as well forget about Kathmandu for today."

I had no way of hiding the disappointment that came flooding in. To be so close, and yet stranded there in Jumla made Kathmandu—not to mention San Francisco—suddenly seem even farther away than it looked from the Langu. I fought off the tears by taking my disappointment out on Rod.

"Oh, great," I replied. "Just my luck. I'll never get out of here; I'll still be sitting on this bench when you get back. If I live that long."

"You'll get out," he said.

"Oh, sure. It's real easy for you to say. You'll be sitting in a restaurant in a couple of hours, guzzling beer and eating pizza. Think about me, won't you, stuffing down another plate of gray rice and shitting my guts out in Pema's wheatfield. I hope that pizza makes you sick!"

Small, persistent flies buzzed in the still air and clung to our bare arms. With the plane due any minute, everyone was listening for the sudden wail of the siren atop the second-story control room—the signal that the plane had been spotted coming in at the far end of the broad valley.

I hadn't the heart to watch, and when the siren began, Jamuna emerged from the office with a big smile and three tickets in his hand.

"You still want that pizza today"? he asked with a grin. I don't know how he got that extra ticket—I didn't want to know—but a few minutes later, when the Twin Otter ran down the dirt strip and lunged with a roar into the air with all of us aboard, the tension and irritation and desperation I'd allowed to build up over the past weeks burst in an instant. As I looked at Rod in the seat beside me, I felt sheepish for letting it all get the best of me. He'd taken so much more in his stride, without a single tantrum.

"I'm sorry I acted like such a jerk, Rodney. I don't really hope you get sick."

"You see," he said, squeezing my hand, "I told you it'd be worth it. We'll be in Kathmandu before you know it."

In an hour and a half, we covered the entire distance it had taken us three weeks to walk five months before. We descended into Kathmandu Valley and stepped out into a warm wash of April air—and back into the twentieth century.

Bike bells jingled, car horns honked in a whirl of dust and modern bustle. Our senses reeled at the cornucopia of open-air shops jammed with goods; the profusion of shapes and colors, ripe fruits and vegetables, bright women in gossamer saris balancing heaped shopping baskets on their heads. Dung smells mingled with woodsmoke and ripe crops in small garden patches as our taxi rattled through the narrow, winding streets to the Kathmandu Guest House, once again our temporary home.

The shower head looked like a drooped sunflower, a big disc with its face to the floor. We stood beneath it, anticipating the rush of warm water. Rod reached out and turned the four-pronged handles. His involuntary howl of delight echoed through the halls as the first clear drops hit his upturned face and turned the color of the summer Langu as they washed over his body. Laughing, now we'd find out how much was tan and how much was petrified dirt. We shampooed our hair three times, emerging long after the water ran cold, scrubbed and squeaking, toes and fingers turned to prunes. Donning city clothes, we stepped out into the swarming streets and headed straight for K.C.'s, where a tourist could get a sumptuous Western breakfast, lunch, or dinner; outrageous pies and cakes; and a big frosty bottle of Nepalese beer. Some hours later we waddled back to the Guest House and collapsed in the shade of the grassy courtyard.

Jamuna, as Rod guessed he would do, resigned. He said that his family's soybean oil business had suffered losses in the months he had been away. But we would learn that Kurt had had a major role in convincing Jamuna to quit, playing upon his affirmed distaste for the study area. Jamuna apparently believed all of Kurt's assertions: that Rod was purely out for personal gain; that he would give no one but himself credit for any

achievements; that the Snow Leopard Project had no shortage of funds; that he could have provided the team with better-quality food and improved living conditions; and that, in any case, the project was bound to fail because of Rod's incompetence. When we returned to Kathmandu with word of "Ek's" capture and radio-collaring, several of Jamuna's associates urged him to stick with it, but by then the damage had been done; it would have taken a miracle to change his mind and kindle an interest in returning to that place.

We were to feel the repercussions of those rumors—which eventually filtered throughout the Nepalese wildlife community—for months to come, particularly in the long-term relationship that would develop with Jamuna's successor. Our agreement with the DNPWC stipulated that we have a Nepalese coinvestigator, and since the department had no one else available who was qualified they helped find Karan B. Shah, an entomologist with the Natural History Museum and a lecturer at Tribhuvan University. He agreed to take over the bharal study in spite of limited field experience and no previous work with ungulates. Once the paperwork to arrange his deputation to the DNPWC was completed, he would make his own way to the Langu, joining us by the end of June or early July, depending on the monsoon and the availability of planes.

The first available Sky Van date was mid-May. We would be allowed a load of about a thousand kilograms (twenty-two hundred pounds), but no one would give us a firm figure in case they had to transport a military passenger or two at the last minute. Much of our weight limit would be taken up with equipment that the Customs Department had been holding for the past five months, so we made up a list of "luxury" items we could leave behind if we had to, such as sugar, canned coffee, powdered milk, and the basket of fresh vegetables for the trail in.

With that done, we accepted a highly appealing invitation to spend some time at Tiger Tops Jungle Lodge, a resort designed for unforgettable wildlife-viewing in Nepal's Royal Chitwan National Park. In 1980, several people involved with Tiger Tops and also interested in conservation in Nepal, India, and Sri Lanka formed a nonprofit organization, The International Trust for Nature Conservation (ITNC). They provided our project with invaluable support, not only in money and logistics but also with a wealth of experience of Nepal from which we were able to draw on many occasions.

Our trip to the jungle lodge served several purposes: to be pampered with a much-needed, luxurious vacation; for Rod to consult with Chuck McDougal, a tiger expert also experienced in remote photography methods; and to borrow a two-person inflatable raft (one porter load) that might make it possible to cross the Langu all year round.

During many years spent in the jungle studying the Bengal tigers that roamed Chitwan, Chuck had perfected a technique for getting tigers and forest leopards to take their own pictures by walking over a buried camera trigger. Rod wanted to try it in the Langu, in an attempt to get pictures of unsedated, wild snow leopards. The chances of radio-collaring every cat in the study area were practically nil, but with good photos different cats could be identified by the unique pattern of spots on their heads. Chuck suggested a practical approach to the problem of how to power the cameras. We couldn't bring enough AA batteries to keep cameras running day and night for weeks on end, but a solar panel and rechargeable batteries might work. Neither, however, was available in Kathmandu, so the problem would have to wait to be solved.

We had taken some sixty rolls of slides illustrating the trek in, Dolphu, and the Langu Gorge. There were also three rolls of the capture of "Ek." Those three rolls contained our hopes for the *National Geographic* magazine being interested in an article. A friend would hand-carry the bag of film to the United States and mail it to the *National Geographic* for developing and consideration by their photographic editor. (Four months later we found out that out of over one hundred frames, there was only one, my shot of Rod with the jabstick facing a growling "Ek," that met the *Geographic*'s high standards for photography. Provided we could follow it with others of equivalent quality, we would have an article.)

The Sky Van is a remarkable machine, looking more than anything like a 1966 Volkswagen bus with wings. The whole back end drops down and makes a ramp over which a Jeep can easily be driven in, parked in the plane's voluminous belly, and flown off over the mountains. Our pile of gear barely began to fill the Sky Van, but it was heavy enough. Every item was placed on the big scale, including Rodney, Lopsang, and me, and for once Rod was happy about the fifteen pounds he had lost in the Langu. There were no extra passengers, and we got the whole allowance. After an hour of loading and arranging our awkward assortment of containers and tying it all down with ropes and straps, the flight crew bolted five canvas and metal chairs to the floor near the front of the plane. Rod, Lopsang, and I were invited to take our seats. The flight engineer and "technician" took the other two, the captain and copilot took their places in the cockpit, the key was turned, and the two engines roared to life—very close to our ears in the uninsulated metal interior.

The ground fog had lifted in Kathmandu Valley, and we took off noisily into cool morning skies dotted here and there with a white cloud. The plane chugged along and the flight crew was easy and relaxed. The engineer produced a large thermos and poured sweet coffee all around.

Thirty minutes out of Kathmandu, the captain turned in his seat and beckoned to Rod. Rod went forward, and for several minutes he and the captain were head to head in consultation. Then Rod returned wearing a look of extreme disappointment. "We have to go back," he said. "It's pouring rain in western Nepal. We have to fly over a high pass, and it's covered with clouds. Captain Rana says we can't do it safely." It had taken that long to get a weather report because the Jumla control tower could be contacted only when the plane was airborne and on course.

The wing dipped as the plane turned and headed back to Kathmandu. We would have to try again another day, and add the cost of an extra hour's airtime to the bill.

The Sky Vans were all booked solid on other business for over a week of fine weather. The next date was canceled at the last minute, and we were left waiting for confirmation of another try, wondering if the weather would hold, and if in fact we would ever get another chance.

At last the word came, and we arose again in darkness to pile our ton of gear into two Land-Rovers for the thirty-minute journey to the airport. We roared off on May 19 into the blue morning with fingers crossed. Our route took us along the southern edge of the Himalayas, and Lopsang pointed out the main peaks, crystal clear and breathtaking in the clear air.

We flew into Bheri River Valley, suspended in the narrow rift between snowcapped mountains, and looked up at the summits on either side of the plane. Then we began to climb, gaining altitude until we could see our breath in the unheated cabin as the altimeter showed 14,200 feet. We cleared Chakhure Pass, a solid knife-edge wall of ice, with what looked like about six inches to spare beneath the plane. Then suddenly we were descending, swooping fast upon the short runway. Lights flashed; the captain worked intently over his instruments, throwing switches, adjusting a lever overhead. We bumped onto the strip and slammed to a halt. A perfect landing.

Jumla was briskly cool and refreshing. The crew stood on the grass near the plane, beamed, and asked for photos, not caring that it would be a year before they saw them, if ever. They ordered tea for us all from the "Jumla Airport Lounge," a wood and mud shack teahouse beyond the barbed wire fence. Then they shook our hands, got back in the plane, and took off in a blast of wind and dust. Once again we had severed our ties to the world of telephones, taxicabs, and flush toilets.

8

How Not to Paddle a Raft

We traveled toward Dolphu at a steady but relaxed pace, taking time to notice how green and lush the land had become in our month's absence. When we reached our last evening's camp at Bailung Stream, something happened that affected Lopsang deeply for the duration of his time with the Snow Leopard Project.

Two of our porters were friends from Mangri. The older one, Tsang Tenzing, had rented space in his house to our people on previous trips between Jumla and Dolphu. He was a large man whose powerful leg muscles bulged below his flowered shorts. His face bore a near-constant smile that crinkled the corners of his eyes, and he seemed to be well known and liked by all.

He was particularly quiet and watchful that evening. Three government men came, on their way to Dolphu on business to do with an election that was in progress. The campaign had not been smooth, and these men were not popular. There was much whispering and sly looking behind their backs. Eventually they went on up the pass, and our camp settled down.

Tsang Tenzing and his friend had run out of food. Lopsang gave them rice and dried vegetables from our stocks and made some arrangement for repayment. Rod and I retired, glad our trek was almost over and knowing Kirken would be glad to see us back.

At 2:00 A.M. we were awakened by the sound of a man in the throes of a terrible nightmare, or something so awful that he could only moan and cry his distress in a chilling, chanting, heavy-breathing song.

Half asleep, Rod mumbled, "What the *hell* is going on?" The chanting continued and he shouted through the tent, *"Sutne! Sutne!"* trying to signal that it was time to go to sleep. It had no effect. He got up, put on his clothes, and went out to find out what was going on and put a stop to it. I heard no words from the irritated sah'b, and soon he slipped quietly back into the tent.

"What happened?" I whispered.

"Tsang Tenzing's sitting in front of the fire, with Karma and Lopsang and a few porters. There's a plate with some grains of rice at Tenzing's feet, and he's in some sort of trance, shaking and sweating."

We lay in the dark for half an hour, nervous and curious, until silence was restored.

Lopsang was hollow-eyed in the morning. He hadn't slept. Apparently Tenzing was a shaman or *jhankri,* a person with powerful ritual knowledge. He had had a vision in his sleep in which he saw that this was going to be a bad year for our Lopsang; he was in danger, and Tenzing had felt obligated to help him in any way he could. In his trance, Tenzing saw things that had actually happened in Lopsang's past. Lopsang, he felt, was going to lose something—either his possessions or his life.

What to do? Lopsang's whole year was to be spent with us, and most of it in the Langu, at best a dangerous place to be, and now he'd been assured that he wasn't likely to live through it. At least that's how Lopsang saw his situation. But maybe Tenzing's prophecy had already happened.

While we had been in Kathmandu, Lopsang's room had been broken into and most of his expedition equipment stolen along with his favorite possession, his radio-cassette player. Then when he was in the bazaar bargaining with a shopkeeper one day, his bag had been slit with a razor and his money stolen. Rod pointed out that he couldn't be in any personal danger, since Tenzing had said either *or.*

"Anyway," Rod said, "I'll bet it was the Kathmandu rice and dried cauliflower you gave him, Lopsang. Tenzing just had a bellyache. He ate enough for an army. His stomach isn't used to it—it was nothing but a nightmare."

Lopsang laughed, but we could tell he took the whole incident very seriously. Later we would have reason to reexamine our own attitude about the abilities of the shamans.

Kirken was glad to see us, telling us excitedly that we had had visitors: Robert and Bobbie Holmes, our close friends from California.

"Oh, no!" I cried. "They *didn't* come, not while we were in Kathmandu!" I looked at Rod; his face mirrored my own shock and dismay. We had invited them the previous year, and Bob, a professional photographer, had been given an assignment from the *National Geographic* to cover our project.

But we had written during our snowbound winter in Dolphu telling them not to come, that the journey was too long, "iffy," and difficult. They never got the letter. They had followed in our footsteps, making the month-long trek all the way from Nepalganj. When they arrived in Jumla, Bobbie recognized our backpacks stored at Pema's Hotel, and they learned that we'd flown out two days earlier. In a magazine article, Bob would write:

On no other trip have I ever experienced such extremes of emotion. To walk halfway across Nepal and miss someone by two days made me sink into a deep depression. But I convinced myself that having come this far, we might as well continue.

They swallowed their disappointment, dried their tears, and walked on to Dolphu. Kirken showed Bob and his Sherpa guide Pemba the way to Dhukyel camp, where they attempted to pick up "Ek's" signal. Bob wrote:

Tracking was not easy and we stalked the mountain sides without success. If the leopard was still in the area it was out of transmitting range.

Experts have spent months looking, so what chance had I? I had never really expected to see a snow leopard in the wild and I felt privileged to have been so close to one. You have to know when to quit, and the following dawn we started the long climb out of the Langu Gorge. . . . Pemba suddenly yelled that there was something moving on the other side of the valley. Below us a group of langurs were agitated and chattering nervously. I looked hard but could see nothing. I snapped a telephoto lens onto my camera and desperately scanned the mountainside. Still I could see nothing. Then I saw it. About half a mile away I spotted a snow leopard, its fur merging perfectly with the landscape, its long, thick tail equaling the length of its body. It was unmistakable. For fifteen seconds the leopard slowly stalked between the boulders on the steep mountainside and then it was gone, disappearing behind a ridge. Those fifteen seconds will remain with me forever.

"They brought you presents," said Kirken, "but they were so sad that they decided to eat one present to cheer themselves up. That was a jar of peanut butter."

We returned to Dhukyel on the last day of May and stayed for nearly two weeks. There was no fresh leopard sign, and Rod could get no signal from "Ek." The muddy river was much higher than normal, flooding with the big winter buildup of snow still melting from the high peaks. Boiling rapids and big waves ruled out a raft crossing at Dhukyel, and we were more or less back where we had begun: stuck. We could accomplish nothing by staying put. Not only the cats, but also the tahr and bharal and even the langurs had all vanished, presumably moving up the mountain slopes as the snow melted and exposed the fresh new grass.

There was a permanent bridge across the Langu below Dolphu; from there, according to the villagers, we could travel all along the southern side, past Dhukyel, all the way to Ruka Canyon, a distance of some ten miles along the river. It wasn't easy, they said. We would have to climb over a high cliff, the one we had named "Tyson's Cliff," but it could be done if we were willing to take a risk.

We decided to send Kirken, Lopsang, and Sonam on a little expedition along the southern-side trail before we packed up all our things yet again and moved our base camp.

They left early one morning, backtracking to the bridge below Dolphu. Lightly loaded and moving quickly, they appeared on the bank opposite Dhukyel Camp at 6:00 P.M.—twelve hours to cross fifty feet of river! We shouted across the river's roar but could make out nothing of what each other said. They continued on upstream and disappeared around the bend. They came back at 6:00 A.M. the following morning, heading downstream, and late that evening arrived again in Dhukyel Camp.

Kirken had made a map showing a few campsites, all with one or more disadvantages: poor shelter, scarce wood, or no water besides the Langu mud. They had gone over Tyson's Cliff using ropes, but there wasn't much to tie on to, just a few bushes and a lot of rotten rock.

A flat riverbar at the near end of the cliff offered what they felt was the best spot for a camp. The villagers called the place Choyap, and they camped there for a few weeks each summer while they gathered and dried *jimbu,* a wild herb that looks like chives and tastes deliciously like garlic. Choyap was relatively safe from falling boulders, the river was fairly smooth, so it might be possible to try the boat. If it worked, we could avoid Tyson's Cliff altogether. But we would have to live with the silted Langu water.

It took two and a half days to move. The southern-side trail made the Dhukyel Trail seem like walking through Kansas. If we weren't picking our way over the rocks we were sliding down gullies where the trail had been washed away, and the lightest of steps sent down a cascade of sand and rocks. Kirken mentioned a "tricky" place. *One* tricky place? It seemed that around every bend there was another tricky place, but every time I asked if this was the spot, he said, "It's a little farther."

We came to Kimding, a deep side canyon with a swift stream at the bottom. We began the descent at the top end of a big rock wall. A little sloping crack was meant to keep our feet from slipping; a stone shelf jutted out in the middle at about face level, just far enough so we'd have to bend out backward to avoid it. Beyond it I could see the top of an old log, with notches, disappearing somewhere below. Also below, about five hundred feet, Kimding converged with the Langu in a roar.

The Sherpas were either behind steering the goats, or ahead cutting steps in the trail. Rod went first, and once across, came back to pry me off the rock. He provided his hand for an illusion of safety. I did have a choice. I didn't *have* to cross that rock. I could go back to Dolphu and wait for four months.

Orkin, a boy in his early teens, came up behind me, and I stepped back to let him pass. He carried a load of sixty pounds and without hesitating crossed over, bent himself around the shelf, and descended the ladder. I took a deep breath, stopped all conscious thought, and stepped out into the crack.

Kirken revealed a sadistic streak. He said that this part of the southern-side trail was about a quarter as hard as Tyson's Cliff.

At first glance, Choyap seemed ideal. It lay on a long bend of the river, a wide alluvial terrace with shady pines and poplars, a large rock for a roofed kitchen, and several places to pitch our tents. Too bad there was no clear side stream for cooking and drinking water. We thought of Kimri village and its people living with the Langu year-round; no doubt we could survive a few months of it. The Sherpas made jokes: "We won't need potatoes. Just add salt and it's soup."

There were no rapids for a good quarter-mile stretch, but the river was moving very, very fast. Could we cross it in the boat? Rod was concerned about one or two standing waves, sure evidence of boulders beneath the surface. He was skeptical of a safe crossing. None of us was exactly a rowing expert. Kirken and Lopsang, however, were gung ho to go rafting.

We unpacked the raft and inflated it with the foot pump. We tied a long rope to one end; Karma and one of the porters held it. Off went the Sherpas, riding high into the current, with Rod shouting directions over the river's drone. On the terrace above, I watched through the lens of a camera.

They would have made it with ease if there had not been that big wave just a few feet from the gravelbar they were aiming for. They hit it dead center, did a slow-motion flip, and slid gradually into the icy, swirling water. The boat turned upside down, but both Sherpas hung on to the sides. The rope went taut and snapped to a midstream stop. The three men onshore held on, but the thin green nylon sliced through the skin on their fingers and palms. They kept their grips as the boat disappeared around the bend where the riffles got bigger and the rapids began.

Rod, fingers bleeding, made himself the anchor while the other two ran downstream, leaping boulders and crashing through think clumps of caragana plants, with their daggerlike, three-inch-long thorns. I, too, ran downstream along the terrace, my eye on the rope stretched just above the water.

Around the bend lay the boat, right side up on the bank, and beside it Kirken and Lopsang stood wet and shivering in the wind. I ran back and called to Rod that the Sherpas were safe, and we all returned to camp, cured of rafting for the duration of the Snow Leopard Project.

As we sat around a big fire bandaging three pairs of bloody hands, Lopsang sighed and said that he'd lost his good rubber boots to the river.

"They have gone to India," he added ruefully.

"You're lucky that's *all* that went to India," I said, thinking of Tsang Tenzing and his vision.

With that, we discovered how they'd kept from being swept away. They had tied themselves to the boat—something absolutely prohibited in professional rafting because of the very real danger of being drowned. If Rod had seen their ropes, he would have made them untie themselves, but maybe it's just as well he hadn't.

For the rest of the summer the boat served as a settling tank for the Langu water.

9

Tyson's Cliff

The summer was warm and dry; by late June, the monsoon should have arrived. In Dolphu and Wangri, even sheltered by the high mountains as they were, low clouds and mist normally would be clinging to the mountains, and enough rain would fall to nurture the summer crops. But it was well into August before any rain came, and by that time the village fields were parched beyond recovery. They would replant, but this year would bring no bountiful harvest to the people of western Nepal.

Karan, the new coinvestigator, arrived in the first week of July. He seemed older than twenty-nine, perhaps because he was bigger and more filled out than the small, thin village people I was used to seeing. He had liked the journey in from Dolphu even less than the rest of us. He hadn't experienced the slight courage-building advantages of the Dhukyel Trail. His first words to me, after "Hello," were, "You should convince Rodney not to take such risks, making Base Camp at the end of such a dangerous trail." His dark eyes reflected his fear; and his assumption that I held sway over Rodney's decision-making reflected a charming faith in my womanly powers! Walking along the brushy terrace and flat riverbar, I pointed out the nests I'd found of Tickell's leaf warblers and a pair of pied wagtails, and we discovered a mutual interest in birds. Walking back, he spied a flock of Eurasian goldfinches, adding a new bird to my list. By the time Rod arrived, we had caught up on most of the events since we'd last met in Kathmandu.

With Karan's arrival, we worked out a kind of routine. The cat spent a great deal of time at the upper end of the canyon, so Rod often stayed at a cave camp near the confluence of Pukchang Canyon with the Langu. With ropes on Tyson's Cliff, he could make his way far upstream tracking the cat, on the opposite bank, as it moved along the canyon. One of the Sherpas or Karma would often accompany him to stock the camp and spend a few days helping wherever needed. But neither Karan nor I could muster the courage to try Tyson's Cliff.

A typical Choyap day began at six with tea brought steaming to the tent by Karma or Sonam—a luxury held over from the original trek in. Sometimes tea would be followed by a bowl of oatmeal, rice pudding, or *tsampa,* roasted wheat made into a good Tibetan porridge. For lunch we might have rice and *dal* (lentil soup or sauce), rice and potato curry, or chapatis with dal. For special occasions we had French fries and powdered eggs (or occasionally fresh ones from Dolphu), or French fries and a hunk off the round of yak cheese we had brought from Kathmandu. Dinner was the same, with the additional choices of fried rice with freeze-dried vegetables, noodle soup, or a chicken if we were lucky.

Mrs. Bhakra went into the pot. She had lost her popularity with the staff; she would never come home at night, and they were forever having to hunt for her and her kid. Finally Karma gave up in disgust and just let her stay out for nights on end, and that got him in trouble with Rodney, who didn't want to provide a free meal to any uncollared cat without its having to run the trap gauntlet. So we ate her. The kid walked around the familiar head lying open-eyed on a piece of wood beside the kitchen. The cooks were saving the head for something special, a delicacy.

They simmered it for hours with curry spices, tending the pot carefully, then brought Rod and me the first aromatic bowls of it out of respect for Rod's position as boss.

"Don't look at it too closely," I told Rod. "It's got pieces of Mrs. B's

107

lips and ears in it; and one of her eyeballs is staring up out of my bowl."

The others thought something was seriously wrong with us, passing up the most delicious thing we'd been offered all year.

When there was no signal from "Ek" when he moved far up a side canyon, or over the high massif of Chaling La, a lesser peak on the northern side at about midgorge, Rod would return to Choyap, and the days would become an open classroom. With Karan, we might climb high to search the cliffs and slopes for tahr or bharal and spend an afternoon learning the horn shapes of males that indicate their age, and how to distinguish an adult female bharal from a yearling male, whose horns are so similar. Or we might "run a plant transect"—a detailed examination of everything growing along a premeasured line following the hill contour, or across it, or down a ridgeline, to determine how the availability of forage plants affected the movements of the wild sheep and goats, and in turn, the movements of the cats.

From Kathmandu we had brought a stack of old newspapers (ten pounds of our planeload), and I began to collect samples of the study area's plants and to learn about their identifying characteristics, taping each specimen onto a separate sheet of paper and pressing it between two crosshatched wooden boards.

Karan had an enormous amount to learn about ungulate biology and the field techniques necessary for his work. Up to now he had never worked with anything larger than a bird or a snake; he had no experience at all with mammals. By reading the scientific books and papers we had brought into the field, by observing the sheep firsthand during identifying sessions, and through conversations around the evening campfires, Rod hoped that Karan would quickly absorb the basics and soon begin to come up with his own ideas and suggestions regarding study methods.

We kept a separate set of radio-tracking gear at Choyap. When Rod was away I would monitor the cat whenever I could pick up his signal. Choyap, however, was poorly situated for tracking, and it was rare for us to get a signal. The northern canyon wall ascended in a series of cliffs, pinnacles, and narrow ledges, topped by rock spires and domes rising many thousands of feet. It was prime, perfect territory for snow leopards, but we had no way of getting at it, either by foot or with the radios.

Rod's stays at Choyap, therefore, were short-lived; he was always anxious to get back upstream, where he might recontact his cat and where he had his traps set in hopes of catching others. Each time he left I tortured myself, watching his progress on Tyson's Cliff, my palms clammy on the binoculars, my throat tight with apprehension as he grew smaller, a toy figure clinging tenuously in the wind to the thin rope on the sheer black rock. How could I *ever* get the nerve to try it? Worse, how could I cope with my failure to try?

From Rod's diary:

June 28, 1982, Pukchang Cave

The start of another week. How odd that concept of time appears as we continue to take each day for itself. I returned to Pukchang this morning, and again crossed Tyson's Cliff. It is becoming less awesome; today I looked down over the precipice frequently, moving up with confidence and with little of the deep fear I experienced previously. Perhaps I've acquired some of the Dolphas' "mountain goatness." Passing heaps of tahr droppings below the long log ladder that spans the abyss, I smiled, pleased to be following one of their routes across this black crag. I recalled Matthiessen's words from *The Snow Leopard* as I gazed across at the red cliffs of Chaling La, "There is so much that enchants me in this spare, silent place, that I move softly so as not to break a spell." Karma's soft songs filled the air, mingling with the sound of wind and the Langu far below us.

Will a leopard visit our goat tonight? It is dark, and having no lamp, we retire early, like primitive or prehistoric cave dwellers. I lie by the cave entrance; above, a black rock arches over, enclosing a sliver of sky against the broken cliffs on the Langu's northern bank. Kirken sleeps deep in the cold but comforting bowels of the cave, further removed from nighttime spirits. A draft of cold air brushes past from inside, like the movement of a cat, and there is the fragrant odor of juniper smoke. This is our temporary home, and in spite of a monotonous rice diet and a dusty floor, I am happy, at ease. If there are regrets, it is that we have little data on the collared cat. No contact for four days now with "Ek." Conjuring images of a female with young, I *will* a cat to visit the rock overhang at Pukchang Stream where our traps, and the goat, wait. My sleep is taken in brief one- or two-hour stretches. I awake, and wonder: Have we caught a leopard? Try the receiver, perhaps "Ek" is near. Then at 3:00 A.M., as the moon sets, reflecting ghostly shadows upon a thin sky devoid of stars, I fall asleep, deeply.

We check the traps in the morning. There is no leopard.

July 3, 11:00 P.M.

Things always change quickly. An hour ago, I picked up "Ek" on Tillisha Mountain, and now I'm settled in for a night of monitoring. As I listen to the "beeps" the moon appears through thick clouds. Across the canyon, light strikes the sandstone and dark bushes, contrast of black and gray. The river is a bright ribbon, curved between steep landforms. Except for its roar, all is quiet. Unlike the jungle, there are no night birds, no roaring lions, barking zebras, or howling jackals.

Moving across Tillisha's high grassland, the snow leopard covers its range, probably aware that a kill in the moonlight is unlikely. Perhaps that is why it did not start moving until after 10:00 P.M.

As the month wore on, we began to lose hope of catching another cat. Day after day passed without Rod's finding even so much as a track in the dust. During the spring, it had been easy to find fresh tracks and scrapes at the river level, especially around the confluences. "Ek's" capture site at Dhukyel seemed to confirm the theory that the chances of catching a cat were best where the sign was so concentrated. But the traps at Pukchang remained empty, and Rod's worries grew.

"There's just no fresh sign along the river anymore," he said. " 'Ek' is staying with the bharal up in the grassland, and I'm sure that's where all the others are, too. We can't do a study with just one cat. And we can't get another grant unless I can prove that catching 'Ek' wasn't just a fluke."

"Why don't we go up there?" I asked.

"I don't think we could do it," he replied. "We'd have to climb up above Dhukyel. You saw those cliffs—they're worse than Tyson's. And what about water? And wood? Even if we found a place to camp, I don't know where in hell I could place a trap in all that grassland. It isn't like the river bottom, where they have to follow a certain path. It's absolutely hopeless, a waste of time. The best thing I can do is to get as much information from 'Ek' as I possibly can, and that means spending even more time at Pukchang."

I hesitated a moment before responding: "And meanwhile Karan and I aren't helping you very much, are we, hanging around Choyap?"

"Not really," he admitted. "There were several times when you could have helped me get twenty-four-hour activity records on 'Ek.' It's very hard to stay awake all night, tuning in the radio every five minutes. Tyson's Cliff is scary, but I know you've built it up in your mind to be much worse than it really is. Besides, it's nice beyond the cliff; don't you want to see how it looks?"

"I do," I replied, "but every time I go up to where the rocks begin, my knees get weak and my palms start to sweat. All I can think about is falling."

"It looks like it's going to be a lonely summer, then," he said with a sigh as he hoisted his backpack for the two-hour walk to Pukchang.

For several days, "Ek" stayed low among the cliffs opposite Choyap, and Rod stayed in camp, monitoring the cat and getting map bearings on his location. It was two months since we had left Kathmandu, and there was a good chance we had mail waiting in Jumla. Karma would soon leave with our outgoing letters, and I sat on a tarp in the shade, writing to our friends and family. I tried not to think about what letters Karma might bring back with him; there was no point in getting excited about an event that was still some three weeks away.

My letter-writing was interrupted by rocks falling across the river. It took a few minutes to spot a group of tahr jumping quickly over a wide gap between two rocks.

"I wonder if they smell 'Ek'?" I said to myself, squinting up at the cliffs, feeling behind me for the binoculars. A movement made my heart jump. It was two more tahr. Moments later, Rodney came rushing to the tent, grinning and saying, "Come quickly."

"Oh," I said. "You've seen the tahr, too."

"Tahr?" he replied, "No, but I've seen 'Ek'!"

He had traced the cat with particular vigilance that morning. The beeps were clear and strong, and he was confident of getting an unusually precise "fix." Picking his way along the roaring river with the earphones on, he was not aware of the tahr passing above and sending rocks down the cliffs. Having gotten an equally good fix a few days before at Pukchang and spending hours searching unsuccessfully with the scope, he didn't think he'd see the leopard this time. But as he homed in on the cat's location, he couldn't resist a quick search with the binoculars. He put them to his eyes, and there—dead center—was "Ek," standing on a big flat boulder, looking intently across the gully where the tahr disappeared.

"It was such a shock to see him," said Rod. "He stood there for about thirty seconds, then he disappeared into the gully. That's when I came to get you. But now we'll be lucky to see him; his signal is inactive and he's probably bedded for the day somewhere behind that promontory."

Rod was right, we didn't see him again. In fact, that was the last time we ever saw "Ek," and one of only four times we saw *any* of our collared cats roaming free.

I worried for weeks over the hovering specter of Tyson's Cliff, and as time went on, it grew bigger, blacker, and more terrifying in my mind. What was I going to do, sit in Choyap all summer? What if we came back next year? Rod had conquered his fear, and he kept encouraging me to come with him to Pukchang. There was much to be done besides monitoring "Ek." If I did it, perhaps Karan would follow suit. Choyap was confining, and I was getting increasingly bored. One evening as Rod packed for an early-morning start, I announced,

"Okay, I'm ready, I'm going with you." I knew I couldn't take it back then. At least I'd have to try. So much for a good night's sleep.

As we made our way along the grass slope, Rod said all his most reassuring words about how we would just go slowly and steadily and he would be right there if I needed a hand, and if I wanted to turn back that was all right, too, but really it isn't as bad as you think it's going to be.

"Right," I agreed, lying, "it'll be a piece of cake."

Once again I made my mind a blank, restricting my eyes to see only my feet and hands and the rope and rock in front of them. I ignored the lump in my throat and the pounding of my heart, concentrating every ounce of energy to control my trembling muscles, to breathe naturally. Above all, I must avoid accidentally looking over the edge.

A series of narrow, small, diagonal ledges led up the rock face. Where one ledge ended, the villagers had leaned a notched tree trunk against the stone, providing a precarious foothold to gain the next ledge. It looked like it had been there a long time. The bottom end was rotten, stuck casually in the ground; the top end leaned against the rock, anchored in nothing but air. I tried to swallow; my throat felt like sandpaper. Rod held the ladder as I placed my feet in the inch-deep notches and climbed up, keeping my eyes on the end of the log. Reaching the top, I held it for Rod, who then took the lead, his hands and feet easily finding small, firm steps in the solid rock.

"Face the cliff wall," he said over his shoulder. "That way it'll be hard to look down. Use the handholds, and don't move your feet until you feel secure. Plan your route and take your time."

The green rope that we had been holding ended at a small juniper near the crest. A path led over the top, set back from the edge of a long dirt slope that plunged abruptly into the void. "How are you doing?" Rod said for the umpteenth time. "Fine," I replied once again. "Well, we're halfway there," he said, "but the next part's a little worse."

We came to the end of the path and stood looking over another edge, into the mouth of Muga Canyon, a narrow tributary cut deep by aeons of cascading snowmelt.

"This is the side the Dolphas call 'Lobur,' " Rod informed me. "I don't know what it means; no one can or will venture to say."

A short set of "steps" took us over the edge and down to a rock overhang, where we rested while Rod described the route. We were faced with a long stretch of smooth, rounded, sloping rock several hundred feet above Muga Stream. There were no steplike footholds. Someone had once hacked a few shallow dents to serve as steps, about a yard apart. Another length of green rope stretched down to a log platform built by the Dolphas five or fifty years ago.

"Go down backward, facing the rock," said Rod. "I'll go first and guide your feet into the niches, since you won't be able to see them. Get a good grip on the rope and lean *out*—away from the rock. Trust your shoes; they won't slip."

"Put that on my tombstone, please: 'She trusted her shoes,' " I said as I tested the rope.

Twenty minutes later we were taking a drink of ice water from Muga Stream, washing the grimy sweat from our foreheads. I was alive. Rodney was right; it wasn't quite as terrifying as I thought it would be. If I had done it sooner, I could have saved myself some nightmares. Still, it was the most frightening thing I had ever done, and though I would never try it alone, I did a dance of conquest there on the banks of Muga Stream. "I *did* it!" We were less than half a mile from Choyap Camp, and it had taken us an hour to get there.

We sat resting on a boulder at the entrance to Pukchang Cave. Below on the flat riverbar, a black and yellow hoopoe pecked in the ground. A long-tailed minivet, brilliant red, perched on a peach tree, and a pair of snow pigeons skimmed low across the river. Blue rock thrushes, rock buntings, and Tickell's leaf warblers flew among the bushes of rose, barberry, honeysuckle, and jasmine.

Here was where Rod had spent so many wakeful nights alone, trying to find practical solutions to our logistics problems that would convince funding agencies to support the Snow Leopard Project. Many of the problems had already been worked out. We had proved that a snow leopard could be radio-collared and that it was possible to establish and supply a long-term base camp in the gorge. With such a good foundation, it seemed only logical to extend the study for at least another year. It was also clear to Rod that another experienced radio tracker was essential.

"And what about you?" he asked as we unpacked our things in the dark, chilly cave. "What do you think about spending another long field season out here?"

"No problem at all," I replied. "What's another winter in the Langu to someone who's just conquered Tyson's Cliff?!"

"Seriously," he continued. "I want to make Base Camp beyond Tyson's and set traps on the northern side at the Tillisha confluence. I'm sure it's a good place, and with a whole winter of intensive trapping we should be able to collar several more cats. But it will mean getting back in and setting up camp early so we don't get caught in Dolphu again, and we'll have to be prepared to be snowbound in here for a few months."

"Well," I said, "you can count me in. I would hate to stay at home wondering and worrying about what's happening, and if you're safe— and missing all the excitement."

"Permanent bridges are the crucial thing," he said, preoccupied with his problem-solving. "Even tracking 'Ek' is a hit-and-miss affair. We need to be able to follow him, to explore the territory where he makes his home and to find out where he goes when we lose his signal. There's just no way we can do that from the southern side. Somehow we simply *have* to find a way to get across the Langu all year round."

We couldn't leave for Jumla until mid-to-late September, when the monsoon was over and planes started flying again, so we had about a month left to gather what data we could. Now the days were gray and muggy; low mist and clouds obscured all the high country, dropping little rain on the parched land. The humid air dampened books and papers, and mold grew among the plant specimens so carefully collected and pressed. The trees acquired hidden voices; concealed among their dense leaves, bird-size cicadas worked themselves into a buzzing, chugging, urgent crescendo, their mating call ceasing only with the dusk. The weather hampered everyone's work. For Karan it was a critical time to watch the bharal herds. In theory, snow leopards preyed heavily on the young lambs, but without numbers the theory could not be proved, and the clouds made observation difficult.

Our treat box had been empty for weeks—no chocolate, no sardines, not even a package of dried cabbage. Certainly no rum. The kitchen stores were again down to chapatis, rice, and potatoes. Karma still had not returned with the mail, and we had long since read the two murder mysteries we had sneaked into the planeload. A bleak depression descended upon us, the worst bout yet of deprivation blues and lunatic cravings. Even the thought of an airline meal, foil-wrapped wedges of pasteurized cheese and cardboard dinner buns, was appealing.

The river level dropped near the beginning of September, and we began to look for likely places to make a bridge. Nowhere was it narrow enough for one tree to span it, so we had to find a place with big boulders midstream to support two or more sets of logs, and where there were trees nearby of sufficient height to reach from bank to boulder and boulder to bank.

From Dhukyel to Pukchang we found just one place, below Tyson's Cliff at Muga Stream. It would take four sets of substantial logs, one set spanning thirty-five feet. The only wood was on the slope high above, a hour's hike up. We held a "board" meeting at which various suggestions were offered for how to get the big, heavy pines down the slope without dropping them in the river, and then how to get them onto the boulders *over* the river. Kirken designed a scaffold to support the logs while they were being maneuvered into place, but it wasn't guaranteed to work and wasn't worth the wood and effort it would have taken.

"I have an idea," suggested Rod. "We'll center a log over a boulder at the river's edge, with Karma perched at one end. Then we'll all leap onto the other end—all at once—and catapult Karma to Tillisha. If it works, you can do the same for me, and we won't need a bridge."

The idea was rejected, even when Rod offered to build a memorial chorten for Karma if it didn't work.

"Don't worry," said Kirken, "we will build a bridge. Five days maximum."

And they did it in three. Plans were made and gear packed for exploring the other side. Then, just before dinner, it began to rain like we hadn't seen for the whole monsoon. The downpour lasted forty-eight hours. At the end, the river had risen two feet, turning the yellow-ocher of the rocks and precious soil it carried with it. All the side gullies were flowing with runoff from Jhobu La, covered again with snow. Not a single log remained of our bridge.

There was no longer any point in staying. Our time would be better spent in returning quickly to the United States, working out the logistics problems, submitting funding applications, finding another researcher, and getting back well before the winter set in again.

Going Home

After eleven months in Nepal, we flew home to San Francisco, somewhat unprepared for the reverse culture shock that waited. Our room, with four walls, windows, drawers, and a closet, seemed utterly luxurious after pawing through plastic bags and duffels in our two-man tent for nearly a year. The vacuum cleaner and even the neighborhood laundromat held pleasures—perverse ones that soon vanished. Never again would I take a bathtub for granted.

In a matter of days, we had left behind a world where pine pitch torches lit our cave kitchen, where the wheel's only purpose was the turning of prayers, and returned to a life where the automobile was essential, if not the drive-up bank or the drive-up hamburger machine. These "modern conveniences" seemed particularly absurd in light of western Nepal's withered fields of grain, where the soil was turned by cattle pulling wooden plows.

Entering a supermarket, we looked, amazed, at its bountiful shelves, seeing food we had forgotten existed. We ate like there was no tomorrow, our friends and family astounded at our capacity to pack it in in spite of a weight loss of some fifteen pounds each.

"Is it possible," said Rod one morning, when jet lag had us both awake at 4:00 A.M., "that just a week ago I was squatting in Pema's field, fertilizing the crops, and here I am today, drinking coffee from a china cup, reading *The New York Times,* and trying to decide what computer to get?"

But for Rod, it would be a swift and hectic break. In a mere three weeks he would be back in Nepal, and Christmas would find him once again beside the Langu River.

First there was the task of finding someone experienced in radio-tracking, a person who was willing to join the Snow Leopard Project as a virtual volunteer, without repeating the Kurt fiasco.

There was actually no shortage of volunteers. We had a stack of letters from people all over the world asking for a chance to be involved. For the wildlife biologists who wrote, the opportunity to study such a little-known animal held great appeal and professional satisfaction. Most seemed well aware that hardships and sacrifices would be required, but we knew from experience that just what constituted hardship could be a matter of interpretation. We knew, too, that there were no foolproof tests of compatibility.

Gary Ahlborn, a local biologist in his early thirties, had studied desert bighorn sheep, distant cousins to the Nepalese bharal, and had radio-tracked the lesser prairie chicken on the plains of New Mexico. He had produced a "job application," listing his virtues and shortcomings, the pros in one column and the con in another. He did this in spite of a warning from a botanist with whom Rod had once worked, and argued, that Rod was nearly impossible to deal with because he had such high expectations and worked continuously. The pros column went on for several pages, comprised mostly of variations on the themes of surefoot-edness and a love of every combination of rice, potatoes, and lentils—especially leftovers. The con was that he had never been to Nepal. At the end, knowing Rod's insatiable passion for chocolate, he asked, "Would I be interested? Does Rodney Jackson eat M & M's?"

He failed to list a "pro" that wouldn't come to light until much later: He was also a mechanical wizard. But when it came right down to it, Rod asked Gary to join us because he liked him. Although I didn't know him, I liked his sense of humor.

There was one serious drawback to Gary joining the team: Roxy, his wife, was pregnant; their first child would be just three months old the day that Gary would leave for Nepal, and he would not be home for some six months. Quite apart from the no-salary factor, the emotional and practical hardships on all of them would be considerable. As Gary wrestled with his dilemma, Rod and I, facing only a few months' separation, knew how hard his decision must be. Inevitably, the Langu won. It wouldn't be easy on Gary, Roxy, or the daughter they named Morgan. Like many mothers of biologists' children, Roxy would do what she must to accept his decision and to adjust gracefully to staying behind, alone, with their infant daughter. We would do what we could to make it up to her, and in the end she and Morgan had a reward of sorts: They visited Nepal, rode the elephants at Tiger Tops, and fell in love with the country and its people.

Gary brought all that Rod had hoped and more to the effort: as a scientist, he was rigorous, imaginative, and thorough; As a friend, he was amusing and considerate. But he was also something of a loner. Perhaps in self-defense against the isolation, he seemed to embrace the long, solitary days and nights in the Langu, making them his refuge, drawing strength from his own widening boundaries. It worked out nicely: the two of them shared complementary scientific skills, and the three of us, thank God, had compatible personalities.

Only after we had at least one more radio-collared cat would proposals for further funding be seriously considered. With what little was left of the first year's money, Rod could squeeze out three more months of study—a late-fall–early-winter effort.

He and Karan would return to the Langu from November through January, making their base camp beyond Tyson's Cliff at Eding. Access in and out would be easy while the river was low and log bridges could be placed wherever necessary. They would go light, using the regular RNAC plane service to Jumla, and take a minimum of food and gear. For planning purposes, we would assume they would collar at least one more cat during that time, assuring the money to continue.

Gary and I would handle the growing tasks of answering correspondence, submitting requests for equipment donations, and coordinating with funding agencies.

Gary had an additional technical task: Find out how to make and install a suspension bridge with aircraft cable, pulleys, and a seat harness; then beg, borrow, or buy everything we needed, and pack it so it could be carried to the Langu on somebody's back.

I, too, had a special mission: earn the money to pay my way to Nepal, with plane tickets costing fifteen hundred dollars. As a "nonscientist volunteer" team member I would have to cover most of my own expenses, as I had during the first field season. In late February 1983 I presented a slide show in the basement "ballroom" of my former employer's home, inviting everyone I knew to come and pay five dollars. When the evening was over I found two thousand dollars in the kitty and a whole new awareness of just how many friends and how much support I had.

Any other cash contributions we received from individual or corporate donors would go toward a small monthly stipend for Gary. None of the granting agencies would cover salaries for the Western team members, and while Rod and I had stored our furniture and eliminated most of our U.S. bills, Gary, with a family, could not.

The Snow Leopard Project paid the Nepalese camp staff and scientists well and supplied them with all the necessary equipment. This was standard practice, and part of our agreement with the government, but we also felt that it was only fair. It made me furious every time I thought about Kurt and his mistaken idea that Rodney was getting rich at the expense of Nepal and the Nepalis. On the contrary, we were all getting poor, but none of us complained as long as we were getting to do what we wanted.

Rod and Karan would come out of the field at the beginning of February to get the Nepalese visas and other paperwork done in time for Gary's and my arrival in early March. We would then, hopefully, charter a Sky Van to get the whole team and all the gear back in.

The sun was rising over San Francisco International Airport as we checked Rod's bags and found our way to the departure lounge. He groaned to think of the long flight ahead, but despite his too-short break he was anxious to get back into the field and to work on the cats.

"Happy Thanksgiving," he said as we stood lingering at the gate. "Eat a drumstick for me, and a wedge of pumpkin pie."

"We'll set a place for you and carve the Rodney Jackson Memorial Turkey Leg. Or maybe I can find some 'turkey jerky' to bring you—Christmas in March. Hang the turkey; I wish I were going with you."

"Four months," he said. "I'll try to send mail from the field—a telegram if the news is really good."

A quick hug and he was going through the doors, my last glimpse distorted through a wash of unbidden tears. He turned to wave, then vanished quickly into the plane.

The coming weeks would pass quickly for Rod. His days and nights would blur, as he fought his way out of a morass of project paperwork and arranged the details of getting people and food into the study area. Those things always took a lot longer than anyone would guess, partly due to our own ignorance of the system and partly due to the different pace and level of modernization in Nepal.

Although we worked through the DNPWC, we were also subject to rules and policies of other government departments: the Home Ministry for visas and trekking permits; the Customs Department for importing equipment (at least until experience taught us the wisdom of hand-carrying our project gear into the country); the Remote Sensing/Topographic Services for maps; Tribhuvan University for Karan's yearly deputation; the Royal Nepalese Army for aircraft charter; and to the Nepal Rastra Bank for a project account.

The bank was a wonderful example of twentieth-century Dickensian Kathmandu. Clerks wore aprons and green plastic visors. They sat behind iron-barred windows with heaps of thick, dusty, leatherbound ledgers at their feet. Faced with a customer who wished to make a deposit or a withdrawal, the clerk would choose a ledger from the pile, leaf intently through its pages, and then dip his fountain pen into a glass well of blue ink to make the entry.

The Nepalese have a normal workweek of six days, but there are numerous holidays throughout the year that close business offices for up to a week at a time. In addition, any event of national importance can cause impromptu office shutdowns. This is, to my mind, an admirable and highly civilized work ethic, but it doesn't make it any easier to get things done.

Often it was easier and faster to rent a bicycle or hire a taxi and go to a particular office in person rather than try to telephone. In the hotel lobby there might be five people waiting to use the one phone. You wait your turn, pick up the receiver, wait for a dial tone—which can take several minutes—dial the number, and get a busy signal. You repeat the process and get a wrong number. By this time, the person in line behind you is drumming his foot on the floor. On the third try, someone answers who doesn't speak English. You get the hotel receptionist to translate and learn that the person with whom you wish to speak has just stepped out.

With the installation of satellite communications, however, phones are becoming more reliable and common throughout the city.

Rod worked his way relentlessly through his "to-do" list, heedless of the months of loneliness ahead or the thought of holidays occurring halfway around the world. But once they got to the Langu, set up camp, and settled into their routines, he would have few defenses against the pangs of solitude.

I would feel his absence acutely from the moment he boarded the plane. The time passed quickly enough, working in the new and unfamiliar territory of fund-raising. But behind my every waking thought lay the questions: Where is he now? What is he doing? What has happened? Is everything all right?

Things were not to turn out as planned. Before we met again, Rod's resilience would be tested by a new set of circumstances that threatened to bring the project to an abrupt end.

Part

2

November 1982–July 1983

CHAPTER

II

Capture!—"Dui"

Karma's rapid progress with English and his quick grasp of the duties of an expedition camp assistant made it unnecessary to have two Sherpas on the winter staff. Knowing Kirken's attitude toward the Langu and its villagers, Rod asked Lopsang if he was willing to undertake another field season, as sirdar. Lopsang accepted, and agreed to direct Karma in the finer points of Nepali-style "Western" cooking.

The following excerpts from Rod's diary describe his journey to Dolphu, two weeks behind Karan and Lopsang, and the three-month prewinter season they spent in the Langu.

November 26, 1982, Dolphu

On his rooftop terrace, Karma Lama's father, Wangchu, sits, making masks for some religious ceremony from old cloth and clay. Karma Lama's wife is nursing their baby, huge mammaries rolling about, while his mother is mixing some awful-looking potion. From the trail below, the Mukyia, Thondup, calls his greetings. There are few people in the village and no staring faces young or old. We are offered yak's milk, at three rupees (fifty cents) for a tablespoon!

I learn that Karan has established a new camp at an abandoned summer house above Shimbu Gulch, near Dolphu, a departure from our plan. He has taken all our equipment with him, both essentials and nonessentials, complicating my plans for porters into the gorge. I feel a flame of irritation, which I suppress until I find out his reasons.

Karan and Lopsang meet us at the eastern ridge of Pamalang Gulch, Karan particularly happy to see me. Walking up to the Shimbu summer house, he reveals exciting news: Eight or ten days ago, one or perhaps two snow leopards killed a goat and three calves. They would have set traps, but no one knew how to tranquilize the cat, so they waited in frustration. Thondup had said he heard the leopard calling at night. He was sure it was a snow leopard, not a forest leopard.

Over dinner in a warm, surprisingly smoke-free hut, we discuss plans and agree Lopsang should return to Dolphu tomorrow to get our goats and to buy two more.

Although the Shimbu camp is very comfortable, we cannot stay, for it is not well placed for the work at hand. It is impossible for me to radio-track "Ek" from here or Dhukyel. The large bharal herds at Tillisha are too distant to study, and only a few animals forage on the Shimbu slopes. I reiterate my plan to establish a winter base camp on the Langu's southern side, at the place the Dolphas call Eding, directly opposite where Tillisha Canyon meets the Langu on the northern side.

Karan is reluctant to go; he feels it is too far from the relative safety and comfort of the village. There is also the problem of moving all the gear. There had been a dispute over Karma Lama's rental fees for the small room in which we had stored some gear, as well as the disappearance of several items; thus the reason for their bringing all our things to Shimbu.

November 30, 1982, Shimbu

At "Ek's" capture site and along the western terrace, large, fresh tracks suggest the cat had returned to the location of its traumatic experience. Also, a medium-size cat had left three scrapes and a few tracks along the terrace. Had one of these animal killed the calves and goats in Shimbu? My instinct tells me no, that it was more likely a common leopard like the one that we encountered last winter. Even though Thondup may have heard a snow leopard calling, no one had actually seen the leopard at Shimbu.

If I am wrong, such behavior is fairly unusual. Unlike areas such as Pakistan and northern India, where instances of livestock depredation by snow leopards—and retaliation by the villagers—are relatively common, in Nepal they are not. Adult yaks and the cattle with which they are crossbred are generally too big for a snow leopard to bring down, and the cats seldom venture into the villages where the smaller livestock are kept. In the Langu, depredations by the common leopard, a more aggressive predator capable of killing much larger prey, are more likely to incur the villagers' wrath and determination to retaliate. Then little or no thought is given to the possible plight of the leopard; upon obtaining consent and ceremonial blessings from the lamas, they will go to any lengths to destroy it. Such was the fate of Kirken's leopard—either that one or another that was in the area at the same time: The villagers tracked it down and stoned it to death in its lair while it was engorged with yak meat and unable to escape. At such times, the villagers' only thought is the protection of their animals and thus their own survival. It isn't difficult to understand their attitude toward wild predators, when their survival is always balanced so desperately close to the edge. They would treat a raiding snow leopard just the same, except that hardly any Dolphu villager has ever even seen one.

We set more traps at Shimbu, near the Dhukyel trail both baited with a goat.

December 7, 1982, Eding Camp

Training Karan in immobilization procedures was a high priority, and we have spent several mornings going over drugs, dosages, injections, the jabstick. We practiced repeatedly, using a cardboard target. To maximize our trapping efforts, he will remain at Shimbu, as he wishes, sending a runner to fetch me if a leopard is captured.

By establishing this second camp at Eding, I can radio-track "Ek," monitor a further series of traps on the terrace across the river, and make excursions up the ridge toward Tillisha Mountain as well as upstream to Pukchang Confluence. Leopard sign deep in the uninhabited gorge is abundant, and I am highly encouraged.

We passed by Choyap Camp, its grass now golden, the thorny

caragana pinkish-beige, vegetation dormant in the late fall transition. There were our bare-earth tent sites from the summer, Darla's bird watching trail. Feelings of loneliness flooded in—I miss her, even her chronically cold feet pressed like sudden ice cubes against my warm calves!

December 8, 1982

We spend the afternoon cataloging leopard scrapes on Tillisha Terrace, above the high bluff running parallel with the river, and in setting one more trap. Returning, I am amazed to see fresh leopard tracks descending the terrace bluff toward the stream. I followed the solitary pugmarks, evidently a medium-size cat, past the hunters' camp and up the ridge. The cat had walked sixty yards from the goat, missed a terrace trap and the ledge trap! Obviously, more traps are essential if we are to avoid these near-misses by such wily leopards. Karma and I returned later to add one more trap to the ledge trail.

December 12, 1982

As if purely to tantalize me, leopard sign abounds everywhere. Hardly a day goes by without fresh tracks being found. But there is still no signal from "Ek." I have checked Dhukyel, Tillisha, and Pukchang and feel certain he was not in any of those areas, assuming, of course, that the transmitter is still functioning. A check for pugmarks of his size revealed no sign fresher than about three weeks at Dhukyel or Tillisha. Has he shifted his territory? I need to climb Chaling La, which will take two or three days, yet I must stay by the traps—a familiar dilemma. Having Gary here will make all the difference.

December 15, 1982

The second leopard is trapped, on Tillisha Terrace, and I'm still reeling with relief and happiness! An adult female, weighing just sixty pounds. As I write, she has nearly recovered from the ketamine, and for the last twenty minutes has been steadily climbing upward away from her "bad dream," and with the benefit of a nine-hour sleep beneath berberis bushes and juniper trees directly opposite camp.

Early, on a colder morning than usual, I climbed the nearby ridge, and focusing the scope, clearly saw the beautiful cat sitting near the terrace bluff. Yellowish-green eyes met mine, the cat watching my every movement, obviously believing itself to be unseen.

I had an immediate problem. Should I risk the delay incurred in bringing Karan from Shimbu? It would mean the cat would spend a full day in the trap. The welfare of the animal—of paramount importance—simply couldn't justify it. I set about preparing equipment, and coaching Lopsang for the tranquilization, and a few minutes later we headed across the river.

In contrast to "Ek," the immobilization was smoothly undertaken with no significant hitches. I injected a larger dose of drug with the jabstick, and Cat #2, "Dui," was fully sedated in less than eight minutes. She stayed under for nearly thirty minutes.

There was much to do, and Lopsang and I worked quickly. With the tattoo kit retrieved from Customs, we put a #2 in her ear. We also had to check for any wounds; inject Flocillin, a general antibiotic; check temperature and respiration; estimate age based on dentition; remove the trap; attach the collar; examine the paws; take photographs; and take measurements.

All her vital signs remained normal, though she had an extended tongue and some salivation, typical side effects of the ketamine and the relatively large drug dose. Her teeth were moderately yellow, with somewhat blunted canines, which helped me to determine her approximate age of two and a half years. Her gums were lacerated from biting at the trap and bushes, and I administered a topical antibiotic in addition to the internal Flocillin. She did not appear to be pregnant, and the difficulty I had in finding her nipples suggested that she never had been.

I was anxious to leave before she recovered any muscular coordination. During the following three hours, she moved about seventy-five yards upslope to a juniper tree by a large boulder, where she remained out of sight. As she moved slowly up a talus slope, unsteady but on all fours, I marveled at her superb camouflage: smoky-gray spotted pelage tinged with yellow, blending perfectly with the surrounding rubble, impossible to see from three hundred yards away without the aid of a spotting scope.

She moved up, crouching, slipping and stopping every few yards to look around with a blank stare of ketamine sedation, instinctively using bushes and rocks as cover, seeking shelter, where she lay resting until after dark. Then she moved steadily with few rests until 1:00 or 2:00 A.M., onto the top of a ridge. There she rested during the cold early-morning hours, until 6:00 A.M., again traveling up Tillisha Gorge. She covered about a kilometer of steep rocks before bedding for the day, around 10:00 A.M.

We did it! Our grant application depended on today's luck. Now I can send a letter to Kathmandu, asking that Darla be telexed immediately. Surely the future of our study is assured, but my desire to celebrate this second leopard capture is tempered by the knowledge that Karan will be upset that I did not send for him.

In a day "Dui" will be out of receiver range, and already she is bringing to attention the serious problem in the stationing of the team and the fact of two widely separated camps: It is not possible for me to track a ranging cat and monitor the traps at the same time.

Politically, scientifically, and personally, it is critical for Karan to be involved in at least one immobilization and collaring, not to mention tracking. But I find myself completely unwilling to consider leaving a leopard in a trap for the length of time it would take to bring Karan to Eding or Pukchang, or myself to Shimbu. The cats' welfare has to come first.

This has worried me all along, though I was persuaded by Karan's argument—more trapping locations the better—and his intense interest in bharal rutting behavior. Now I will simply have to convince him that his future as well as mine depend upon our ability to get data on snow leopards.

Deactivating the Pukchang traps, I returned to Shimbu with Lopsang to discuss needed changes. Karan was pleased about the capture, yet did not attempt to hide his dejection at not being summoned for it. At the same time, he was completely against packing up the Shimbu camp and moving to Eding, stating that he would go only if I order him to. He would not talk further, and I went to bed wondering how to resolve this serious problem.

In the morning, I discovered that he was even more upset than I realized about not being present for the collaring of "Dui." He felt that not only had I broken my promise to send for him, but I had placed him in a bad position with Wildlife Department officials, who expected him to participate in immobilizing and collaring the cats. Here was an example of something that had been bothering him all along: that I don't keep my word, that I'm always saying one thing and doing another. Why couldn't I make a clear decision and stick to it?

I explained again my dilemma: the necessity of searching for the still-missing "Ek." The inability to keep traps active while working away from Base Camp. I mentioned the good bharal and tahr herds deeper in the gorge and their more direct relationship to the collared snow leopards and the fact that an intense concentration of traps in one area is most likely to catch a cat; I also reminded him that my study area centers on Eding, and if we have to make one camp, then that is where it must be. I didn't want to act like a dictator; I wanted him to share in the decision-making, but also I wanted him to accept that decisions are never cast in concrete; flexibility and adaptability are essential for doing fieldwork. In this instance, I had tried to adapt to his needs, and it hadn't worked. The plan had to change; I had to do what I felt was right for the study as a whole. At last, still reluctantly, he agreed to move.

December 23, 1982

Karan, Karma, and I returned to Eding, leaving Lopsang to follow later with the porters. We removed the Shimbu traps on the way and found signs of another capture and escape. The size of the pugmarks and the fact that the trap stake had been bent suggested to me that it had briefly caught a forest leopard, perhaps the raider of the livestock. But Karan had caught a glimpse of what he was certain was a snow leopard the previous evening, and now he staunchly defended his opinion that this trap had nearly caught it. The brief sighting had vastly improved his mood. "Now I can at least go back to Kathmandu and say I saw a snow leopard, even if we don't catch any more," he had said with a smile.

Lopsang brought thirteen porters carrying the gear from Shimbu. The porters gathered around to put on the earphones and hear "Dui's" signal. They were not impressed, describing the beeping as "tok . . . tok . . . tok."

Young Orkin wrinkled up his forehead and exclaimed, *"Sabu chaina!"* meaning, "That's no snow leopard." One man commented, *"Ah, kaam sidyo"*—"Your work is done."

Now, as I write in the candle glow, I wish in some ways that he was right, that my work was done. Light snow flurries fall intermittently on the peaks, and it is colder than usual. As Christmas approaches, I long for a hot bath; a bottle of wine; and Darla's optimism, bright smile, soft body.

December 30, 1982

Karan has not recovered from his depression at leaving Shimbu. He finds it very difficult to cross the Langu on our log bridges, to climb up the steep slopes, or to walk long distances carrying the equipment necessary for his work. He has little experience of the rigors that make up the life of a field biologist, and he seems to have little interest in exploring, or pushing, his physical limits. Rather, he feels that I have selected the wrong study area; that if we cannot all work here without fears for our personal safety, then we should be somewhere else. What can I do? There isn't anywhere else that's any safer and still has snow leopards. I get irritated with his unwillingness to challenge himself, especially since I, too, have had to overcome many fears. I wonder how we can ever resolve this critical conflict.

January 9, 1983, Eding

January 7 was a disaster for Lopsang. He and I set off for Dhukyel to clear a dangerous trail section for Karma, who was expected back shortly from Jumla.

Near Choyap, Lopsang climbed a riverside boulder, checking it for possibilities as a future bridge anchor. Without thinking, he jumped down, facing forward, hoping to land by his heels on a small piece of jutting rock lower down on the boulder. His boots slipped and the next minute blood was spurting everywhere, Lopsang nearly knocked out by the impact of his teeth hitting the ice ax he was holding in his hand.

He felt his mouth—a big gap where two teeth had disappeared—and started to wail, flailing his hands against rocks, whimpering, "Oh, God,

I have lost my teeth." I grabbed his arms and pulled him toward camp and medical attention. He refused to come, crying. He finally calmed down enough to begin the thirty-minute walk, silent now, though I kept reassuring him his teeth could be replaced. As evidence, I showed him my own dental plate, the result of a childhood encounter with a baseball bat.

The pain, physical and emotional, must have been great, and poor Lopsang dove immediately into the solitude of his tent. Karan and I inspected the damage and gave him a strong pain-killer: Two teeth had been broken in half and one was loose, almost ready to fall out. He would have to leave for Kathmandu, but he was very reluctant to go, pointing out that he would have trouble finding a porter to go with him since Dolphu was busy preparing for Tibetan New Year; that the plane at Jumla would be full and he would never get a ticket on his own; that he would be okay for the ten days until we would all leave; and finally, in desperation, that he was too weak to walk.

I couldn't help but recall Tsang Tenzing and his night of prophecy regarding our Lopsang. If he delayed getting treatment, the long-term effects might be serious, and I certainly didn't want that to be added to his misfortunes.

In the end, I convinced him it would be best to go, that he would not be causing us undue trouble. I thought surely he would find one man in Dolphu willing to accompany him to Jumla. As he left, he broke down in tears once again.

That afternoon, I met Karma on the trail. He had made the round trip in just thirteen days, walking through knee-deep snow on Gurchi and Danphe and waiting out two days of bad weather in Dolphu. He had delivered my telegram and our outgoing mail, but there had been no letters waiting for us—a big disappointment to me, for my homesickness is becoming acute.

I was to leave for Chaling La today with Sonam, to look for "Ek," but something is bothering him, too. He faked a leg injury and is most reluctant to go. He gives reasons—he will walk like a cripple, he will freeze to death—but it is likely that Lopsang's accident affected him psychologically and superstitiously.

January 13, 1983

A leopard has again walked within a yard of the Muga trap. I immediately placed two more out, taking hours to find places where the metal stakes would go in the ground. We have only a week left, and I desperately want another cat.

Next morning, loud signals warned of a captured cat on Tillisa West terrace. "Dui" had crossed the stream, avoiding the traps the first time, but then had returned, perhaps attracted by the "bobcat potion" (a commercially bottled scent lure, popular with sport hunters), and got herself retrapped.

Finally, Karan had an opportunity to perform an immobilization. Taking Sonam, eyes aglow with "hunt fever," we made our way across the Langu. We loaded the jabstick and Karan moved toward "Dui," who hissed and spat and growled. Sonam, alarmed, grabbed Karan's arm to prevent him from moving closer and getting hurt. Only a little of the drug went in, and I followed it with another injection.

She was down for fifteen or twenty minutes. Measurements not taken last time were performed, photos taken, and the cat released. She moved to some rocks about two hundred yards away, resting until around 2:00 A.M. the next morning. Then she hightailed it for the slopes of Chaling La and Pukchang. Today we will follow.

Karan was ecstatic: The third immobilization in the wild was performed by a Nepali. Of his comments, one especially stands out in my mind: "It is easy to read and write what should be done; the practice is very difficult." Truer words were never spoken!

Karan's mood is greatly improved after "Dui's" second capture, and with Lopsang gone he and I should be having talks in the evening around the kitchen fire. His attention is no longer captured by the Sherpa's familiar Nepali conversation, and I wish we could establish a more companionable relationship. But there is still a wall between us that neither of us seems able to penetrate.

Perhaps my obsession with work is part of the problem. I find it difficult to banter, to tell stories or jokes, and I don't enjoy the card games that I've often watched the others playing in the evenings. In my past research work there has always been a great deal of discussion: what methods work best and what kind of results were emerging as the research progressed. Naturally, I expected the same free exchange of ideas to develop with Karan. But for him this is an alien way of learning, vastly different from the rote method by which Asian students are taught, and I think he just feels threatened when I ask him questions, as if he's being tested or put on trial. If we both gave in a little more, tried harder to get to know one another, perhaps we could make more of this opportunity, here alone, to become friends.

Our hopes for catching another cat face an imminent deadline, but I am ready to leave despite good success at data-gathering. There has been no news from home for three months, and I want to see Darla.

January 22, 1983, Dolphu

As we left the study area, we pulled up the Muga and Dhukyel bridges, saving the long logs for future use. Too much effort had been expended in felling and shaping them to let the Langu carry them off "to India" with the spring snowmelt.

At Dhukyel I lay in bed listening to "Dui's" "tok-tok" as she walked along the broken cliffs below Choyap. I wondered why we hadn't caught more cats. After all, there was no shortage of snow leopards in the area. The failure of the southern side traps could simply be ascribed to bad luck; several cats had been briefly caught but worked their way out of the snare. Trapping sites on the northern side were limited by access up- and downstream, but with Gary's help we would be able to cover a broader area in the spring. Hopefully, funding would be assured by the collaring of "Dui," and we could work to improve our trapping techniques.

Again, I considered the obstacle topography has posed to our study in substantially limiting our ability to "follow in her tracks," to find prey remains, to catalog scrapes made in a known time frame by a known individual.

With its large paws; short, stout limbs; powerful muscles; and long tail, the snow leopard is well adapted to moving across precipitous cliffs, smooth ledges, or loose talus. The name "rock leopard," if less romantic, is more descriptive for the species.

I had one final contact with "Dui" for the season, made as we crossed the Pamalang Ridge overlooking Dolphu, and over my last piece of "birthday cake," one of Lopsang's specialties, a tasty sweetened quick-bread made with nuts and bits of dried fruit. With a line of sight far up the gorge, the signal came in loud and clear. I wish I were a chough or lammergeier, adept at overcoming gravity and hurtling upward on a thermal, or upcanyon on the lower echelon of the jet stream!

CHAPTER

12

Permission Denied

From Rod's diary:

February 6, 1983, Kathmandu

Arrived this morning, near-freezing, and made my way to the Kathmandu Guest House, anticipating my first hot shower in months. Alas, there was no water, hot or cold—the pumps were out of order! I settled instead for a cup of "cappuccino" at K.C.'s and set off to see the folks at Tiger Tops.

I had had no mail since leaving in November. Waiting for me in the office of John Edwards, General Manager of Tiger Tops, was a pile of letters and a telex from Darla. When I opened the telex and read, ". . . National Geographic funds, in hand, $34,016.00," John had to dash behind his desk to avoid getting kissed!

With the collaring of "Dui," the National Geographic Society's Committee for Research and Exploration had approved Rod's application. National Geographic would continue to provide about half of each year's budget, with the balance coming from the International Trust for Nature Conservation, the New York Zoological Society, the World Wildlife

Fund-US, and a variety of other conservation organizations and individuals. Such financial support was an affirmation of Rod's improved credibility, but along with it there were also words of encouragement and support from established and well-respected wildlife authorities.

But that day, begun on such a high note, was to end in despair. A bombshell fell—one that brought Rod close to canceling the project. The application for Gary was denied, and though I had been given an official visa the previous year, it would not be renewed.

The fact was that we should never have been allowed into the Langu in the first place. Lying within twenty-five miles of the Tibetan border, it was included in Nepal's "Restricted Zone" and therefore was off-limits to foreigners.

Upheaval and turmoil feature largely in present-day Tibet, and its culture is highly threatened. In the so-called Cultural Revolution the Chinese all but wiped out the Buddhist shrines and monasteries in Tibet, forcing the Dalai Lama, the Buddhist spiritual leader, into exile. The underlying issues in this territorial battle are complicated and ancient. Today the arid, barren, and windswept region still is governed by the People's Republic of China, but the Tibetan people are proving that they will not willingly abandon their independence, their historic Tibetan Buddhist religion, and their loyalty to their exiled Dalai Lama.

True, we were in Nepal, not Tibet, but the more radical members of some border tribes tend to make their opposition to Chinese rule fiercely and actively known. In the past they have roamed the northern mountains, sometimes skirmishing with the Nepalese Bhotes and creating unsafe conditions for tourists. Although no recent conflicts had been reported from Mugu District, Rod's 1976 visit had been approved by mistake. The oversight was carried through when our initial visas were issued, but now the Langu's restricted status had come to light, and with that discovery the project's future was suddenly in extreme jeopardy.

As mentioned previously, the Snow Leopard Project was administered by the DNPWC, a subdivision of the Forestry Ministry. Major planning and decision-making were supervised by the Royal Palace Wildlife

Committee, headed by His Highness Prince Gyanendra, Nepal's Patron of Conservation.*

The Royal Palace Wildlife Committee had welcomed the Snow Leopard Project. His Majesty's government was anxious to promote sincere efforts to preserve the cats and their fragile Himalayan habitat. Because of the National Geographic Society's involvement, newspaper articles had been published in Nepal, in the United States, and elsewhere around the world. It was clear that the Snow Leopard Project would attract worldwide attention and that it could not be terminated without loss of national esteem. But the Langu *was* restricted. If an exception to the rule was made for our group, then a precedent would be set, and other Western scientists and adventurers would beleaguer the Home Ministry begging for permits to visit those immensely intriguing, forbidden areas of northern Nepal.

While Rod and Karan had spent their winter in the Langu, a compromise was proposed in Kathmandu. By substituting two Nepalese for Gary and me, Rod would be the only foreigner in the restricted area.

Rod knew that there were no qualified Nepali biologists available and that there was no time to train anyone, even if someone could be found who was willing to accept the physical difficulties. The training of Nepalese biologists in field study techniques was admittedly an important aspect of the project, but he simply could not give another trainee the attention he would require. As it was, he was being pulled in too many directions. In addition to radio-tracking, he had to perform the jobs of administrator, teacher, accountant, diplomat/politician, and fund-raiser.

In fairness to our sponsors, the original study goals had to come first. Even with qualified help, the radio-tracking itself was more than a full-time job.

When the committee heard Rod's argument *in absentia,* they made a further concession, reluctantly agreeing to admit me, quietly and unoffi-

---

*Nepal's first non-governmental conservation organization, The King Mahendra Trust for Nature Conservation, was formed near the end of the Snow Leopard Project, and administration of our project was then shared between the DNPWC and the new trust.

141

cially, but maintained their stance that an additional Western scientist was out of the question.

Late at night, a few days before Gary and I were due to get on the plane, I got a phone call from Rod in Kathmandu. His voice broke as he relayed the news that had kept him awake for several nights.

"I've done everything I know to do," he said. "I'm sorry to lay the job of telling Gary on you. I feel like giving up, myself. There's no way I can take on another student, not without jeopardizing my data-gathering. Besides, it wouldn't be fair to Gary, who has given so much already. You should come ahead as planned, but don't be surprised if I cancel the whole thing."

Rod, despondent, turned to John Edwards and his Tiger Tops "moral support brigade," and not for the last time, John saved the day. Long experienced in interpreting the mysterious ways of the Nepalese bureaucracy, he produced a bottle of good Scotch, unhooked his phone, cleared his desk of its chronically urgent papers, and sat Rodney down for a pep talk rich in wisdom, candor, and encouragement.

"Don't give up," he urged finally, "You have too much invested to end it now. Okay, you lost a round today, but the issue isn't closed forever." He made a suggestion that at first seemed unlikely to have any effect but that in the end made all the difference.

Rod sent a telex asking me to bring a selection of the Langu slides, recently processed and duplicated for our use by National Geographic, to Nepal. Meanwhile, he and the people at Tiger Tops organized an evening gathering of everyone in Kathmandu who had an official interest in the project.

Karna Sakya, owner of the Kathmandu Guest House, author of *Dolpo: The World Behind the Himalayas,* and ardent Nepalese conservationist, reiterated John's advice:

"Your work is important to Nepal," he stressed. "Hang in there, Rodney. Tomorrow the whole picture could change for you."

The presentation was held a day or two after I arrived, and when Rod showed the slides, it was clear that despite all our verbal attempts to describe the study area, no one involved in revoking our permits had been fully aware of the Langu's harsh conditions and Rod's justification in asking for help.

As slide after slide flashed upon the screen—perpendicular cliffs; snow-covered mountains; steep hillsides of barren earth and rock; and wobbly log bridges spanning the brown, turbulent river—the audience felt the full impact of the Langu's vastness and remoteness, and the strength and endurance of the villagers who made their homes in that seemingly hopeless, inhospitable land.

"How," asked a Forestry Department official, "can anyone *live* in such a place?"

In the audience were two of our Nepalese friends, Hemanta and Susma Mishra. Hemanta had the ability, if he chose to use it, to act in Rodney's favor. But a great deal of effort would be required in Rod's case, and a sign hanging in his office mirrored Hemanta's reluctance to involve himself:

Getting things done around here is like mating elephants: (1) it's done at a high level, (2) it's accompanied by a lot of roaring and screaming, and (3) it takes two years to get any results.

We had spent an evening in the Mishras' home, sharing a delicious curry dinner, but Rod had been unsuccessful at convincing Hemanta to help.

Susma also was a scientist, and it was clear that Hemanta loved, admired, and greatly respected her. I watched her, sitting serene and lovely through the slide show. Even then she seemed somewhat celestial, radiating the Nepalese virtues of compassion and a great love of peace. That night, on their way home from the slide show, she asked a simple question of Hemanta, seven words that turned the tide for the Snow Leopard Project.

"Why don't you help that Rodney Jackson?" In the discussion that followed, Susma herself convinced him to take on Rodney's problem. At least that's the way we heard the story several months later.

With time, Gary would be given permission. Hemanta would let him know by mail that the wheels were once again in motion for him to join us. We would leave for the Langu thinking that he would arrive shortly, but the sign in Hemanta's office was more accurate in Gary's case than anyone would have guessed. It was to be four months before we saw him again—four months in which we had no way of knowing how things were unfolding in Kathmandu and the United States.

CHAPTER

13

Lovers

The day before I left San Francisco, Gary had brought over all the bridge-building equipment. But in his bitter disappointment at being denied permission to join us, he had not written down what he had learned about the construction. I arrived in Kathmandu with two big spools of aircraft cable and several bags of hardware, among other things in the eight duffel bags that made up my luggage. Rod emptied the bags of bridge hardware onto the floor of our Guest House room. He arranged each group of like pieces into small piles and attempted to assign a purpose to each.

We spent our last day in Kathmandu with members of a Canadian expedition, sketching out a "working drawing" of what parts went where and how best to use them.

Lopsang would not be coming back to the Langu. In his place would be Nema, a Sherpa in his thirties who had spent several years on Colonel Jimmy Roberts' pheasant research farm near Pokhara. Nema was to prove an extremely capable and reliable sirdar who did not let his opinion of western Nepal interfere in his dealings with the village or his running of the camps. His warm smile had etched deep squint lines around his brown eyes, and he seemed at peace with himself and his surroundings.

Though he was accustomed to separations from his wife and four children, in the coming months he would feel acutely the Langu's particular isolation, from which even our Sherpa guides were not immune. For the Sherpas, I think the crux of the problem was the lack of interaction, socially and professionally, with people who held them in high regard. They got it in Kathmandu, and along the regular tourist trekking routes. Indeed, throughout most of Nepal, there is a deeply entrenched respect for the Sherpa people. They seemed to measure self-esteem by the prestige they were accorded, but in the far West of Nepal, where the Bhotes had no tradition of dealing with Sherpas, they were treated just like any other outsider. Nema seemed to work it out in his daily prayers, in the blue-gray incense of burning juniper, in the flags and chortens with which he graced our camp.

As if to balance out our recent difficulties with some good luck, the Sky Van was arranged without a hitch, and it flew us on schedule to Jumla on March 14, 1983. We were treated once again to hot sweet coffee and the spectacular snow peaks of Nepal's famous mountains from our winged green "VW." The weather was perfect, and we touched down to a sunny Jumla Valley.

At the airport we were greeted by the Wangri woman Guru.

"You won't find Karma in his village," she informed us. "He's taken a Mangri man's wife and eloped to Surkhet."

"He's done *what*?" said Rodney, speaking to Karan, who was interpreting Guru's brow-furrowed gossip.

Karan couldn't help laughing at first. This form of "kidnapping" wasn't all that odd in Nepal's "Wild West," except for the fact that Karma already had one wife.

Karma was supposed to choose a go-between who would arrange compensation to the husband, usually money. Until the debt was paid, neither Karma nor the wife would dare go near Mangri. According to village law their lives were in the hands of the husband and any friends or family members who may choose to be his avengers, and that could be the whole village, for if there is one thing they all love, it's a good scandal.

Once compensation was made, the lovers would be safe. But it was widely known that *our* lovers were anything but safe. Karma had neither a go-between nor the cash to make the exchange. He had given all his project wages to his father.

"Just bloody terrific" was about all Rod could say. Not only had Karma opened a huge can of worms for himself, he also had left us quite in the lurch. We had counted on him as cook for this season, and to arrange reliable and trustworthy porters to get us to Dolphu. Also, we really needed the pressure cooker he had stored at his house. You couldn't buy a pressure cooker in Jumla, at any price. There weren't any trained expedition cooks in Jumla either. Who could we get to take his place? How could Nema manage on his own in unfamiliar territory? And *what* was Karma planning to do?

"He's lost his mind," said Rod. "Surely he doesn't think we'll just take him back when he decides the coast is clear."

"If he *is* planning on coming back," I said, "how will he get past Mangri? The way news travels on the Mugu Trail grapevine, they'll know we're back and everyone will be on the lookout. He must *really* be in love to take such a risk of getting fired—or maimed."

Wangri Guru knew a good thing when she saw it. She suggested to Karan that Cinon, her oldest son, might step in to help Nema. Since his father had died, he was the man of the family, and he turned out to be a fine, responsible young fellow of about eighteen, on whom we would call regularly for part-time help in the months to come.

Guru was with a whole group of Wangri people, and they were all willing and eager to interrupt their work to carry our loads to Dolphu.

Seven of the porters were Jumlis, not so strong as the Bhotes in either will or stamina, but we had promised them jobs before we discovered that all the Wangris were in town, and we couldn't go back on our word. The Wangri Bhotes—two of whom were carrying double loads of about 140 pounds—referred to them disparagingly as "the Nepalis."

We left Jumla on March 18 at the usual late hour of 10:30 A.M. The sky had clouded up, and it started to snow just before we began the ascent of Danphe Lekh. We made a crude camp right where we were, to avoid being caught on the windswept crest.

The spring storm passed quickly, but intermittent rain and snow were to follow us all the way. I had given my heavy leather boots to Karma, whose feet were the same size as mine, and this time I'd brought only lightweight boots and running shoes. It was one of the best things I ever did, for never again did I experience the agony of blistered feet, no matter how far or hard we might travel.

Making the long ascent up Ghurchi Lekh, we arrived at the Bulbule teahouse, near the crest of the pass, just ahead of an intense overnight storm. Other travelers were there before us. In the two squalid structures there was one room available: space for six at a pinch, and we were thirty-one, with twenty-seven loads and four backpacks.

A cow shelter back down the trail seemed to be a possible shelter for the porters, and so dumping the loads in the teahouse "public area," they went to investigate. We were loath to pitch the tents, fearing that the howling wind would rip them to shreds. Icy sleet was blowing horizontally up the mountain. We thought the back room might do as an alternative for Rod and me, Karan and Nema, plus the old man who had gotten there first. As we were discussing the matter, all the Wangris came trooping back. They refused to share the cramped cow shelter with "the Nepalis," and anyway it wasn't much of a shelter.

So much for Rod and me sleeping inside; during a lull he and Cinon pitched one tent on the roof. Karan remained indoors.

"I would prefer to be squashed like a sardine in this smoky room rather than squashed in my tent by a falling pine tree," he remarked. To this day we do not know where or how he, Nema, and the twenty Wangri porters slept that night.

It's quite likely that they *didn't* sleep, for out of the storm around dinnertime appeared the familiar form and voice of our Karma. The porters' passion for gossip probably kept them up all night needling him for the details of his adventures.

Rodney and I certainly couldn't get much out of him. He explained briefly that he had been "delayed" by a sick porter he had hired to help him bring rice for his family from Surkhet, that otherwise he would have met us in Jumla on time. He had met a Wangri villager on the trail below Jumla, and learning that he was in big trouble with Ronney-Sah'b, had taken a shortcut via Sinja to catch up with us.

Rod let him know he wasn't yet *out* of trouble, but for the time, no mention was made of Mangri, money, or women. That could wait until tomorrow, away from the suddenly large Bhote ears all tuned to our conversation.

In the morning, Rod suggested that Karma return to Jumla, get the pressure cooker and other things stored at his house, and make his way to Dolphu, keeping a low profile. Already, one could almost feel the grapevine humming, the amazing verbal communication system that moves information between Jumla (if not Nepalganj) and the remote mountain villages. But waiting at home were a father *and* a "first" wife, neither, presumably, in much better mood than Mangri, and nothing would persuade Karma to face his family.

The storm, a little less intense, was still blowing, but there was no question of staying another night in that awful place. We prodded and poked the Bhotes into activity. The Nepalis, reluctant in the extreme, came up late, and we set off up the last stretch of exposed meadow. Once we crested the pass, the wind was magically and wonderfully cut off, and we made the long, long, steep descent in light, intermittent snow, looking forward to a comfortable, warm lunch stop at the bottom.

With the high passes behind us, we made good time in the following two days. We would have to bypass Mangri. Fortunately, it sat on a high hill, on a branch of the main trail. Most travelers climbed up to overnight in the village. As we approached closer and closer to the trail junction, our line of marching men and women turned more and more of their attention to Karma. All eyes watched, twinkling, as he struggled to maintain his "Mr. Cool" image.

The loose muscle in his left cheek defied his attempts at control, twitching and vibrating faster with every step closer to Mangri. A Mangri man approached and nearly passed us by before calling out to Karma and chuckling in a most unpleasant way.

Karma stopped at the next bend in the trail and put down his load. Off came the brown jogging pants Kirken had given him, revealing a second pair of blue Nepali-style baggy trousers. On went Nema's blue windbreaker. Around his head went an orange and white dish towel, wrapped like a turban. Thus disguised, he still looked just like Karma. He might have known he would get no mercy from our group as we "sneaked"—now thirty-two in number—along the Jumla trail, attempting to hide him among the line of porters.

We camped in a little-used trailside shelter, Rod and I fully expecting a horde of kukri-wielding vigilantes to descend in the night. Whether or not Karma got any sleep, he was still alive and in one piece in the morning, and we wasted no time in moving off, under a blue sky and a hot sun.

At lunchtime we stopped by a stream and washed our socks and bathed for the first time since Kathmandu. I envied the men, who simply stripped down to their underpants and stood in the water, giving themselves a complete wash. I had to do it away from the others, if I could find a place, and even then awkwardly, under a too-small towel. I should have brought a dress that would do for the purpose, as I'd seen women of the low-lying areas wearing. But still, there comes a point when any kind of bath is better than none!

Now all that remained was to coax the Nepalis over the Kartik-Dolphu Trail—no easy task. Pointing at the cliff edge, rolling their eyes, and clutching their throats, tongues hanging out, they begged just one last cigarette from Rod before facing certain death. They got the cigarette.

We arrived in Dolphu well before lunchtime on the twenty-fifth. Receiving their pay, the Nepalis left for Jumla immediately, not even stopping to eat. They said they would make the return trip in three and a half days, so badly did they want to be back in their own familiar homes. For our part, "home" was the farthest thing from our minds. We were eager to plunge in the opposite direction, deep into the gorge, to contact "Ek" and "Dui," and to see if we could cross the Langu on a bridge of aircraft cable.

CHAPTER

14

Capture!—"Tin"

By the beginning of April, Rod, Nema, and I were set up at Eding Camp, with Karan, Cinon, and Karma working at Dhukyel. Though traps were out at both camps, radio-tracking would have to wait while the two critical bridges were quickly installed at Dhukyel and Eding before the river rose. Though we found several possibilities, none of the sites was exactly right: Either the span was quite long, or the trees rather small. Without Gary to consult, Rod was reluctant to try bolting into rocks, and we hadn't enough cable to wrap around any of the big boulders at the river's edge.

I didn't think much of Rodney playing bridge engineer with the kind of "crash" course he'd had in Kathmandu as his sole reference, apart from a hastily scrawled note from Gary about how many thousands of pounds of stress the average person will place on each end of the cable when he or she travels across. "Be sure it's anchored well," he wrote, "and you'd better leave some slack."

Rod kept clutching his temples and saying things like, "I wish I knew what the hell I'm doing," and "I sure wish Gary were here."

I made myself scarce during the construction. But when they got the first cable up and ready for the test, I had to get the camera and not only watch, but also be sure to get dramatic pictures.

First Rod sent a duffelful of rocks across. The spindly young trees to which the cable was fixed seemed to take the load all right. They hauled the duffel back, and Nema stepped forward saying, "Let me try, sah'b." Rod, remembering the rafting episode, replied, "No, if anyone is going to get dumped in the river, it's going to be me this time."

He buckled the seat harness around his waist and clipped the big, oval mountaineer's carabiner from the sling to the pulley. He tested his weight on the cable, bouncing once or twice with his feet off the ground. Everything felt secure. Sending a farewell wave through the air between us, he pushed himself off the bank with a great leap, coasted out to midstream, and reached for the towrope. It seemed to take forever for him to work his way across, hauling on the rope, dangling over the water like a fish on a hook. But he made it; he turned around and launched himself again, this time sailing down the slanted cable in a free glide all the way across. He landed with a big grin. "It's fun," he declared. "Better than Disneyland." There was no way the villagers would go anywhere near such a flimsy-looking setup. They were convinced that Rod was demented; they went back to Dolphu with tales of the "mad sah'b." Even Karan refused to take a turn.

"I'm heavier than you," he said to Rod, but the real reason slowly came out. He had a phobia about drowning, only slightly less intense than his fear of heights. Even the log bridges had given him nightmares. If Tyson's Cliff was not enough, the cable bridge confirmed his determination to stay away from Eding when the river was high. He so hated the thought of being "stranded" in the gorge that he would do everything in his power to come no closer than Dhukyel.

Early on the morning on April 4, while Rod was at Dhukyel working on the second cable bridge, Cinon came rushing into Eding, shouting to Nema and me that a leopard had been caught at Dhukyel. He thrust a message into my hands from Rod telling us to bring the cameras and the drugging gear and come as fast as we could.

The three of us raced back along the trail, arriving at Dhukyel in midmorning. The leopard was trapped on the terrace west of the stream, opposite where "Ek" had been trapped a year and a day before. We approached to a large concealing boulder, where we stopped to prepare the blowpipe syringe with the drug.

Karan and I followed as Rod crept slowly toward the trapsite. Suddenly Rod straightened and stiffened; the trap was empty, the leopard gone, a circle of demolished bushes and grasses all that was left behind. The cat had been there when they had looked eight minutes earlier.

Karan had been first up that morning to check the traps—the sites he had chosen and the traps he and Rod had set together. Delighted and proud to find his first success, he called Rod.

"What to do? Shall we tranquilize and collar it now, or send to Eding?" he asked.

Rod wanted to give the blowpipe another try, after discussions with the manufacturer about its problems. It and some of the other equipment they needed to do the full examination and record-taking were in Eding. And we badly needed more photographs.

Still, he and Karan could immobilize and collar the cat; the emergency kit was there for that. Was it an emergency? How securely was the cat trapped? That was the key.

We had brought new stakes from Kathmandu, made from shorter rebar (metal concrete-reinforcing bars), to see if they'd be easier to place in the stony soil, but they had used the old long ones, and Karan said that he had pounded them into firm ground.

They approached to within thirty feet of the trapped cat, and Rod could see that the cable had caught well above the cat's paw; the two inches of stake showing aboveground were no more than on the other two occasions. The cat looked to be in good condition in no danger of overstress or injury. Rod made the decision to wait the two and a half hours, and Cinon was dispatched to Eding.

It was easy to say, looking at the empty trap, that that was the wrong decision. The cat had worked the stake out of the ground and escaped, dragging it, with the cable around its foreleg, across the terrace and up Dhukyel Canyon, where vertical cliffs rise hundreds of feet on either side.

For a mile upstream we followed the track, Cinon's hunting skills coupled with Rod's desperation, until the trail of dragging metal vanished on impossible cliffs.

Rod leaned against the hard rock, and tears joined the sweat streaking his face. "What have I done?" he said with a groan. "I don't know what kind of a chance that cat has, and there's nothing I can do to help it."

I took his hand, having no words to ease his remorse, and we walked back to camp, where we found Karan sitting by the hearth, equally disheartened and apprehensive.

"We will have to let the Wildlife Department know what has happened," he said. "If we can't prove that the leopard will survive, then meetings will be held to determine if the dangers in trapping snow leopards outweigh the benefits of being able to radio-track them."

"I know," Rod replied. "Right now we can't prove anything. All we can do is double the stakes at every trapsite and pray that it doesn't happen again."

He took a stake and snare from the trapping kit and began to experiment with the cable. He found that with the loose stake offering little resistance, he could work the cable off his wrist without using his hands. But what if the stake got wedged in the rocks above Dhukyel? Dragging from the eye end as it was, the chances of that were slim, but if it did, then it would be the cat whose chances were slim. We could never find it, even with climbing gear, among the perpendicular cliffs of Dhukyel.

"If it can't get the snare off, it'll have a hard time hunting," Rod continued. "We'd better put goats out, with traps all around. If it gets hungry enough, it may come back—if it doesn't altogether leave the area."

It was too late to return to Eding, and we made our bed under the stars, drawing small comfort from the ease with which Rod had been able to remove the cable from his wrist. In the following weeks, Rod found tracks of the correct size around Dhukyel, and new activity at the scrape sites—reasonable indications that the cat freed itself from the snare and stake.

"Dui" ventured down the cliffs opposite Choyap one day, to take a drink from the Langu. She left clear tracks in the wet river sand, and we got our first chance to make plaster casts of wild snow leopard tracks. Rod, ranging upriver as far as Pukchang, was still unable to recontact "Ek."

As Rod emerged from our tent in the early-morning calm of April 21, he looked up on the terrace to see bushes waving wildly.

"Ohmi*god*, we've got another leopard!" he called as he ran for the storage shed, where the spotting scope was kept.

In minutes the three of us had grabbed the gear and made our way one by one over the cable bridge, across Tillisha Stream, and up the terrace bluff. When the syringe was ready, Rod and I approached, to find another empty trap. The cable snare lay twisted and broken beside the metal stake, still buried to the hilt in the hard yellow ground.

Rod knelt to examine the snare. The cat had twisted it several times around the eye of the stake; the loop was bent and kinked, but a whole new factor had allowed it to escape. The small block of metal, clamped on to the end of the cable, was gone—broken or pulled off. Without it, the snare was useless; there was nothing to keep it looped. Rod stood up, looking down the empty trail.

"I just don't see how a cat could have done that. Are they so strong, or are my traps inadequate?" he asked. The ground was hard from the cold night, and there was no sign of where the cat went, but it was no doubt up, up, onto the cliffs, well away from Tillisha Terrace.

Out of seven captures, four cats had escaped. Two of those were inadequately snared to begin with; their reflexes were quicker than the spring and cable. Some of that was to be expected, but two escapes were directly attributable to faults in the system.

Rod had been certain that the leghold snare was the best of all the options, both for its likelihood of success and for the welfare of the cat. Only by radio-collaring the cats could enough information about their habits be collected to attempt to preserve them and their habitat. Other big cats, even delicate-boned fox, had been harmlessly but securely trapped by this method. But now Rod's confidence in it was seriously undermined.

With the materials available to us in the Langu, we could never have built a strong enough box trap. Anyway, it seemed unlikely that a cat could be enticed to enter a box. Rod would simply have to modify the snare system during our next summer break.

Rod and Nema crossed the Eding cable to set the last of our traps on Tillisha Terrace. They followed small, fresh cat tracks up the bluff trail. There was a fresh scrape at the place were the big cat had escaped on the twenty-first; and farther on, at the last trap, they found the scene of yet another escape.

The leopard had not been caught very long; the bushes were barely disturbed, and there were no kinks in the cable—only a few hairs left clinging to the wires. It had rained in the night, and beaded silt in the pugmarks indicated that the trap had been sprung around 2:00 or 3:00 A.M.

We were glad to see the end of April, hoping that May would bring a turn of events and a lift to our sunken spirits. There still was no signal from "Ek."

Rod made a run to Pukchang Cave, tracking "Dui," and saw a pair of Brahminy mynas, birds we thought were a record sighting for our area. They weren't; the birds' range has been greatly extended since the second edition of *Birds of Nepal*. But I wanted a chance to see them, too, and we planned to go back the following afternoon to look.

We didn't see the mynas. We didn't get to Pukchang. We got as far as Eding Knoll, where we stopped to do the usual binoc search for bharal. We found a herd on the slopes opposite, and Rod was setting up the scope to classify them when Nema appeared, sweating.

"Rodney, Didi, come quickly—I found one big leopard! Tillisha trap exactly catch him!"

"Oh, God," said Rod. "Here we go again." We were off and running before Nema got the words out of his mouth.

He'd gone across the river, onto Tillisha Terrace. Cresting the bluff, he found a cat busy trying to get out of the trap. Two leaps got him back down the seventy-five-foot bluff, or so he said. He stood at the mouth of Tillisha Canyon, whistling to us and waving his jacket like a wind-whipped flag. We were too far away to have heard him over the noise of the river, and neither of us happened to look back at camp.

He made it back over the river, not bothering to buckle the seat sling, past camp on the run, up across the landslide and to the knoll in something less than fifteen minutes.

Now here I was trailing the others, last as usual, hating the unstable earth and rocks of the great landslide, slipping and sliding as fast as I could over boulders perched treacherously in the path.

I allowed myself just one thought: "Stay trapped, cat; please, stay trapped." I knew from sad experience that to give in now to the persistent waves of excitement could be a setup to crushing disappointment.

Rod crossed over the Langu first and hurried to climb the bluff while the rest of us took turns on the cable.

I made my way slowly across Tillisha Stream, holding my breath—and then there was Rod, nodding and beckoning.

"Yes, it's still there," he murmured. "Get the cameras ready; I'll load the drugs here. It may be yesterday's escapee. Let's be quick."

There was no question of keeping cool, both of us now pleading with the unseen cat not to get away as we did our best to scramble quietly up the bluff.

It was raining. Not hard, but misty-wet, with low clouds. Nema waited just below the terrace edge; Rod and I continued up. The trap was only a few feet from the top of the trail, and Rod, carrying the blowpipe, went quickly. The leopard lay right at the edge of the terrace, the drop abrupt. As Rod maneuvered for position and I maneuvered for pictures, the cat lunged, snarled, and growled low in its throat, showing ivory teeth in a blood-red mouth.

On the opposite ridgeline, above Tillisha Stream, seven langurs watched, wild with nervous excitement, screeching and chattering and bounding from boulder to boulder.

I heard Rod's heavy puff of breath and saw the syringe fly out of the pipe and stick in the cat's flank. We moved back, motioning Nema to come up.

But again, for some reason the syringe didn't deliver the drug; we found it later, still full. We had a makeshift jabstick carved from a tree branch, and with that Rod moved in again for a second try. He had to be careful not to injure the cat by sticking the needle in its ribs, or worse, but it wasn't easy. The animal lunged around, twisting and turning—only inches from the edge of the bluff drop-off. On the third try the cat finally went down, wide eyes blank, the tip of his tongue protruding.

The cat was firmly trapped at the left forepaw, the stake still well in the ground. He could not have been trapped for long. Nema found him sometime between 10:30 and 11:00 A.M.; he wasn't there when the traps were checked at 7:00 A.M.

He must have come *that* close to our camp in broad daylight, probably while we were eating lunch. We might have seen him walking along, had one of us looked up at the terrace.

We didn't know how much, if any, of the first two shots had gone in. The last dose was a light one and we had the usual extremely short immobilization time. The cat's gums were abraded from chewing on bushes, but it was nothing serious; in fact, the bushes were barely disturbed compared to the usual destruction. The injected antibiotic would help the surface cuts to heal quickly.

As the drug began to wear off, he crept away from us to rest, going only a few feet up the slope, rolling and tumbling, mind and legs still out of synch.

We left him and returned to camp, and watched much later through the scope as he emerged from his resting place and slowly made his way upward, following an instinctual urge for the security of the high cliffs above Tillisha Stream. We held our breath; he was still so unsteady on the narrow ledges and protruding rocks that a moment's loss of balance could have been disastrous. Stopping at last on a high, deep, protected ledge, he settled down for the long rest that would completely restore his senses.

He looked healthy and strong, even with mud on his rich coat. In the morning he would no doubt groom himself, removing the scents and traces of his capture—all but the collar, which he would grow used to quickly. Finally, we had *caught* one; perhaps the reign of bad luck was over with the capture of "Tin," our third collared cat.

Jimbu People

Rod and I climbed high on the western side of Tillisha Stream scouting a place to make a temporary tracking camp. We followed a "knife edge" ridge formed by the confluence of Tillisha Canyon with the Langu.

We were looking for a spot flat enough to pitch a tent permanently, with some kind of shelter for cooking, and, though we would be lucky to find such a thing, a seep or spring. We would need more than one tracking camp now that there were two cats with functioning collars to follow. Working just from Eding, it was too hard to stay with the collared cats, especially with a backpack full of the essentials: a tarp for shelter, sleeping bag, mattress, extra clothes, leopard receiver, short-wave radio, batteries, cameras, film, scope, tripod, notebooks, measuring tape, compass, and altimeter.

Several camps stocked with tents and food would make a big difference in our mobility. Maybe, too, we could find out what happened to "Ek."

We found only one place in the whole day of looking where a tent platform could be made, a small knoll at the bottom end of the knife-edge ridge. At 12,500 feet there was still a bank of gritty snow on the north-facing, shaded side of the ridge, but when that was melted there would be no water at all. It would have to be carried up. A small grove of pine trees grew on the shaded side, offering a frugal supply of wood to cook with, but the southern, exposed side was dry and rocky, with stands of thorny caragana, mats of dwarf rhododendron, and here and there a dusty juniper. One such juniper, old and shaggy, formed support for a kitchen tarp suspended from its branches. It also provided a shaded place for hanging food in a duffel bag, where we hoped in vain that the mice would leave it alone.

Pine Camp was a crow's nest of sweeping views, in contrast to the canyon bottom at Eding. Far across the gorge, the spires of Kanjiroba rose into the blue. At the end of the valley stood the blinding white barriers of Jhobu La, ramparts shielding Dolpo and the Tibetan Plateau. Directly south were lesser peaks clad lightly in the snow of our mild winter, exposing the forests of pine and birch that distinguish the southern banks from the barren ones to the north. Though anyone who stayed at Pine Camp would be roughing it in the true sense of the word, it came to be our favorite of all the tracking camps.

On the way down we found that one of the traps had been sprung during the night. For a few brief minutes it had caught a snow leopard. It also answered our question of whether "Tin" had been the April 30 escapee.

The tracks around this trap were those of the April 30 escapee, and it had foiled our system for the second time. Probably its finely tuned reflexes had saved it again—reacting before the cable tightened around its forepaw, caught by one or two toes.

The cat wanted nothing more to do with Tillisha Confluence. Its retreating tracks, back up the canyon the way it had come, were clear evidence of that. Nearly a month was to pass before we saw sign again that could have belonged to this clever, or extremely lucky, "Houdini."

On May 4, "Tin" got caught again, on the Tillisha Terrace trail, a hundred yards from where he'd been caught the first time. We had been monitoring his activity all that night. Several hours before dawn, the signal became active, emanating from the trap site, so there was little question that he was trapped again.

"What's he doing back here again so soon?" said Rod, with more than a tinge of exasperation. "Why do the same cats keep getting caught?" There wasn't anything we could do until first light, so Rod stewed

Self-portrait

Snapping candid shots of snow leopards in the wild presented a complex challenge, including extreme temperature variations, dust, and constant servicing of equipment. After selecting a site marked by scent sprays, droppings, and scratchings on Tillisha Terrace, the team placed a pressure pad of the type used for security systems. Wires led from the pad to the camera assembly, prefocused at thirteen feet, as seen in the diagram (right) that shows how the jacket photograph was made. In the glare of the flash, this cat's eyes glow with a greenish hue reflected from a mirrorlike membrane behind the retina that enhances night vision.

© *National Geographic Society*

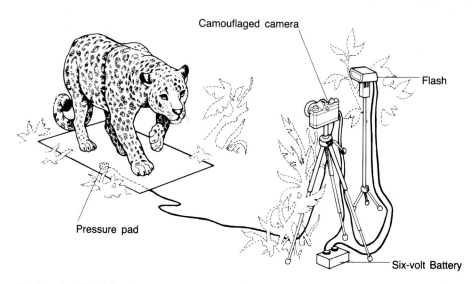

Camouflaged camera

Flash

Pressure pad

Six-volt Battery

During the 561 nights that a camera was in place, only two dozen or so cats ventured near the pad.

The Army Skyvan at Jumla, with a pile of gear and food to last eight months

Jumla's main street

Yaks on the high trail from Jumla to Base Camp

Leopard 5 ("Panch") in the trap, prior to being jabbed by Gary

As Lopsang Sherpa tries to distract Leopard 1 ("Ek"), Rod lunges with a jab stick tipped with a sedative.

Self-portrait

© National Geographic Society

Leopard 2 ("Dui") in the trap for the fourth time. Note the facial scratches.

After its recapture, Rod and Meelan move Leopard 3 ("Tin") away from the bluff drop-off to the shade of a tree so the cat can recover after immobilization and radio collaring.

Still groggy, Tin's initial attempt to leap away ends in a spill.

Houses at Dolphu

Inside Karma Lama's house (one of the
wealthier families in Dolphu): (Left to right)
Karma Lama's wife and son, his mother, his
father, his daughter, and Karma Lama wearing
a red "Western" jacket

Jimbu harvesters

With a last look back, Leopard 2 ("Dui") prepares to steal away, following the attachment of a collar.

Eding Camp. Tillisha Terrace is across the river.

Overview of central study area, seen from
Pine Camp trail, showing Tillisha Canyon
mouth, Eding Base Camp, Tillisha Terrace.

The author looks out at the Langu Gorge from Tillisha Cave at 14,475 feet. Gary (right) works on tracking equipment.

Kirken Sherpa and the author climb down the "easier" side of Tyson's Cliff, facing Choyap Flat.

Gary on the more difficult Lobur side of Tyson's Cliff

Sonam crosses the Langu on cable bridge.

Nema Sherpa pays the porters at Dolphu.

Lopsang Sherpa cooking a meal in the
base-camp kitchen

The author and Rod get their first mail in many months.

In winter, when water was lower, the Langu could be bridged with logs, but the only suitable trees were found high above the river and were very difficult to cut and haul down.

Karma and his second wife, Kartol

Orkin of Dolphu, photographed on Rod's 1976 trip; note his fire-black hands.

Karma Lama's father, Wangchu—respected village herbalist and high Lama—in his private gomba

Victim of age, a bharal judged to be thirteen years old and weighing 125 pounds is hoisted by 110-pound Karma with the help of Karan. After an autopsy is performed back at camp, it will be carved up for the cook-pot.

Pine Camp: As Gary radio-tracks, the author taps water "bladders," taken from wine-in-a-box containers in the United States. Lightweight and strong, they proved excellent for storing water, but had to be covered when crows took a liking to the bright silver foil and started pecking holes in them.

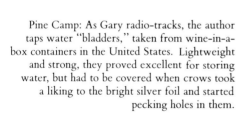

Radio-tracking near the river was impeded by the Langu's rugged terrain.

Gary finds a collar lying in the grass, bolts intact, and no sign of leopard remains. Scratches on the collar and bharal bones nearby indicate that the cat pulled the collar off during a struggle to make a kill, perhaps hooking a horn or hoof.

Leopard 3 ("Tin") remains calm under
sedation while Rod makes a final check
of the radio collar.

Although poaching for pelts is no longer considered the biggest threat to the species' survival,
snow leopard coats are still sold, even on the open market. Rod discovered this abandoned
carcass in 1977.

through the final dark hour of the May morning, until we could see to cross the river and send "Tin" on his way again.

Taking Sonam, Rod made an expedition to "Tillisha Cave," high above Pine Camp on the flanks of Tillisha Mountain. He wanted to know how radio-tracking from the highest possible elevation compared to lower points in the gorge. He also wanted to see if the grassland offered any prospects for trapping, and finally he needed to expand his search for "Ek."

While they were at it, they would try to approach the large herds of bharal we had seen grazing on the long grasses. Photographing the sheep was proving to be as hard as photographing the cats; but maybe the grassland would be different.

The three-mile journey took a whole day; they climbed up more than four thousand feet on slopes that were near-cliffs. Every time Rod asked Sonam how much farther they had to go, he kept saying "Little bit more, sah'b," until Rod began to think the place didn't really exist, that the whole expedition was just Sonam's elaborate joke, his way of paying Rodney back for making him give away all his hunting secrets! For the last several hundred yards they slogged through dense stands of knee-high caragana bushes with three-inch dagger thorns.

The "cave," at nearly 14,500 feet, was really just a rock overhang, deep enough to pitch two small tents. And the weather was awful—cold, misty, and almost always either snowing or raining.

Dwarf juniper grew in sparse patches here and there in the vast expanse of grassland, offering a scant supply of deadwood. But there was so little that it could be used only as an emergency fuel supply. A warming campfire was out of the question. The only warm place was inside the sleeping bag. They had Rod's camp stove, with watered-down kerosene purchased in Jumla. Potatoes took two hours to cook; the rice never did. Sonam, cold and sore from the long day of climbing with a heavy load, burned fragrant sprigs of green juniper to placate the gods, certain he was pushing his karma (or fate) to the limit. Still, they managed to stay for four days.

Despite an abundance of bharal—forty-five in one herd—the leopard sign was slim, and the options for travel routes made successful trap placement virtually hopeless. They were well above "Dui" and "Tin" and picked up signals from both, maintaining contact for long periods of time. But they couldn't always get good fixes because of signal bounce from rocks on opposite sides of the valley, and it was impossible to place the cat's position on the slope; the best Rod could say was that they were "somewhere below." They still could find no signal from "Ek."

From Rod's Diary:

May 20, 1983

Tillisha's grass slopes are a lot steeper than I expected. Seen from below through the spotting scope, they look like gently rolling hills. The air is thin, and it takes a lot more time to get around. Just getting up in the morning is an effort.

Still, it is incredibly beautiful up here. Across the Langu's dark chasm, fluted snow peaks of the Kanjiroba Range gleam icy-white in the sun. Instead of the Langu's springtime roar, here there is only the distant trickling of water in a gully below, and the roar of the winds, descending in furious determination to scour Tillisha of its grassy mantle—if not its two human intruders. I look downslope, into a gully that disappears in a deep rift, plunging straight down into the Langu. Far, far upstream I can just catch a glimpse of the red rocks of Ruka, marking the upstream boundary of the study area. Standing on the roof of the cave, I can see the dark slash of rocks above Wangri, reminders that other humans do indeed share this planet with Sonam and me.

I was sick the whole time they were gone, with vague, flulike symptoms of aching bones, back, and head. Then the backache went away, leaving an intense headache and a 102-degree temperature. The medical book was with Karan, which was just as well. Reading it was worse than staying ignorant; it was guaranteed to foster hypochondria. Looking up a simple pain usually unearthed several possibilities for what it could be, all terminal, given that we were virtually beyond rescue.

We did have an extensive medical and first aid kit, with some fairly fancy ingredients, like cement for filling teeth, wire splints, and a range of drugs for just about every conceivable ailment, including enough injectable ampicillin to get out in time, probably, if one of us got appendicitis. But since we were not doctors, we had been unable to get morphine or an equivalently strong painkiller in case one of us got badly injured and had to be carried out, or even to lie around for the minimum of five days it would take to get rescued, if a helicopter could even get in at all and land. We all did our best not to break any bones.

The wild herb jimbu had not done well in the dry year, but the villagers came anyway at the end of May to make the best of it, laying claim to their favorite drying rocks by placing sprigs from nearby bushes at the corners of all the wide, flat boulders. The crop was too valuable to pass up altogether. A measure of dried jimbu was worth a double measure of Jumla rice, and the enterprising woman Wangri Guru had once traveled all the way to Kathmandu with two of her sons on the proceeds of a good year's harvest.

Jickchor, a fellow in his midtwenties who seemed to be the village comedian, led a happy band of three women, including his wrinkled mother. They informed us that they intended to make Eding their "base," working at Pukchang, where the jimbu was most abundant, if not the entertainment.

In her first breath, Jickchor's Ama (mother) pointed to the stack of three empty Mountain House dried-vegetable cans, hoping that, perhaps out of respect for her "elder" status, we would present her with them. We ignored her hint, needing the cans for our own purposes.

They had spent the previous night at Dhukyel and then proceeded boldly across our cable. Jickchor, gregarious and cocky, was a natural for the job of "bridge guinea pig." He must have been coached well on technique by Sonam, who had made his first crossing only after drinking several shots of our best brandy and allowing himself to be buckled into the seat sling and pushed off the riverbank. I wondered how the women, especially Ama, at age sixty-something, got their long bulky skirts and aprons into the seat sling.

They all acted particularly blasé about the whole experience, concealing whatever difficulties they may have had, for they had not asked our permission to use the bridges and they suspected that we might be less than happy about it.

We should have known this was coming, but Sonam's initial terror had led us to think that the villagers wouldn't come anywhere near it. We had even used it as a threat against petty thievery around our camps. When Nema had discovered some plastic containers missing, Rod had declared: "Anyone caught stealing will be hung by their toes from the cable."

Our threat was suddenly impotent and worse. If anyone got hurt using it, we would be blamed and held liable for compensation through their version of "workers' comp" or, God forbid, "death benefits." They were unwritten laws but enforced all the same.

In any case, we certainly didn't want anyone to get hurt. All we could do for our own protection was to issue a "use at your own risk" disclaimer, for now that the Dolphas had taken the first step, neither village would be content to use the arduous and long southern side trail to Eding and Pukchang. For their protection, we would at least have to see that they were using it properly.

Jickchor's Ama brought us a bottle of chang and four boiled eggs—peace offerings—and I felt suddenly stingy, remembering the empty Mountain House cans.

Jickchor brought a note from Karan. He had recently moved his camp from Dhukyel to Shimbu, and Nema had joined him there, trading places with Karma. The note started off with the opinion that Shimbu Camp had the worst weather in the whole Karnali Zone. They hadn't seen the sun since they moved, and the wind blew a constant gale "enough to operate a windmill." They had seen leopard sign, but all the village yaks grazing on the slopes between Shimbu and Pamalang hampered trapping. The bait goat died, "maybe strangled on its rope, or from eating a poisonous plant. Its stomach was swollen and the rope had gotten twisted around its leg."

Soon after we read Karan's note, the villager Yangyap appeared, carrying our share of meat from the dead goat. Nema had given him bridge-crossing instructions; he had assured Nema and Karan that Jickchor had told him all about how to do it, and off he went on his merry way, our goat meat wrapped up in a plastic garbage bag slung over his shoulder.

He came to the cable, buckled on the seat sling, and pushed himself out over the swirling water. Midway across, his launch momentum expired; the anchor tree was higher on the other bank. He had reached the point where he had to catch the towrope and haul himself the rest of the way across.

He released his grip on the pulley rope to grab the nylon towrope—and promptly found himself hanging upside down, pulled off balance by the heavy meat on his back. Struggling, he righted himself and tried again, with the same result. He decided he'd better turn back, make the journey with Jickchor or Sonam. But he couldn't manage that, either. Every time he let go of the rope suspending him from the pulley, he lost his balance and ended up dangling by his bottom, his close-cropped head only inches from the water. He could hear the thumping and roaring around the bend downstream where the river churns itself into a rampant, frothing tumble of terrifying rapids.

He got across in the end, somehow, and by the time he reached Eding, he was sufficiently recovered to tell his story, winning the Eding Camp Comedy Award of the Week. And he was ready to go back the same day.

Crossing the cable with a heavy load or pack was eventually prohibited, because everyone who tried it had the same problem as Yangyap. A minimum of two people would have to go together, to haul the loads across one by one.

At dinner that night, as we chewed on rubbery pieces of meat, a better explanation for the goat's death was suggested: old age.

Before long, there were nine "jimbu people" in residence at Eding Camp. Our "kitchen" was crowded with the four of us. With thirteen it was a madhouse. The Bhotes have a different notion of space requirements; they happily gave up half the kitchen to us, squashing themselves into the remaining six square feet of dirt floor. They were joyful at being away from home, released for a time from their normal daily tasks. The jimbu harvest was a big party, an excuse to stay up all night singing and talking, laughing and joking.

They were up and out by 6:00 A.M., often stopping at our tent door mosquito net to look in, giggle, and rattle off some comment about how we should be up and working at that late morning hour, or pointing out things they wanted, or speculating with brazen and hilarious pantomime about Rodney's private parts and how he might put them to use.

Then off they would go, combing the hillsides all day, stopping only to munch a chapati or two left from the morning meal, cutting the clumped jimbu with small curved knives and flinging it over their shoulders into the dokos on their backs. Some young and beautiful, others toothless and wrinkled, they all sang as they worked. When a basket was full, it was carried down to one of the flat rocks and upended; at day's end they all came down with the final load, took up short wooden clubs and pounded the fresh piles into a rough pulp, and spread it out to dry. As dark settled upon our camp an almost overpoweringly pungent odor of garlic pervaded Eding.

They brought their usual complement of fleas, which abandoned their blankets and clothing in delighted hordes for the tender, fresh taste of our "foreigner blood." All night long they explored our sleeping bags, springing from thigh to arm to feet to back, never stopping long enough to let us catch them.

One night when a big moon rose over the canyon wall, Rod, unnoticed by the others, took a walk to Eding Knoll, tracking his leopards. Later, slipping back into our tent, with sparkling eyes and a look of delight on his face he whispered, "I found the jimbu people's dokos on the knoll trail and hid them all behind a bush. That should pay them back for bringing all the fleas!"

Rod and I never could decide if we preferred the spring and summer moons to those of the crackling frozen winter nights; blue-white fluorescent snow, juniper branches crystal-coated with clear ice, and the sound of snow crunching underfoot. But one thing was certain: Never had we been so keenly aware of the soft flux of our days and nights, of the moon and its phases, of the heat of the sun and the lengthening days of spring, of the colors on the hills as the seasons turned. Our lives were attuned to the natural rhythms of the gorge, our senses were sharp with the long months of outdoor living. We had three collared cats, and at last the balance had begun to swing away from the wearying, seemingly perpetual adversity.

CHAPTER

16

"The *Guest*"

"Dui" spent ten days near a large landslide in Tillisha Basin, followed by a long, looping circuit down along Tillisha Stream to the canyon mouth and up onto the tall bluffs of Tillisha West. The leopard followed almost exactly in "Tin's" tracks made a week earlier, stopping at almost every prominent ledge and rock overhang to scrape the ground and leave an occasional scat on or near the places marked by "Tin." Some of the scats were mere "tokens," a small bit of feces left as a marker.

Here at last two radio-collared leopards were providing information on how they interacted and shared the territory of the Langu. How different life must be for those researchers who are able to observe their study animals! With these leopards, we would have to be content to learn from the radio signals and sign they left in the environment.

Apart from radio-tracking, clues could be gathered in several ways. Scats could reveal the snow leopard's diet, and we collected enough to fill several cardboard boxes—and to win us sideways looks, not only from the villagers but also from the Customs inspectors when we came back to the United States! Pugmarks of uncollared cats had proven of little value, since we seldom found a good set of tracks that could be followed for any distance in the rocky soil or river sand. The poor tracking medium also made it impossible to distinguish among individual cats, although their varying sizes served at least as a rough indicator of the local leopard population. Sign transects along paths that the cats regularly used revealed a tremendous amount of information. A sign transect was established by noting every place along a measured length of pathway at which a cat had stopped to scrape or leave a dropping. Each site was assigned a number and unobtrusively marked by tagging nearby bushes. Each scrape was measured and assigned a "visibility" number on a scale of 0 to 4, 0 being just barely recognizable and 4 highly visible. A detailed sketch was made of each site, especially since some sites had been scraped and re-scraped many times. Once the chosen length of pathway, or transect—which varied from about 750 yards to over eighteen hundred yards—had been marked and sketched, then any subsequent marking activity could be monitored.

Scraping obviously played an important role in communication, for as many as 235 scrapes per kilometer (1.6 miles) of pathway were found, with up to twenty-four individual scrapes of varying ages at a single site. Later, scent-sprayed rocks and raked trees would be added to the cat's repertoire of sign monitored on the transects, but it would be the following field season before the key was found to identifying such markings.

Rod was in biologist heaven following the sign left by "Dui" and "Tin." The ability to radio-track and then follow up on known leopards was the best of both worlds.

From Tillisha West bluffs, "Dui" embarked upon a bout of extensive travel, moving from the ramparts of Dhukyel Canyon, back past Eding Camp in deep night, pressing on to Pukchang.

A few days later, "Tin" returned upstream, using a higher route in the subalpine scrub below Pine Camp.

"Dui" spent almost no time at Pukchang, turning around and heading back downstream again, following the Tillisha Terrace trail. There, a few yards from her other two capture sites, the cat was trapped for the third time in five months.

Rodney was tracking from the tent near midnight as her signal, loud and clear, beeped from the direction of the trap. But it was the slow, "inactive" signal.

"Surely she'd be struggling if she were trapped again," I said.

"Not necessarily," Rod replied. "She didn't struggle much when we caught her the second time last winter. She must be resigned to her fate, just lying there waiting for her shot of ketamine."

She was caught by one middle toe; when we approached, she was literally in a cotoneaster bush, where she remained, chewing branches, while Rod almost casually gave her a shot in the flank with the jabstick. She carried on biting the bush until the drug took hold, as if telling herself, "Maybe if I just stay here and keep chewing, this bad dream will go away."

She had fought so little that the cable was as good as new. There was a healing wound on her flank; she had licked off all the fur around a two- or three-inch abrasion. The wound may have explained her long stay at the Tillisha landslide, especially if she got it making a kill; she was slightly heavier than she was in January. Rod doctored what was left of open skin and we watched, when she moved off, to see that she had no limp.

The bolts on her collar were so loose that it would soon have fallen off. The hard resin coating surrounding the transmitter unit was scratched and pitted, and the corners were worn. Obviously the units took a beating as the cat jumped from rock to rock, or tumbled with a bharal or tahr. When we had caught "Ek," the tool for tightening the lock nuts was with some of our other equipment being held by Nepalese Customs, and Rod had had to use a pair of pliers. Now, looking at "Dui's" collar, it seemed very likely that "Ek's" could have fallen off, somewhere out of range of our receivers.

Rod had no intention of trying to recapture the collared cats when the transmitters expired, especially since they would fall off naturally within a few years. Now we hoped that it didn't happen *too* soon.

While the docile, cooperative—and possibly retarded—"Dui" lay trapped during the night, the young cat "Houdini" also came back to Tillisha. Walking right up the bluff trail to the top of the terrace, it must have become aware of "Dui." Instead of walking along the terrace, where it might have been caught, it went up onto the cliffs and presumably back into the canyon.

* * *

At the beginning of June, Rod had a conference with Karan at Shimbu. Our plan was to leave the Langu by mid-June, to catch the last scheduled flight out of Jumla. For the second season, there would be no data collected on the birth of the blue sheep lambs, due to begin any day, unless Rod could talk Karan into coming to Eding and remaining behind for several weeks after Rod, Nema, and I left. Nema was needed at his home in the eastern mountains. As it was, he was already too late for the spring planting. I had to be back in Kathmandu before my visa expired, and Rod's fund-raising commitments in the United States precluded his staying behind.

Karan agreed reluctantly to stay through the end of June. Not only would he have to overcome his fear of Tyson's Cliff *and* the cable bridges, but also he, too, had conflicting commitments at home. No one could say if the end of June would be long enough; we could only hope the lambing began soon.

Returning from Shimbu, Rod took a day off. He sat in the shade of the camp peach tree, writing his notes. Reaching for the cup of tea I offered, he asked,

"Do you think I'll go to hell for admitting I'm glad it's nearly time to leave? I'm so tired of walking up and down, and down and up. My knees are sore, and I'm ready for a break."

"I wonder what's happened to Gary," I replied, as one of us did nearly every day.

Late afternoon found us still lazing by the big boulder. Voices and footsteps drew our attention to the pathway. Into camp walked Nema, and close behind him was Lhakpa Norbu, the Sherpa Warden at Rara National Park in the mountains above Gumghari.

Lhakpa's visit instantly earned him the title "*The* Guest," a title he would hold for the duration of the study. Since we had missed Bob and Bobbie during the first field season, he was the only person from the "outside" we saw over the whole four years.

He had spent a day with Karan and Nema at Shimbu, seeing his first bharal through the scope, fascinated by the rugged gorge. He almost

171

didn't come to Eding; he had so little time, the weather looked like rain, and Karan warned him of the dangerous trail. But he was inspired by seeing the little-known bharal, and he knew he was unlikely ever to find himself in prime snow leopard country again. So in he came, bringing some news that sent us into a tizzy of speculation.

"I heard that permission has been approved for Gary," he said. "Some-one—I don't know who—said, 'Rodney will have his American friend with him.'"

"When?" demanded Rod, his eyes big with amazement. "What else did they say?"

"I don't know. He could be on his way right now, or the permit could be for next year."

Rod invited Lhakpa to take a walk before dinner along Eding Terrace. I left them alone, knowing that this time with Lhakpa, who was so outgoing and enthusiastic, would help Rod revive his own flagging energy. A stream of conversation floated back down the trail. Over his shoulder, Rod carried the scope on its sturdy tripod, hoping that he and Lhakpa could spot a herd of bharal grazing on the western Tillisha slopes. Later that night Rod wrote in his diary:

June 5, 1983

For almost an hour we scanned the slopes; no sheep to be found. I moved the scope back and forth, up and down across the iron-red cliffs and outcrops, nearly overlooking the low, white creature traversing a wall of stone. Blinking lest the image be illusory, I exclaimed to Lhakpa, "I have a snow leopard!" Without moving my eyes from the scope, tracking the hurriedly moving feline—which has a remarkable ability to vanish instantly and reappear as suddenly—I directed Lhakpa to the spot. He saw it and shouted with joy.

The cat crossed a band of rock high on a ridge, leaping easily across the broken slabs, its coat ruffled by a gust of wind. Its huge pads gripped the coarse stone, its tail spiked the thin air and whipped softly against rock fire-red in the setting sun. At the top of the rise the leopard paused, gazing out over its domain, looking perhaps for a herd of bharal. Seeing no telltale movement of gray hide or curling horn, hearing no whistle of alarm, the cat continued on its search, moving rapidly down the ridgeline, zigzagging among bushes and tall rocks, disappearing finally into a deep gully thick with obscuring boulders, brush, and juniper.

They were sitting stunned and silent when I came up to join them, drawn irresistibly by the novelty of a visitor. Lhakpa found his tongue first.

"It's incredible. I've just seen a snow leopard."

"We both saw it," said Rod, "so it must have been real."

"I'm so *glad* I came after all," Lhakpa continued. "I so nearly stayed in Shimbu. I just *never* thought I'd ever get to see a wild snow leopard."

We stayed on in the deepening dusk, searching the ridge, the slope, the gully for another glimpse of the cat. We were ready to give up when Lhakpa gasped.

"Oh, Rod, I see it!"

The cat had traveled three hundred yards from where it had disappeared. Now it was rapidly descending a ridge, a black-and-white blur of taut muscle and rippling fur, palest smoky gray dark-dappled with charcoal spots.

For all the times we had held them, drugged, in our arms, this was the grand prize—a wild, free snow leopard, all its senses fully engaged, completely unaware of us. We watched for perhaps a minute, transfixed, as darkness descended and the cat vanished, mingled with familiar shadows, to stalk its prey in the watchful silence of the Langu night.

Rod, knowing that somewhere up there an uncollared snow leopard might be coming closer to Tillisha Stream, crossed the river to scent liberally the western Tillisha traps with powdered, freeze-dried urine taken from a captive female snow leopard in heat. Hopefully, the wind would waft it to the cat, and perhaps the cat was a male. "Yum," it would say to itself, sniffing the potent aroma, and it would come to investigate and get itself trapped. But here it was June—way out of season for a female to be in heat. Would the cat be fooled?

We floated back to camp feeling as if we shared the most marvelous secret, to a celebration dinner of freeze-dried chicken chop suey, delicate water chestnuts, and bean sprouts only lightly touched by Karma's curry powder.

The canyon seemed enchanted, our spirits elevated by our rare experience. Now we knew the joyful side of the Langu's mountain gods. What were the odds against Lhakpa, our friend Bob, and Pemba Sherpa seeing a snow leopard, when all of them had come into the gorge for just twenty-four hours? In all of our seasons in the Langu we would see among us only eight uncollared free-roaming cats.

Rod was up at dawn, training his scope on the traps, quiet and empty in the stillness. After tea he crossed the river to inspect the West Tillisha Trail. No cat had come anywhere near his scented traps.

CHAPTER

17

Gary

Karan went with Lhakpa on a short vacation up the Mugu River. He would return directly to Eding, where he and Rod would then spend the few remaining days going over the lambing data needs and work program.

There were last-minute jobs to complete and lists made of gear we would leave behind in Dolphu or hidden in the rocks across the river.

Rod and I did a final plant transect on the slopes of Tillisha West, working in a line cross-slope, measuring off plots and in every other one counting, aging, and estimating the density of each plant and noting whether it had been eaten by the bharal and tahr.

With no guide to the mountain flora for reference, we developed our own system of identification. For the notebooks and for my pressed collection, we gave each new species a number, but for our own purposes we had rather less scientific descriptions.

There were several species of awful thorny bugger—all so good at puncturing holes in people that Karan was highly concerned about getting lockjaw. Rod and I were more concerned about them poking holes in our mattresses, so we kept them outside, along with our lone specimen of foul-smelling sucker.

The first lambs were spotted by Rod on June 10—four in the East

Tillisha herd. Perhaps a week old, already they were quick and agile, making long jumps from rock to rock, running over the loose slopes with their mothers. They were especially pleasing to watch—black-kneed miniatures, always alert for a chance to suckle, tails vibrating in bliss.

How many would become an easy catch for the stalking leopards? How many stalking leopards were pregnant females, ready to den, just when a fresh supply of tender lambs might help to keep them fed? Karan would soon be able to get the study's first data on how many lambs were born to a herd and what percentage of them were taken in their first few months of life.

Nema had been climbing up Tyson's every afternoon to watch for Karan and help him over the cliff, but somehow he managed to miss his arrival, with Cinon, at Choyap.

Rod had gone looking for two pieces of his radio-tracking antenna that had fallen out of a mouse hole in the bottom of his backpack. So he missed Cinon's early-morning arrival in our camp. Cinon brought a message from Karan. The paper, unread and heavy with portent, lay smoldering on the camp boulder, awaiting Rod.

Inside was the news that Karan had tried twice to get over Tyson's. The second time several jimbu people joined Cinon in offering help and encouragement, but he couldn't find the "mental or the physical strength" to reach the summit. For him, it would be utterly impossible to come to Eding. Instead, he would stay as long as Rod wanted—anywhere downstream of Tyson's Cliff. Returning at midday, Rod read the note and erupted.

"Oh, Jeezus," he fumed, his eyes rolling. "This is just great. Where in the hell does he think he's going to stay? Choyap's no good—the canyon walls are like a box. And Dhukyel's not much better. He's going to be outside the study area, getting lamb counts on a bharal population that our collared cats have nothing to do with. He agreed to come, damnit. He *has* to come. He's responsible for the bharal study. Every one of us has had to face the same fears; what makes his so special? He's reneging on a promise—on a *contract,* for that matter!

"Where's the ketamine?" he demanded finally, stalking off toward the storage shelter where we kept the capture gear. "I'll tranquilize him, load him into a duffel, and Karma can *carry* him over the goddamn cliff!"

The note had other news, which nearly got lost in the heat of the moment. Several days earlier, on the way back from Mugu, Karan and Cinon had met some Gumghari people on the trail. The Gumgharis mentioned to Karan that they had seen "an American and a Sherpa" below Mangri. They said they were on their way to Dolphu.

Karan retreated to Thondup's house. It wasn't worth setting up camp again in Dhukyel or Shimbu. In the remaining days of the field season he would work on getting counts of the Pamalang lambs.

By June 14 there still was no word or sign of Gary. One of the jimbu women showed up in Eding to collect a load she'd left behind earlier. As far as she knew, no "Amrikans" had been seen on the Dolphu Trail.

My Nepalese visa, issued separately from Rod's, was to expire at the end of June, so Nema, Karan, and I would leave immediately, with fingers crossed that we could get out of Jumla quickly. Rod would stay behind with Karma to get the Eding lamb counts.

The night was warm and Rod and I lay close together with nothing but a sheet for cover; even that was too hot. We talked far into the night, sometimes with lumps in our throats so big that we could hardly speak. During the past months we had experienced few of the strains and petty irritations that being in such constant close proximity might have produced, and it was clear to both of us that we were suited to this camp life and to each other.

In the Langu's wilderness we were discovering a powerful self-reliance. We had realized, through an opportunity few people in the Western world will ever experience, how very little we require to be content and how easily we could do without most of our former trappings. I would never succeed in erasing the worry of illness or accident, but the threat had lost its sharp edge, softened by the pleasures of a life free from calendars, of deadlines and commitments to be met, free of the rush to be transported somewhere else. Neither of us was ready to be wrenched apart so abruptly, even if it was only for a couple of weeks. The Langu being what it was, any departure left a nagging emptiness and the reminder that one must never take the other for granted. Now the need for openness seemed doubly important, to plumb the depths of our feelings before the sun came up and to feed our hearts well for the journey ahead.

"Promise me you'll take very good care of yourself and come to Kathmandu as soon as you possibly can," I said, knowing he would do both of those things without my asking.

We walked in the morning to Choyap, Nema and the three porters, Rod and I. Then he turned to go back alone up the dark monolith of Tyson's Cliff. Walking down the trail, salt tears softly blurring the stones and blades of grass, a sudden chill of fear raised the hair on my arms. I ran to catch up with Nema, brushing at the tears. Placing a strong arm around my shoulder, he hugged me hard, and then we walked in silence down the smooth beach of Choyap Flat.

We went quickly and steadily, the men determined to reach Dolphu in a day. The only rest stop was the hour it took to get us and our loads across the Dhukyel cable. I was glad of the grueling pace. I welcomed the total exhaustion at the end of the day, and the black curtain of sleep that descended as my head hit the pillow.

About midway on the Kartik-Dolphu Trail, the path goes through a deeply overhanging section of rock. Before the trail was improved as a "Far West development project" it had been a particularly nasty place. The base of the rock sloped sharply, and it was always slick with a mixture of livestock urine and manure, snow and ice, or a treacherous combination.

I was thinking about how dangerous it must have been in those days for Dolphu and Wangri people to travel for trade or even to visit Kartik, when I came around the corner into the overhang, and there was Gary sitting on a rock, surrounded by our porters, talking to Karan.

"Ho, Didi!" shouted all the Dolphas. "Sathi! Sathi chha!" Indeed. The fact that Gary and I were *sathi* (friends) was confirmed to their immense delight when we stood in the trail and hugged and exclaimed and planted kisses on one another's sweaty cheek.

The equivalent Dolphu greeting is rather more formal and subdued, at least between members of the opposite sex. The woman takes the man's hand and bows down in front of him, or sometimes men will show respect for an older male, and always for a lama, in the same way. This, despite the spirited, lusty antics of the villagers at play. They always thought it was hilarious to see Westerners embracing, and an innocent kiss was license to howl.

There were too many questions to ask and to answer, and too much ground to cover.

"Would you like a dried apricot?" I offered.

"Yes," he answered with no hesitation. "I've hardly had anything to eat since we left Jumla. I got sick the first day, and the teahouses were so gross that I couldn't bring myself to eat anything they had to offer." He'd been living on the nuts and chocolate and specialty snacks he'd brought from Kathmandu, like ramen (oriental noodle soup).

When he'd received word that his visa was approved, there was precious little time left in the field season. He knew he might miss us, but he took a chance and came on to Kathmandu.

He and Gumbu, his Sherpa guide, had had five Jumla flights canceled. Once, they had taken off from Kathmandu and gotten within fifteen minutes of landing in Jumla before being turned back from the cloud-obscured pass.

Succeeding at last, they had walked steadily from Jumla in five days. Whoever the Gumghari people had seen on the trail, it wasn't Gary.

I hated having to go on down the Kartik Trail and miss the grand reunion at Eding Camp, the fireside nonstop talking, the details and gaps that would be filled in and forgotten long before we were all together again.

Rod would be amazed and pleased to see him, even though they wouldn't have much time. At best Gary would get an orientation—provided they could find enough food to keep them there for a few more weeks.

I lay in my bag for long, sleepless hours that night. A few lingering Dolphu fleas flung themselves against my skin, but I was hardly aware. My head was crammed with reruns of the day's events, thoughts of what I forgot to ask or tell Gary, all the variations of how their plans might work out, and when I might see Rodney again. On that last thought I closed my eyes, and sleep came at last.

Jumla in the Rain

From the top of Danphe Lekh, the Jumla Valley, spread out below, looks much closer than it really is. On the knee-crunching walk down the mountain, the suspense builds with each step: Is there any mail? Does the wretched bazaar have something interesting to eat or drink? Will the planes be flying? Will there be any seats?

As we rested on the grassy summit on June 24, Karan looked wistfully into the valley and remarked, "If only people had the power of fleas, we could have made Jumla from Dolphu in ten great leaps rather than ten long days!" When the laughter died down, we heard the distant engines of a Twin Otter taking off; a symphony with violins could not have sounded better.

Pema's hotel had a new improvement: electric lights. A naked bulb of about five watts hung in each of the four rooms. The United Missions had recently finished their hydroelectric project, and Pema had been among the first of Jumla's "private citizens" to take advantage of it. There still was no toilet.

Karan secured tickets for the four of us on the Kathmandu flight scheduled for the day after tomorrow. He also made reservations for Rod and Gary for June 29, just in case they couldn't get food in Dolphu and came out immediately. The flight on the twenty-ninth was the last scheduled flight of the season, and it would be very crowded.

I pitched my tent on Pema's roof, one place where there were no parasites. But in the morning I took it down and packed it up for storage. We would have to be up early the next day, ready to go. Because Pema was short of space, I would have to share Nema's room for the night.

We awoke at five-thirty on the twenty-sixth to a leaden sky and the sound of pouring rain. No possibility of a plane landing in that. All flights were canceled.

Karan asked the ticket agent about rice charters to Nepalganj. Were they still flying sacks of "government" rice in for the local civil servants? Was it still possible to get a ride to Nepalganj on the empty plane?

"No" came the reply. They were using the big Avro, which couldn't land at Jumla. Instead, the plane would circle over, dropping the rice by parachute onto the runway.

"Well," I said, "it's a good thing you booked those tickets for Rod and Gary. If the weather clears and a plane comes, we can use their reservations."

"I only hope this isn't the beginning of the monsoon," he replied. "If so, then we may be walking to Nepalganj in any case."

On the twenty-seventh, the downpour was unabated, and I awoke with itching bedbug bites wherever my body had come in contact with the bed. Awaking also with a full bladder, I dashed out into the streets.

The rain continued to fall and the lanes ran thick with smelly streams of muddy dung, animal and human. As my visa got closer and closer to expiring, I wished more than ever that I'd stayed behind with Rod and taken my chances with the Home Office. Said one of our friends in Kathmandu: "They simply fine you if you're late—or hang you."

I decided to overcome my shyness and reluctance to bother anyone with my problems and go visiting the missionaries. It would help just to have someone to talk to. I would warn them that I was a walking bedbug factory and simply ask if there were any books I could borrow until either a plane came or we started walking to Nepalganj.

The United Missions had been operating in Jumla for several years. Having completed one trade school in central Nepal, they meant to repeat their success in the remote West, bringing electricity to the town, offering village boys training in agriculture and animal husbandry, and educating the general public in basic hygiene, and in pre- and postnatal care for mothers and infants. A government-imposed condition for their working in Nepal was that they would agree not to attempt to convert the Hindus and Buddhists to Christianity.

When we first arrived in Jumla, the school was in its earliest building stages; by the time we left, it was finished, a big celebration had been held, and King Birendra had attended the official opening ceremonies. The project took many years of dedication by a remarkable handful of people; they would supervise the operations here only until Nepalis were trained to take over. I had to change most of my preconceived notions about missionaries (gaunt, straitlaced, narrow-minded Bible-thumpers hell-bent on saving the souls of the world's "primitive savages") when we got to know the kind, nonjudgmental people involved with the Karnali Technical School.

I walked up the hill toward Danphe Lekh until I reached the school complex, where the buildings were nearing completion. Beyond the school was a combination house and barn.

I knocked on the door and was greeted by a roomful of warm, cheerful, friendly, beautiful, sympathetic, English-speaking women. They gave me coffee to drink and homemade bread and jam to eat. The following evening, if the plane didn't come, I was invited for dinner, bedbugs and all, to a house in town where Judy Henderson, an Australian pediatrician, and Jenny Sutton, an English nurse, lived and ran their clinic.

The rain continued throughout the twenty-eighth, and after reading my way through the day, I walked across town to Judy and Jenny's. Their house contained two small bedrooms, a storeroom, and a combination kitchen-sitting room. They cooked on a wood-burning stove, which also provided heat in the winter. There were no indoor pipes; water was hauled from the community spout a short distance away.

It was a toss-up what the best thing was about Judy and Jenny's: the toilet downstairs or the absence of bedbugs. Homebaked bread and jam came to be high on Rod's list. But, with all that, we came to love Judy and Jenny's most as an oasis of warm hospitality and friendship, especially at the end of a long field season.

That evening they made pizza and salad from their garden! As the table was being set, Judy produced, from the recesses of their storage room, a bottle of clear, bubbly, delicious homebrewed beer. She'd been to Kathmandu recently, visiting the Jesuit priests, and to her delight they had given her some hops. Not being sure, or perhaps being *quite* sure, how their fellow missionaries might view the brewing of booze in the house of two single, attractive women in their thirties, they didn't publicize the operation taking place in the back room!

"Move out of Pema's and stay with us as long as you need to," said Jenny. "Could we tempt you with a mission house nearby that has a solar shower?"

On the twenty-ninth, there were patches of blue among the clouds, and on the radio an announcement that two planes would attempt the Jumla route.

Karan and I met at Pema's and hurried to the airstrip, crossing our fingers that the weather would hold for the three or four hours we would have to wait. He stepped up to the ticket window and then changed his mind. He handed me the tickets and said it was best that I present them, since they were for the canceled flight of the twenty-sixth.

My heart stopped beating. Surely he had arranged for us to use Rod and Gary's tickets. He wanted to get out of there as badly as I did.

Biting my tongue, I passed the tickets through the window, to be told that they were no good. Since Rod and Gary had not arrived, their tickets had been canceled, and all seats on today's flights were now filled.

All at once, and for the second time in Jumla, my self-control deserted me, taking with it the small reservoir of strength that had been filled by my visits with the mission folks. Right there in front of the RNAC window, and in front of all the people standing around—some of whom would actually understand the words to my high-pitched, slightly rabid performance, and all of whom would understand the gist—I ranted and raved at Karan. I flung my arms around and got red in the face. Spitting saliva, pacing back and forth in front of him, I repeated, "I just don't *believe* it—I just don't believe you could let this happen!" over and over again, until I realized that all I was doing was providing entertainment for the crowds.

Karan, stock-still and devoid of any expression, was evidently in shock. I realized, too late, that I had gone too far, shouting at him in public.

Nema and Gumbu stood to one side, trying not to look as if they belonged to our group, while I burned up a short length of grass, trembling, smoking a cigarette, trying to cool off, determined not to drop a single tear.

Karan found that he could actually move without splintering into a thousand fragments and that he could speak as well.

"It doesn't work like that," he explained. "We were never entitled to Rodney and Gary's tickets. There was already a waiting list for them."

"But why did you let me think that we could use their reservations?"

"I didn't know you were thinking that we could."

"Well, there's no point in hanging around here," I said with a sigh. "I certainly don't care to watch the plane come and go without us on it." I wanted to get my things; go back to Judy and Jenny's; and have a long, private wash and cry in that solar shower they had mentioned. I got my backpack and headed down the road, but soon I heard Nema's piercing whistle and turned to see him running after me.

"Didi, come back!" he called. "Karan has two plane tickets." I could see that he was angry. He caught up and reached to take my pack. "What about me and Gumbu? How will we get home?"

He and Karan held a short discussion, but I couldn't hear what was said. The sky was still full of clouds, and I wondered if any of us were going anywhere that day. Were we being ripped apart by bad feelings for nothing?

Should I offer Nema my ticket? After all, he was as late as I was, and he had more than a fine to face if his crops didn't get planted. But he would never accept. The siren began to wail, and a black dot on the horizon grew into the Twin Otter approaching from the far end of the Jumla Valley. Only then did I seriously begin to court thoughts of Kathmandu. I went to get my boarding card from Karan. As he gave it to me, he said, "It isn't for sure. We can go only if the plane is low on fuel. If the tanks are full, it will be too heavy and there will be no need for it to go out via Nepalganj to refuel, so they won't take us."

What did that mean? Did it mean *anything*? Had Karan, out of all good intentions, "found" a ticket merely to provide a few minutes of hope in a hopeless situation? I felt the foam forming again in my mouth and the urge to jump up and down, pull my hair out, and eat the airstrip. Would the RNAC give me a mercy flight away from Karan?

A few minutes later we were airborne, leaving a forlorn Nema and Gumbu below on the green, flying high in bumpy clouds south to Nepalganj, to refuel. On the blacktop at Nepalganj the plane was like a tin oven. Late that morning we landed in Kathmandu.

Standing in my room at the Kathmandu Guest House, I looked in a mirror bigger than four square inches for the first time in over three months. I expected to see a ravening beast, fanged and glowering, not the thin face, two blue eyes, sunbleached eyebrows, red nose, and bedbug scabs reflected back at me. I was not happy with myself. I had let it happen again. The mental strain of being so *close* to those longed-for modern conveniences and yet so utterly dependent on a fragile network of "ifs" had proven too much. Sure, I could live for months in a tent in the middle of nowhere. It's a fine life, with no expectations of better. But get me near an airstrip, just let me know that I'm an hour and a half's plane ride from Kathmandu and see how fast I fall apart.

My blowup on the Jumla airstrip was never mentioned again. For the duration of the project, the relationship between Karan and me would be cool but cordial. Professionally, he and Rod also arrived at a polite impasse.

I have since asked Karan in correspondence to express his thoughts on the study, good and bad. He replied, ". . . whatever bitter things happened in the past should be forgotten and we should remember only the sweet and significant things."

But since I had specifically asked, he went on to outline what he felt had caused the rift between him and Rod. In his opinion, Rod showed a lack of openness in his thinking and decision-making, and a lack of clear judgment and direction, and that these things had weakened his position.

Karan felt, too, that Rod lost sight of his main responsibility as principal investigator, that he spent too much time on the politics and business of the Snow Leopard Project, to the detriment of the scientific leadership.

"People are alike throughout the world in many ways," he wrote. "Whatever good and bad customs I saw in our society, the same things were also exhibited by your society. It depends person to person, but one's behavior is also affected by his social status and family background. It is too bad if a biologist (or person belonging to any academic subject) completely forgets his main duty and behaves like a politician or businessman. I have to say I have the same opinion about the entire human race, whether Asian, foreigner, or whatever else."

I strongly feel that Kurt's legacy of falsehoods influenced Karan but that the innate differences between his and Rod's characters would have led to problems no matter which culture or country they happened to find themselves in.

Asked how he would have done things differently had he been in charge, Karan replied that he "would have set a good example of leadership by providing all kinds of facilities to my project members, *more* than I was getting myself." He felt that he could have completed the study with only 75 percent of the budget "by using a proper way of operation." And finally, that he "would have developed good friendships, not only between project members but throughout all concerned."

From Rod's point of view, the issue was one of expectations. At first Rod was excited about Karan's participation. And Karan felt it, too. "We had two sessions in the field," he wrote. "The first was one of the best . . . in terms of the relationship between us, but the scientific achievement was not satisfactory, as I was layman and Rod had wrong selection of study area. The second session in fall and winter was also very successful in terms of our relationship and productivity, but after that it never got any better."

Karan might have felt that Rod expected too much of him, since he was schooled in Asia, where educational standards are below those of the West. But Rod did not demand that Karan perform to Western standards. What he did expect was for Karan to expect more from himself. To meet his own standards, he pushed and prodded himself. Before the Snow

Leopard Project, he had a reputation as a workaholic, spending days and nights and weekends on the job, though it was not, perhaps, in his nature to be a forceful leader. He took it almost as a personal failure that he did not, by example, inspire Karan to overcome his personal barriers to working within the core study area. When Karan stopped short of the invisible line that to Rod meant acceptable progress, he was disappointed. He couldn't hide that disappointment, or his frustration over the lost data on the study area bharal, and it came out, unfortunately, as a rejection of friendship.

But in the final analysis, Karan did learn and grow. Certainly, he returned to the Langu on his own, to earn his doctorate on the Dolphu herds. He is by now the Nepalese expert on bharal.

What were the good things he remembered about the Snow Leopard Project?

"Seeing a snow leopard pair hunting on a large herd of tahr in Kimding, excellent academic achievement, national and international recognition and publicity, and a good gain of wildlife knowledge."

Gary, guided by Sonam, had arrived at Eding in early evening, surprising Rod out of his wits as he walked along the river to get a fix on "Dui."

They stayed for nearly two weeks, returning to Tillisha Cave, where, as we waited in Jumla, it rained or snowed the whole time. They explored all the accessible territory between Dhukyel and Pukchang, getting a peak lamb count. And then, faced with the food shortage and the difficulty of getting leopard data during the monsoon, they left.

Karma had the responsibilities of sirdar on their journey to Jumla. There were still some concerns about his Mangri problem, since no one knew the status of his elopement negotiations, and he certainly wasn't talking.

When they neared the Mangri branch in the trail, Karma insisted that the whole group *must* go out of its way to spend the night in Mangri. He left Rod and Gary with no doubt that something was fishy when he appeared that morning dressed in his Sunday best.

"He *wants* to go to Mangri?" asked a skeptical Rodney.

Yes, Karma wanted to go to Mangri, and when he had Rod and Gary settled in the village guest house, he disappeared. It all became clear when he came back some hours later, well fortified by a number of bowls of chang and the moral support of several villagers. In an obvious state of agitation, Karma sat down and announced to Rodney:

"Now give me two thousand rupees."

Technically he was due two thousand rupees and more. But that wasn't a very good way to get it. A little verbal digging uncovered the fact that two thousand rupees was the asking price for Kartol's freedom and that Karma had agreed to pay it to the soon-to-be-ex-husband.

Probably unwittingly, Karma had created a scene that would make it appear that Rod was paying for Kartol, thus condoning the union and making it appear that the Snow Leopard Project was henceforth willing to be involved in the staff's personal business. It simply wouldn't do; the situation was too open to misinterpretation, false rumors, and future hassles.

Had Karma explained his plan and asked for his wages anywhere along the trail before Mangri, everything would have been fine. Rod and Gary could have stayed out of it altogether. But Karma wanted the status of being seen by the Wangris talking business with the "Amrikan sah'b." It was an irresistible opportunity for him to strut, and once again he had strutted himself into a tight corner.

Rodney called a Village Council meeting. He made sure that the whole cast of important characters was gathered, in their red lama robes or homespun chubas, silver earrings and basketball shoes. As they all looked on in solemn concentration, two thousand rupees were counted out into Karma's hand—the *wages* honestly earned and honestly due—money with which he could do as he pleased. And the matter was settled. Perhaps . . .

The happy couple—and they *were* happy—had their *mah chandra maa*, if indeed the Bhotes have such a thing as a honeymoon, en route to Jumla. After that, I guess the bride had some interesting adjustments for a Bhote newlywed: life with the mother-in-law, the father-in-law, the first wife.

I heard a taxi drive up to the door of the Kathmandu Guest House. Taxis always are coming and going, but for some reason this time I looked out the window. The door opened and Rod and Gary got out. They had left Eding on June 30 and arrived in Jumla on July 7. They had dinner with Judy and Jenny, and the next morning a rice charter came in. It was the first plane to fly since the day after my big scene, when Nema and Gumbu flew out. Rod and Gary landed in Nepalganj, spent three hours sweating at the airport, and caught the connecting flight to Kathmandu. Their swift journey would have been a record in any season; for the height of the monsoon, it was something of a miracle.

Part

3

November 1983–July 1984

Close Encounter

Twenty of our friends sat around the big dining-room table. Outside, summer fog engulfed San Francisco's Richmond District, dripping from the branches of cypress trees and eucalyptus all along Nineteenth Avenue. At one end of the table stood Gary, giving a demonstration, with a fifty-pound bag of granola before him.

"Okay," he said. "You take one of these quart-size plastic bags, scoop up the granola with a cup, and pour it in. Meanwhile, the team at the other end of the table will have measured the powdered milk into those baby-bottle liners. Put one portion of milk into each bag of granola. Then bunch up the top of the bag, suck as much of the air out as you can, and tie it up with a rubber band. If there's too much air, the bag'll burst in the unpressurized hold of the airplane. Anybody have any questions?"

"Yes," someone called from the end of the table. "What're you gonna do with that big bag of dog food in the corner?"

"That's not dog food. It's soy protein, beef flavor. It goes with the spaghetti dinners. We'll do those next."

Gary had come up with the idea of putting together a selection of lightweight, fast-cooking meals for use in the tracking camps. He had spent several summers as a mountain guide, and he knew a lot of recipes and how to prepare them without spending a fortune on commercially packaged backpacking meals.

Besides the granola, we could do up pancake mix and several varieties of hot instant cereal for breakfasts. Dinners would be mostly variations on a theme of pasta, using packaged sauce mixes, the "dog food" soybean meat substitute, spices, and grated parmesan cheese.

We had invited our friends to help us measure, fill, rubber-band, and pack the one- and two-person meals for the long journey to the Langu. We knew it was a labor of love, but we never saw them sneaking into the back room and typing up individual "granola fortunes" and "pasta proverbs." Much later, sitting on a mountaintop, we would pour out the cereal or open the chili-macaroni to find a little scrap of paper that said, "Who needs Hawaii when you've got the Himalayas?" or "Look forward to another morning stretch workout!" As yet no one has admitted to typing "Cabernet Sauvignon would be a perfect complement to this meal."

Rod and I were looking forward to having five whole months in the United States in which to recover our enthusiasm for outdoor living. I knew we also had a heavy work load facing us, but I thought for sure that we would take a week or two just to relax. I had in mind a country inn with a stack of books beside the fireplace, or a North Coast cabin where we could hear the waves crashing and the seals barking on the rocky shore.

But I was in for an unexpected and dismaying revelation: Rod, positive that there was hardly enough time to do the things we had to do, let alone play, would work nonstop for the whole time we were home. Though, of course, we would eat, and bathe, and even see a movie now and then, I soon began to realize what the word "workaholic" meant. The Langu had held few alternatives; there I had been just as happy as he was to keep fully occupied, but here at home even our friends were noticing his reluctance to take even one day off. "He's driven," they said, and I had to agree.

I could do little else but help with the work of following up funding applications, writing progress reports, delivering slide shows, and rounding up gear to replace broken or worn-out items. Though much of our equipment was donated, it was not a simple matter of pointing out items in a catalog, or visiting a store. In a slumping economy, the days of wholesale sponsorship were gone, forcing us to approach a string of companies, asking each for a short and carefully selected list of requests. Letters and evaluations of previous donations had to be written and followed up. It could take months for applications to be processed, and the timing was always tight, but we depended on our retail sponsors for such things as sleeping bags, mattresses, and the fifteen tents we wore out over the study's course.

The National Geographic Society would continue to provide major funding, but even with that assurance, each field season found us searching for ways to cut costs enough to make it through. Sadly, we could do without Nema. His duties could be split between Karma and Sonam, but we would miss Nema's warmth, kindness, and competence.

The *National Geographic* magazine was now seriously considering an article on the project. We had a base of publishable photographs, and if we could fill in several gaps, primarily close-up shots of free-roaming leopards, we would be assured of publication. But how to get the shots?

The solar-powered remote cameras had been a good idea, but the flash units necessary for nighttime photography kept burning out. We had twice found tracks of a leopard leading over the pressure pad, and the camera's exposure counter was advanced by several frames, but the film had turned out black.

National Geographic's Photographic Division went to work on the problem, but until we were back out in the "boondocks," we wouldn't know if they'd solved it. Working with the idea that the more tricks we had, the better our chances would be of getting a picture, they added another item to our growing arsenal of shooting options: a remote-control camera unit. If we found a fresh kill, we could rig a camera so that one of us could watch from a distance and use the triggering device to take a picture of the cat if it returned.

* * *

Gary returned to Nepal in November, understandably a little apprehensive about all the little pieces of the big picture that would have to fit together for the field season to go right. For a start, he would be traveling with fifteen duffel bags weighing seventy pounds each. He would have a thirteen-hour plane ride between San Francisco and Bangkok, a six-hour layover, and then a morning's final leg of the journey to worry about what he might do if a duffel, or all the duffels, didn't make the plane change. Then there would be the official errands and paperwork in Kathmandu, the food shopping, the arranging of the charter.

Through it all, even in the Langu, he would be virtually alone. Already, he had experienced some of the difficulties of living with campmates whose backgrounds, and whose deference to the sah'b, for the large part seemed to exclude familiarity or friendship. Gary would find them just as inscrutable and difficult to get along with as Rod and I had, but for him there would be no one with whom to commiserate when things went wrong or to share the adventure and the good times.

Like Rod, his obsession with collecting sound scientific data occupied his every thought and waking hour and left little time for socializing with the others. Gary would set off for a two-day expedition up the gorge, carrying an eighty-pound pack, and work until it got dark, then cook his dinner by the light of a meager fire before falling into his sleeping bag.

Often Karan's backpack was carried by Karma or Sonam. Karan worked only within walking distance of Base Camp and either returned for meals or had them delivered. Saturday was always rest day. If Karan gave one of the Sherpas an order, the Sherpa might well in turn order Karma to do it, and if Cinon or one of the young Dolphu men were around, Karma would order *him* to do it. They were all acting according to rules of prestige and caste that have been in existence far longer than our American rules of conduct. For example, as a member of the Shah caste (the caste to which King Birendra belongs), Karan could not be seen carrying his own load. We were visitors to Nepal; perhaps the onus was on us to accept the rules and work within them, but sometimes it was hard. Gary's way of dealing with it was to stay away from Base Camp as much as possible. But his diary reflected his wish for more satisfying human relationships.

From Gary's diary:

December 8, 1983

I was shocked by Dolphu when I saw it for the first time last June. All I could see were the unbelievable differences between our standard of living and theirs. But lately I have begun to notice the innate human similarities; what cheerful, generous, and hospitable people they are, and how much they add to the richness of this whole experience. Their toughness and tenacity are matched to the harsh environment in which they live. In a way, working in the gorge is no different than working in the United States. I don't actually know what the people think of me, but I can guess that they view me in much the same way that a New Mexico rancher might view a biologist spending sixteen hours a day studying lesser prairie chickens on his land: skeptical, suspicious, useless, unnecessary. Odd as it might seem, that's comforting, and it always cheers me up to see their warm, expressive faces. I think that it is really only language and time that prevent us from knowing, understanding, and appreciating one another.

Physically, Gary was fit and strong, well suited to the Langu's terrain. At home he liked to run several miles a day, and his muscular limbs showed the benefit. I was not alone in admiring his physique, but at least in western Nepal I might have been among the few who did it silently! According to reports by Rod, when Gary had appeared wearing shorts for the first time in Dolphu, the women went wild with delightful if rather shameless displays of appreciation. Could that, too, have been partly to blame for his difficulties with the other males in camp? If so, it was misplaced jealousy, for Gary's attention was on work.

December 8 [continued]

Apart from working on the camps, I have to lay out four sign transects, making detailed drawings and measurements along nearly five kilometers of rugged mountainside. Without access to aerial photographs, we will also have to map all landforms and vegetation types. That means making short trips to all possible vantage points for various perspectives. With all of that, I have to set out traps, because catching snow leopards is our highest priority. Who was it in Kathmandu who said, "I can't meet with you today, Gary, I'm spread thinner than a fart in a bottle!"? Now I know exactly what he meant, and how Rod must have felt for the last two years.

If Gary felt stretched, lonely, and depressed, he was about to receive his reward for perseverance. There are, as he already knew, advantages to being alone, but he could never have foreseen what awaited him when he made the cold and arduous journey to fix up Tillisha Cave.

From Gary's field notebook:

December 30, 1983

2:30 P.M.: Tillisha Cave High Camp, 14,334 feet. Sky clear, wind steady 10–15 mph. Morning spent cutting thorn bushes to water supply and collecting the slow trickle, which froze immediately in the can.

3:05 P.M.: While looking for firewood, I spot a herd of eleven bharal feeding in the alpine grassland about 450 yards above me. Some of the animals appear concerned, directing "warning chirps" and long gazes in my direction. However, they aren't *that* bothered, perhaps because I'm downslope from them and the wind is carrying my scent beyond their noses. Two adult males with massive curved horns show absolutely no concern with me, failing even to lift their heads when warning chirps are sounded. They continually circle the females, their heads in a "low stretch" posture, repeatedly sniffing each female's rump in an attempt to stimulate urination. ("What stage of estrus are you at?") Rut is on and these males are definitely thinking with their balls rather than their minds. I started to move toward them, using the small knoll above as cover.

3:27 P.M.: Three rapid sets of warning chirps and I see a female and lamb dart out from behind the knoll. Less than a second later one of the big males came plunging over the right side of the knoll, down the steep

198

slope and directly toward me. Right behind him was a snow leopard.

Both were traveling at top speed, taking huge strides. After a chase of about a hundred yards, the leopard make a quick lunge forward, catching the male on the left side of its rump with its left forepaw and jaw. This sent a cloud of pelage into the air. The bharal's rear dropped nearly to the ground and its knees buckled as it turned into the slope and absorbed the leopard's blow. The leopard's momentum forced it straight down-slope, all its limbs off the ground and outstretched. Its long tail flung into the air and around to its left side, causing it to twist sidewinder-fashion in the direction of the bharal and regain its control. The bharal made several more direction changes, then just above a large boulder it again turned sharply into the slope. The leopard, not able to turn quickly enough, went over the top of the boulder, spun halfway around, and landed in a spray of fine soil several yards beyond. After it regained its footing it walked in the direction of the fleeing bharal, sat down, and licked its forepaws and the air in front of its nose.

The pursuit had brought the leopard within a hundred yards of me, yet its intense concentration on the hunt had not yet allowed it to notice me standing upright. For a few more minutes it groomed its forepaws and looked in the direction of its intended prey. Finally, when it did notice me I became the focus of *all* its concentration. The leopard stared at me intently, and at the same time went through a remarkable transformation. It pulled its ears back tightly against its head and almost imperceptibly melted into the short grass.

From my human point of view, the leopard appeared very uncomfortable, as it had unknowingly put itself in this very unfamiliar and potentially threatening situation. Now, how to solve the problem? I recall my first thoughts, stimulated by the cat's potent stare, were to tell myself, "I'm not a bharal, I don't look anything like potential leopard prey," and I tried to recall who it was that said there has never been a substantiated report of a snow leopard killing a human. I also filled my lungs, trying to puff up in size as much as possible. Who was threatening whom?

After five minutes of staring at one another, the leopard was finally able to make his move. It slinked off slowly, in the same direction the bharal had escaped.

For the first seventy-five yards it barely lifted its belly off the ground, moving in a "stalking-like" fashion through the short shrubs and tufts of grass. Then, with a glance back at me, it stood up and broke into a full run. As it approached the ridge on the horizon it stopped again, looked back at me, and walked over the ridge and out of view.

Tibetan New Year

Rod and I left San Francisco on January 2, hoping to beat the first major storm of winter to Base Camp. We arrived in Jumla to find the whole town in a state of excitement and anticipation. King Birendra was coming, on a tour of the whole western part of Nepal, and Jumla would be headquarters. Pathways long neglected were being paved with big flat stones, buildings were being painted, fancy archways constructed, and every day, sometimes twice, a long parade of officials marched out from the bazaar, inspecting progress on this or that bit of face-lifting. Even the school had specially flown in the closest thing to a red carpet they could find, a purplish rug, in preparation for His Majesty to make the grand opening. The only thing that wasn't being built, as far as we could see, was a single toilet.

Official nerves were taut with anxiety that things must be exactly right; you could feel it in the air.

Karma arrived, three days late, with six porters, including Kartol. She was lovely and sweet and downright hopeless as a "kitchen boy," the job for which Karma had hired her (on our behalf, of course). Probably it was his fault she seemed hopeless. He had risked a great deal to elope with her, and he paid more than a month's salary to win her. His eyes were still filled with stars because normally he would have a kitchen boy running his legs off.

It snowed before we even got over Danphe Lekh—not the dreaded big storm we were trying to beat, but the nights were getting colder, and it would be good to get the two big passes safely behind us.

Below Ghurchi Lekh's squalid teahouse at Bulbule, we discovered just how far-reaching was the effect of even the *prospect* of a visit by the king.

Making our way up the winding streamside trail, we rounded a bend and stopped quickly to avoid bumping into a chartreuse stuffed sofa, six feet long, with four little wooden handturned legs, moving slowly up the trail.

It looked at first as if it were traveling under its own power and that the young boy walking beside it was carrying on a lively discussion with a couch. But two bowed and spindly Bhote legs were just visible beneath the green baize, and when we drew even, we could see a whole man beneath the heavy, awkward load. He was carrying it to Gumghari, to be installed in the chief district officer's meeting room, for the beloved king—if he came—to sit upon; and his son was carrying their food and bedding. We couldn't find out where the sofa was made, but the man had carried it from Jumla, a three- or four-day trip to Gumghari, and he was being paid a flat fee of eight hundred rupees. Our porters got three hundred rupees to carry a load for ten days, from Jumla to Dolphu.

"Sofa Man" asked Rod for a cigarette. There was no place to put the thing down, so Rod lit the cigarette and the man stood there in the trail, happily puffing away, while Rod took his picture. Knowing the downside of Ghurchi, the treacherous and narrow places in the trail, we wondered if the sofa would ever get to Gumghari in one piece. Surely all the legs would break off.

Our camp on the other side of Ghurchi was to be a rude shelter on a windy promontory near the bottom. It was getting late, and though even the porters protested at the awful prospects for an uncomfortable night, they agreed it would have to do. When we looked inside, there was a group of Dolphas sitting around a fire, slurping watered tsampa from the "pie pan" plates they used on the trail. The slurps stopped all at once when they saw our faces; then they were on their feet, shouting recognition and greetings.

They were especially happy to see us, because they thought we might have some medicine to help the villager Tsewong, who had taken ill on their trading trip. We were amazed to learn that the man was Tsewong, for he was completely unrecognizable, sitting on a blanket close to the fire, swollen from head to toe, complaining through puffed lips and eyes of pains in his legs and groin. He had portered for us many times, a gentle and likable man of whom Karan was especially fond. The Dolphas were convinced he had become so ill from eating a squash. For all we knew, they may have been right. Certainly we could not diagnose his problem, or risk giving him medicine that may do more harm than good.

There was no room in the falling-down shelter for any more people, and we had no choice but to continue on in the fast-fading light. We camped at a small trailside teahouse farther down the mountain. Early the next morning the Dolphas passed by, saying they were taking Tsewong to Gumghari, where he could rest for a few days. The others would take his load of rice on home for him and he would continue when he could. Later that morning we came upon him sitting by himself on a rock in the sun.

He got to his feet, but he could only manage to walk a few yards before he stopped, leaning on his walking stick, moaning softly. He was obviously seriously ill, frightened, and in pain.

For the first time since coming to Nepal, the life of someone we knew and cared for was in danger. If it were one of us, a helicopter could be summoned. In a week, perhaps, the ill or injured person would be safe in the best hospital in Kathmandu—or home in the United States if need be. No helicopter would be coming for Tsewong. Rod loaned him fifty rupees, to pay for his food in Gumghari, and we left him sitting all alone beside the trail.

Arriving at the next teahouse, the first thing we saw was the green sofa, all in one piece, perched on the rock wall, while Sofa Man and his son, their work nearly finished, drank cups of tea on the shaded porch.

* * *

Rodney spent his fortieth birthday in Lumsa, where we camped at the newly constructed Lumsa Hotel. Having again caught up with the Dolphas, we all shared the straw-filled loft. From our stores of provisions from Kathmandu, Karma and Kartol produced the closest thing they could to a birthday cake, with tidbits of orange and apple, cookies and dates, and candles, all arranged on a plate covered with a clean plaid dishtowel.

In our after-dinner fireside chat, Karma brought up potato prices in Dolphu, saying they had jumped an alarming 100 percent, in spite of a good harvest. We wondered if the price rise was part of Karma Lama's revenge tactics. And then Karma added a most puzzling bit of information.

"Geddy-Sahb . . . not eat. Big duffel tent in. Launch, not eat. Dinner not eat. What to do?"

"What?!" I said. "Is he sick? What do you mean, Gary's not eating?" But Karma would say no more. We would just have to wait to find out what was going on, and we were still at least five days from Eding.

Nestled in our corner, isolated from the dogpile of Dolphas by a row of duffel bags and two feet of walkway, we made a birthday dip into the expedition brandy and surveyed our circumstances.

"Look," I said, "you can see the stars through the gaps in the roof thatch. Why don't you make a wish?"

"My only wish is that we can get to Eding quickly," he said, as we tucked the warm sleeping bag around our shoulders and lay on our backs, staring up at the cold night sky. "Karma has made me extremely nervous with his mysterious talk over dinner."

At Mangri we stayed in the Panchyat Guest House, where Karma and Kartol were united last summer. Kartol seemed happy to visit her family and show off her finery, including Karma's black polyester sports jacket, which he was letting her wear, and my canvas boots, which she had talked me out of below Danphe Lekh.

A government health worker, Mr. Bogati, and his wife had recently arrived in Mangri to set up a clinic. Perhaps they could help Tsewong.

On the trail the following day we met Karma Lama's father, Wangchu, who was the village herbalist; Tsewong's wife; and his brother. They knew about Tsewong and were hurrying to Gumghari; the grapevine on the Mugu Trail would rival any telegraph. The brother asked Rodney for a hundred rupees. Karma was behind with the porters, so we asked them all to sit down on the trial to wait, for we couldn't handle this meeting without him to interpret.

All three were distraught, and when Karma came there was a chaotic discussion about abandonment, Tsewong's symptoms, and money. All the while Tsewong's wife was streaming tears and clutching my hand to her forehead. I couldn't tell if she was seeking my help or my sympathy.

Karma asked for a pen and paper to write a note to Mr. Bogati; Rod produced the hundred rupees, on condition that it eventually be repaid; and we went our separate ways. Rod didn't really care if he got the money back; the sum was worth only about five dollars, but we had learned that simply to give whenever asked, thereby promoting the impression that we had an unlimited source of money, was bad both for us and future foreign visitors. Neither did we want the villagers to think that we were lacking in compassion, so it seemed best to give what we could with the understanding that it was a loan.

We were happily surprised, upon seeing the chortens of Dolphu, to be greeted warmly by Thondup and family; we were even glad to sit at their hearth, drinking bowl after bowl of chang. Lhosar (Tibetan New Year) was only a week away, and Thondup showed us two huge urns at least four feet tall by three feet wide full of chang, brewing for the occasion.

Thondup wouldn't hear of our leaving in the morning for Eding. "You must stay, rest, talk, and drink chang. There is no chang in Eding. We haven't seen each other for five months." Rod tried to explain the urgency of getting to Base Camp, the likelihood of snow, the need to see Gary and Karan, and the need to get some more leopards trapped. But Thondup announced matter-of-factly that it would not snow for at least seven days (he was right) and that rest, and chang, were far more important.

Rod said, "We'll come back for Lhosar, but I have important letters for Gary."

"Do come for Lhosar," said Thondup. "But you must rest at least tomorrow."

With the Langu at its friendly low level and three good log bridges, there was no need to face the ordeal of Tyson's Cliff. Still, the walk in—following our rest day—took two days, and the trail was slick and scary in shaded places. We walked into Eding Camp through patches of snow not yet melted, (just four hours of sun warmed the flat each day), past Gary's green tent, already faded, pitched at the edge of camp, and Karan's and Karma's close together near the kitchen shelter.

The place was empty except for Sonam, strumming his "guitar" by the kitchen fire. He jumped up in amazement, beaming with happiness to see his friends, and shaking Rod's hand and mine. We soon learned that Karan was at Pukchang for the afternoon, observing bharal. Gary was at Tillisha Cave, his schedule unknown.

We built a huge bonfire that night. Sonam played music, and all the porters danced and sang around the fire, trying to outdo each other with the intricacies of their steps and the volume of their singing.

We unpacked our new tent and set it up. "Jeezus," said Rod, "it's huge. It's embarrassingly big."

The tent was eleven feet tall by nearly twelve feet across—a vast contrast to the two-person dome tent we had before. I couldn't even reach the ceiling, and it had more than twice the floor area of any of the others.

"You could fit the entire population of Dolphu inside, isn't it," said Karan, adding, "and there'd still be room for some Wangri people."

Our idea had been for it to serve both as our room and as a storage shelter for the more delicate equipment. When everything was arranged inside, there wouldn't really be much space, but it felt big, and being able to stand up and walk around in made it seem luxurious.

Karma built us a "bookshelf" from straight branches and seedling poplars. It wouldn't win any design awards, but hopefully it would help to organize our cardboard boxes of papers, stationery, books, tools, and scientific gear. This would open up floor space for the sleeping bags, the plastic garbage sacks that held our clothes, and the locked metal trunks of vital equipment and money. We could spread a woolen "Dolphu rug" on the floor for warmth and for conferences as an alternative to working out of the dirty, cramped kitchen.

In midafternoon, as we were sorting and stowing our gear on the shelves and into the trunks, a hairy, dusty, brown figure appeared in the doorway. It looked only vaguely like Gary—but it *was* Gary! He didn't look like he'd been passing up dinner or living on crackers, but he was definitely starved for conversation.

"I had a funny feeling you had arrived," he said. "I started smelling phantom chocolate bars, and I could swear I heard Morgan's voice. It was only the wind in the junipers, but I could no longer concentrate on work. Welcome to Eding. Did you bring any mail?"

Rod handed over a packet of letters. "I don't know if there's anything from Roxy," he lied, knowing she had needed a manila envelope to hold her letter, photographs, and small Christmas gifts.

Karma's odd comment on the trail had arisen, evidently, from Gary's habit of leaving camp right after morning tea, often not returning until dark. When he wasn't at one of the high camps, he ate dinner with everyone else. There was little wood above fourteen thousand feet, and the quick-cooking backpacking food, kept in a locked duffel in the storage lean-to along with the kerosene and stove, was reserved for use by those at the high camps. Karma must have thought Gary had brought his own supply of food for the entire field season.

We were all beginning to accept that the language and cultural gaps were more like chasms here in the Langu. Some could be ignored, some would simply never be resolved, and others would get worse as time went on. I don't think any of us—Westerner or Nepali—could say who displayed the most baffling behavior. We were all candidates at one time or another.

Anyone tuning in on an Eding Camp lunch hour or eavesdropping on the occasional "staff meeting" could have overheard some mighty peculiar conversations. Ghosts, serious business to the Nepalese, got us going every time.

Almost from their first breath, Nepalese children are threatened by grown-ups with monsters that lurk in the shadows, ready to eat them if they misbehave, or at least to carry them off, never to be seen again. Even adulthood is no defense against these spirits of the dead who call at night, their eerie voices a dreaded sound for anyone caught out alone after dark. Perhaps the ghosts were partial to their own countrymen, and left the less appetizing Westerners alone on purpose. Rod tried appealing to the common sense of our campmates.

"Think of all the nights I've been by myself," he said, "throwing down my sleeping bag on some lonely ridge, staying awake to monitor a cat through the moonless night. Look at me, I'm still alive."

Rod—and Gary, too—loved bedding down knowing that somewhere out there the leopard stalked unseen. Did it ever see the solitary fox or the little jungle cat, neither of which had ever showed more of itself to us than tiny tracks in the powdered dust? Rod liked to imagine the huddled langurs and the small groups of bharal tucked quietly into the cliffs' comforting folds, their ears alert to every sound, waiting out the darkness. The call of a tawny wood owl may have pierced the night, or with luck, he might have heard the winter mating call of a snow leopard echoing down the canyon. The cat's call, heard so rarely and sounding so human, made us wonder if at least some of the stories of the yeti, Nepal's "Abominable Snowman," hadn't in fact been inspired by the snow leopard.

Rod talked about these night sounds around the campfire, but it was useless to think that we could ever hope to change their minds about ghosts. "It will never happen," said Karan, "and you must simply let it be." And so we did, leaving them to their beliefs and wondering what aspects of our behavior they saw as strange, irrational, and unexplainable.

We ate the last two chickens, with slightly wilted cauliflower and cabbage brought "fresh" from Kathmandu, and discussed the possibilities for going to Dolphu to attend the Lhosar celebrations.

I was torn between going and not. Rod and Gary weren't; they wanted to stay and work. Karma wanted to go; he was counting on a short vacation with Kartol before seeing her off again to Jumla. Sonam also wanted to go; Lhosar is the biggest holiday of the year, and all that chang was waiting to be consumed. But Karan wasn't sure; if the big snow came, he might be stranded in Dolphu.

Rod pointed out that he and Gary could fix a rope over Shimbu Cliff if it snowed and everyone could make it back okay.

I decided not to go. I might miss some good photographs, but I didn't have much faith in being able to make any sense out of the proceedings, if in fact the proceedings would make any sense at all, what with all those full-of-chang giant urns that soon would be empty. The others promised to return in five days.

It didn't snow, and no one appeared on the fifth day. Or the sixth, or the seventh. Each day, Rod was getting more irate. "Our high camp work is being delayed, Karan's work is being delayed, and I want to know what's going on."

On the eighth day, Karan and Karma walked into camp near dark. The biggest of the Lhosar celebrations, Karan explained, had taken place the day they were supposed to come back. Thondup was insistent that they stay. We knew how insistent Thondup could be, and Rod made no protest while we waited to hear Karan's story.

"Everyone gathered by the gomba for the big dance. It was a windy, cold evening, and the villagers asked permission of the lamas to move the festivities inside. The lamas said it was all right as long as the fire was well away from the small 'altar' area and as long as they were careful."

Rodney laughed. "Careful? How careful can one hundred fifty drunken Dolphas be?!"

"Everything was fine until Karma Lama arrived and demanded that everyone clear out of there with their fire. They said that permission had been given and please to let them go on with their dancing, that it was cold outside. But Karma Lama would not listen. He even ignored his revered father, Wangchu. He jumped into the circle of dancers, where the children were gathered, and kicked at the fire, sending logs and sparks in all directions. Sparks fell on the children, making them cry and burning holes in their chubas.

"Jickchor's child was in there; he and other fathers became enraged. They hoisted a burning log and aimed it at the central statue of Buddha. Fortunately, it missed.

"At that, everyone joined in, shouting at Karma Lama that they had built this nice new gomba by the sweat of their backs, literally, carrying

209

the huge stones and beams one by one. And where was the government money that was meant to pay for their labor? *Where* was it? In Karma Lama's pocket. Who did he think he was, telling them what they could and couldn't do in their gomba?!

"Then Karma Lama's wife came and dragged him away, while the villagers vowed that if he came back, each and every one of them would take up a stick and beat him. He didn't come back, and the dancing resumed—until 4:00 A.M."

Bitten!

Our Lhosar celebrants had planned to start for Eding the next morning, stopping off for a day or two at Dhukyel to catch up on bharal observations; but they left Dolphu very late due to another fight, this one between Thondup and the villager Geltgyen. Geltgyen said that Karma Lama intended to have Sonam arrested and sent to jail. Even though Jickchor had been the leader of the previous evening's "attack" on the Buddha, Karma Lama was accusing Sonam of doing damage to the gomba.

It then became clear to Karan that Karma Lama was mad at Thondup for befriending us and that, using Geltgyen, he was trying to taunt Thondup. It worked. There was a heated argument; Thondup's wife joined in, and Geltgyen clobbered her over the head with a stick, knocking her out cold and opening a gash over one eye.

"Sonam wailed from the rooftops that his mother was dead," Karan explained. "Thondup went berserk. He stood in the middle of his home, raving, throwing anything and everything he could get his hands on: food, pots, blankets, sticks, and stones. He decided to kill Geltgyen and went in search of his kukri. Karma tried to stop him and got bit on the head."

" 'Bit'?" I interjected. "Or did you say 'hit'?"

"He was bitten," said Karan. "Thondup's friends joined together to calm him down, and eventually they discouraged him from the idea of murder."

Karan administered first aid to Thondup's bleeding but now conscious wife, and with Karma carrying an egg-size lump on his head they started for Dhukyel, where they did the sheep census.

Those of us who stayed at Eding had kept busy repairing all the broken things. Rod and I thought we were pretty good at emergency repairs, but Gary was downright amazing. He got the high camp stove to burn the watered-down kerosene from Jumla, figured out and rewired the burned-out solar panel connections, reattached a tracking antenna rod that had sheared off, and sealed the leaking plastic jerry cans, needed for hauling water to Pine Camp, with tennis shoe glue. He never threw anything away: Empty medicine bottles, matchsticks without heads, bent paper clips—you name it, he had it, stored either in the heap of debris in the corner of his tent, or in the pile just outside the door. And he knew where everything was.

"Your camp looks like pack rat paradise," I told him.

"I need all this stuff," he replied. "You never know what might be useful." In summer, when the flies threatened to take over Eding, he dug around in his pile of spare parts and made "Big Stinky" fly traps for our tents. One time he made a light table for tracing topographic maps.

I worked on the tents, reapplying seam seal, patching holes, and sewing Velcro to replace all the broken zipper doors. Our big tent had a definite disadvantage: It was freezing cold inside the airy, unheated nylon walls. The first after-dinner conference was held with everyone wearing down parkas, wool hats, and mittens while shivering in the −5 degrees Celsius temperature.

We set several new traps, with modified snares held by rock bolts fixed into boulders instead of the unreliable rebar stakes.

Meanwhile "Dui" was in close range on the cliffs above West Tillisha. For five days the beeps were mostly inactive, indicating that she might be sick or wounded, or her collar might be giving out. Rod and Gary decided to go up to see if they could find her.

They climbed as far as they could up the cliffs where the signal was coming from. The leopard was so close that even with the antenna disconnected from the receiver they could hear her "inactive" signal.

In the afternoon Rod and I crossed the Langu to climb Tillisha Terrace. We hoped that from the eastern side we would be able to look with our binoculars directly into "Dui's" hiding place.

Rod led the way up the crumbling bank and crested the bluff to face an angry, growling, trapped, collared cat. It looked like "Dui," but her signal, which should have been blasting through the earphones, was only moderate.

From Rod's diary:

February 14, 1984

. . . We ran back to camp for the tranquilizing gear. About thirty minutes later, Gary moved in to dart the cat, using our new air-powered blowpipe. The syringe, red tailpiece a blur, flew through the air, hitting the cat squarely in the rear flank but breaking in two.

Seven minutes passed and the cat was still active and aggressive, unlike "Dui's" behavior during her three previous captures. We tried again, and the second shot failed even to reach the cat. On the third try, the needle entered the cat's flank; the cat turned, bit the syringe, and removed it. Had any of the drug gone in?

We waited. After five minutes the cat was still way too lively to handle. I moved in with the trusty jabstick, and after some maneuvering got the drug injected. By now the leopard should have received a record dose of ketamine. Another five minutes and it was down, but I was worried; Gary, too. . . . The cat resisted handling, its muscles were rigid, and it was able to move, however slightly. Obviously it had too little drug in its system, over too long a time.

We had no choice but to go ahead. To give it more drug might have been dangerous, considering the significant time lapse between the first and last injections.

The cat was "Dui," her collar worn through to the metal transmitter. I worked quickly to change it for a new one, while Gary did a general body check and prepared to take a vaginal smear, a new step in the program, to investigate later if the cat was pregnant or in estrus. He remarked on the number of facial scratches, on the thinness of the animal, its somewhat dull pelage; and then, in three words, added a new dimension to an already unnerving experience: "A pap smear?" he asked. "The cat has testicles and a penis. . . ."

My mind went blank in the urgency of the moment. "Don't think about anything except getting this cat on its way," I told myself as I felt its muscles straining beneath my hands. We abandoned an attempt to weigh him. Heading for a juniper about twenty-five yards away, we carried the quickly recovering leopard away from the steep bluff.

Less than a yard from the juniper, as we stepped over a boulder, I heard a growl and felt canines clamping on to my hand. Panic! Without thinking, I dropped the cat, pulling my hand from its teeth. Feeling no pain, I expected to see a few clean punctures, but what met my eyes were deep, ragged gashes and blood pumping from the wounds.

Numbly, I walked back, applying pressure at the wrist, calling to Darla, "I've been bitten, badly." I looked away as she washed it with water kept in case the cat overheated.

Leaving Gary to watch "Dui" and collect gear, we returned to camp for first aid. As long as I didn't look at my hand, I was okay. The pain began and I swallowed a Darvon while Karma boiled water and Darla rushed to get the medical book. What to do about deep punctures and torn flesh between two fingers, knuckle and bone exposed?

All I could think of was smoking cigarettes. Displacement behavior, just as the cats chew bushes when snared. My mind was not on my hand; it was on that penis and those testicles. How could I have made such a mistake? Karan, too. Three times we had immobilized that cat, and three times we had called it a female. From its size, I had assumed it was an older cat, assumed we would be able to see testicles; neither of us had felt for them in the dense fur. Even now, a year since the third capture, the sexual organs had not been obvious. I was going to have to account for an error that I should not have allowed to happen, and I was going to have to take a whole new look at my data on "Dui" and my interpretation of it.

As for my hand, I felt certain that a few days of rest and daily dressings would suffice—wishful thinking. Darla and Gary thought otherwise.

"What did I do to deserve this?" Rod asked in the darkness, breaking my fitful sleep. The painkiller had worn off, and he was wide awake, writhing. We had been at Eding barely two weeks. A trip to Jumla, now, in the dead of winter, could take three weeks or more. All that field time would be lost, and it could be a nightmarish journey. A person needs at least two hands on the Eding-Dolphu Trail; snow could delay or strand us anywhere. He knew that he would have to leave, but as he lay in the darkness, racked by pain and self-torment, the only way he could deal with the events of that day was to abandon himself to his misery.

By morning his hand was swollen, ugly, and painful. Infection was guaranteed. The slim possibility of rabies could not be ignored. If there was tendon damage, he could lose the use of his right hand or a finger. Light-headed with lack of sleep and fear for the journey ahead, I helped Rod to dress, buttoning his shirt and pants, my own movements clumsy and slow. We made a sling to support and cushion the hand against shocks and bumps, and I was glad for Gary's calm directions and help. By noon we had the bare essentials packed and ready to go.

Going slowly, we spent the first night camped at Dhukyel, where we got some much-needed rest before facing the most difficult part of the trail. We started early the next morning, and when we came to the cliffs at Shimbu and Pamalang, Karma acted as Rod's right arm, using his compact and sturdy body as an anchor between Rod and the abyss.

We arrived in Dolphu near noon. The villagers, seeing Rod's bandaged hand and hearing Karma's rapid explanation, rallied in record time. Sonam was enlisted to cook at Eding during Karma's absence. His mother packed tsampa and potatoes to add to the little food we had brought from Eding; Jickchor and Lundup would come with us, carrying light loads so we could move fast. We set off an hour and a half later for Jumla.

We camped that night on the flank of Murki Lekh, above the frozen Bailung Stream. Rodney was feverish and in pain, and we were both deeply shaken. Before, it had just been a theory: What happens if one of us gets hurt? We were lucky this time; Rod could walk. But it wasn't going to be an easy trek. What lay ahead? What could I do to help him? If our luck continued, the army helicopters would still be shuttling rice to Gumghari. Perhaps Rod could be flown out, at least as far as Jumla. Thinking of helicopters, I inevitably thought of Tsewong and how much more fortunate we were.

We reached Mangri in midmorning of the third day, just as it began to rain. Mangri's elevation was about seventy-five hundred feet; the rain would be snow higher up. Mr. Bogati took charge of Rod's now extremely swollen and infected hand and did what I couldn't bring myself to do, squeezing out the yellow fluid while even the crowd of villagers looked away at Rod's distress.

In spite of the rain, Rod wanted to continue on after lunch. No helicopters would be flying in the storm; obviously we would have to walk all the way out, and now we would likely be breaking trail over Gurchi Lekh. There was no time to waste.

"Please, stay at least tonight," urged Mr. Bogati. "I think it would be better for you, and I would have the opportunity to treat your wounds again." Karma, Jickchor, and Lundup had no desire to walk in the pouring rain, and it seemed to me, too, that the rest would do Rodney more good than the half day of walking. So he agreed, reluctantly, to spend the night in Mangri.

In the morning, his hand was much better; the swelling was down, and there was little fluid for Mr. Bogati to drain. We left in the rain, which came and went all that day and the next.

We camped just below the mountain in high, gusting winds and light snow and awoke to more of the same, dreading the walk ahead.

We came upon a group of Mugalis, camped in a rough cave just this side of the pass. They'd tried going over the previous evening but were beaten back at the top by the wind. That morning they'd tried again, with the same result. They warned us not to go; the wind was too strong and cold.

The cave was crowded, and none of us particularly wanted to go all the way back down again. The snow had stopped, and looking up toward the pass we could see the clouds beginning to part. We were better dressed than the Mugalis. We had given Karma a warm parka with a hood, and we had extra clothing that Jickchor and Lundup could wear. We decided at least to give it a try.

Luck was with us. We topped the pass during a lull; by the time we reached Bulbule, half an hour down the other side, the wind had picked up again. Even at Bulbule, the snow was knee-deep in places, the trail barely broken by one or two brave travelers.

The eighth day found us plodding up Danphe Lekh, following in the footsteps of an unknown traveler, narrow cylinders in the knee-deep snow. The sun was out now, in full force, and I was the only one who had brought sunglasses.

At the Tharmare teahouse we learned that the steep trail over the pass was open. But Karma, Jickchor, and Lundup could not continue. They had neglected to cover their eyes against the glare, and both were on the verge of snowblindness. We realized that Jumla was a mere four or five hours away. Knowing that home comforts awaited us with the United Missions folks and knowing that there might be a doctor, we decided not to spend another night on the trail. Rod and I took one sleeping bag, our mattresses, and a jacket, and went on ahead. The others could come the next day.

We crossed the broad meadow against the wind. For once I was in the lead, stumbling in windblown, frozen footprints. Rod trudged close behind in my shadow with a red bandanna draped over his head, squinting against the intense glare of sun on the snow.

The trail led up through forest and then along a ridgeline before dropping steeply down into the valley. Snow had blown up against the ridge, forming a giant cornice, and at the top of it the wind was like a hurricane. We were determined to have dinner in Jumla, and we slipped and slid as best we could over the snow and ice and down the other side, until we found enough shelter from the wind for a hard-earned rest.

We knew then that we would make it before dark, but the steep trail was snow and mud all the way. We were like horses going to water in the desert. After falling for the third time, looking like a mud pie, I stopped caring if I slipped, but Rodney's instinct for self-preservation kept him upright and relatively clean.

Coming to the school, we knocked at the door of the barn. We were paralyzed with exhaustion and relief, and I drew a blank when we were offered coffee and spice cake. Spice cake? Coffee? Would we like some?

We washed our hands and faces and sat on wooden chairs that could be easily cleaned when we left. When the words came, they came in a rush, and for the first of many times, we told the story of Rodney getting bitten by a snow leopard.

We were told that Dr. Sibley, who had practiced surgery before joining the United Missions, had recently come to Jumla. We probably would find him at his home down the hill close to town. We did.

"Come in, come in," he called in answer to our knock. New to Jumla, he was probably expecting mission visitors, certainly not us. Stooping to avoid a collision with the doorsill, he stepped outside with his eye on Rodney's hand, his gray hair and beard ruffling in the breeze. He was slender, in his midfifties, and at least six feet tall.

"I've never treated a snow leopard bite before," he remarked as he inspected the damage to Rod's hand. "Looks like someone's been doctoring you, though." We told him about Mr. Bogati at Mangri. "Soak it in a pan of warm water for an hour, clean it out real good so I can see under all that dried blood and Mr. Bogati's multicolored medicines."

After he had examined it closely, he said it would probably be okay to stay in Jumla, taking antibiotics and exercising the fingers regularly. But if there was infection deep in the wounds, he'd need to make an incision. He didn't want to have to do that with Jumla's poor facilities. He didn't think there was tendon damage, but in Kathmandu they could be sure. And in Kathmandu there would be vaccine for the highly unlikely possibility of rabies.

"If I were you," he said finally, "I'd go."

There was the usual hassle over tickets, with two or three prospective passengers for every available seat. Dr. Sibley fashioned a splint for Rod

out of cardboard, newspaper, and plastic sheeting that would have convinced even the most hard-nosed ticket agent to find him a place on the
plane. I would have to be satisfied with a later rice shuttle via Nepalganj.
The idea that I could go at all was good enough for me.

We spent ten days in Kathmandu, where Rod got excellent treatment
from a Nepalese surgeon. While we waited for tickets back to Jumla, we
weren't idle. I spent several hours in the food bazaar. We had arrived in
Kathmandu with literally nothing but the clothes on our backs, so even
with the RNAC's strict baggage allowance, we could get sixty pounds
of goodies on the plane. We met friends and got invited to parties. Rod
became a most reluctant celebrity.

"Oh, Mayor Lindsay, I want you to meet Rodney Jackson," said the
hostess at one cocktail party, introducing us to that ex-mayor of New
York. "Rod's been bitten by a snow leopard!"

Chuck McDougal was in town, on a break from his tiger studies in
Chitwan, and he and Rod discussed "Dui's" mistaken identity. Chuck,
too, had had difficulty sexing young tigers, news that went a long way
toward relieving Rod's acute embarrassment. "I'll still squirm every time
I think about it," said Rod. "But if I had to make a dumb mistake, at
least no harm was done."

Exactly a month after leaving in a rush, we were back in Base Camp,
Rod's hand somewhat stiff but almost completely healed. On the journey
back we met a group of Kartik people below Gumghari. Tsewong, they
said, had died in Dolphu the previous week. Mr. Bogati had treated him
for several days and told him that if he stayed two weeks in Mangri he
could be completely cured. But Tsewong's wife was convinced that he
was dying, that nothing would save him, and she insisted that they return
to Dolphu, for Tsewong had said that if he was dying he wanted to be
at home.

For Mr. Bogati, a man born and raised in the far West and who was
so dedicated to helping the people of his district, it must have been
tremendously discouraging to lose Tsewong. His death brought home the
fact that the struggle to bring modern medicine to Nepal's remotest

inhabitants involved more than overcoming the problems of stationing people and supplies in such rugged terrain. The Bhotes themselves, through their reluctance to accept and put their confidence in Mr. Bogati, erected invisible barriers that would take years of patience and perseverance to overcome.

CHAPTER

22

Capture!—"Char"

Two weeks after Rod and I left for the doctor, "Dui" was captured—for the fifth time—in a trap set along the Pine Camp Trail.

"He's done the whole tour now," said Gary. "He's sampled every one of our trap sites. We should have named him 'Bonehead.' Karan and Sonam wouldn't come anywhere near, so I had to get the drug in him by myself. I didn't want to take any chances either, so I used the jabstick, gave a good dose, and made sure the needle went in the first time. Once he was out cold, Sonam helped me weigh him, and then Karan found a wound on his tail. It looks like 'Dui' really is having a hard time making a living, or establishing his range. But he's gained five pounds, so that's a little bit encouraging."

Recapturing "Dui" wasn't the only excitement while we were gone. On February 25, Gary heard a leopard yowling from Tillisha Terrace. He was in bed and nearly asleep, still reveling in the aftereffects of his first shower since Thanksgiving, taken with the vinyl "solar shower" (a ten-dollar improvement in our standard of camp living that was worth a hundred dollars, except it was seldom warm enough in winter to use it without freezing). Early the following morning, with all the others still away observing sheep at Dhukyel Camp, he heard it again—or perhaps a different cat—calling from the same area. It was none of the collared cats, according to the lack of radio signals. The calls were reminiscent of an alley cat in heat—"aaoowh"—but more varied in pitch and length, sometimes throaty, muffled, and sounding quite human. He heard rocks falling from the bluff, and looked up. The observation period that followed lasted three and a half hours.

From Gary's field notebook:

February 26, 1984, 6:37 A.M.

Snow leopard sitting tall at midterrace; sees me and steps back from the terrace edge. The cat doesn't appear very large, but its body is filled out as one would expect with a mature cat.

In the following hour and twelve minutes, the cat called fifty times. Gary once had a clear view of it sitting like a dog, head thrown back, mouth barely moving as it yowled. He held his breath, goose bumps rising along his arms, when the cat approached a trap and without hesitation made a detour to the left.

8:16 A.M.

Cat is now at the west end of the terrace at the base of a cliff. It circles several big rocks, then stops facing a four-foot-tall boulder, stands upright on its hind limbs, and balances against the rock, using its right forepaw. It throws its head back and appears to sniff the air, then drops to the ground on all four paws, turns 180 degrees, and sprays the boulder with urine and scent. The cat holds its tail erect and rapidly twitches and shakes it as the liquid ejects.

For months and months Rod and Gary had searched for such scent markings, certain that snow leopards did it, like other cats, to communicate signals about their location and possibly their breeding condition; but they had never found proof. This leopard demonstrated that they simply hadn't been looking in quite the right places. By the time we returned from Kathmandu, Gary had found more than two dozen sprayed rocks.

Never looking back, the cat walks, without hesitation, past two traps to the river side of the terrace. It stops abruptly at a clump of grass as though it smelled or saw something that startled it. The leopard lays on its side with its face jammed into the grass. Several times it rolls back and forth onto its back as it alternately "mouths" the grass, then smells it and finally rubs its entire face and head in the vegetation. It is not eating the grass; rather, it is transferring messages (at least saliva and all its implications) to and from the spot. This clump of grass is about a foot from an established group of scrapes.

With his eyes glued to the leopard, Gary had moved slowly up onto the terrace west of camp. Now he was in an awful quandary. He should go back for the cameras. But if he left now, the cat might move and he'd have no idea which way it went. For once he was sorry the others weren't in camp.

8:30 A.M.

Finally, the cat sits up erect, and staring off into the distance, tilts its head back and calls several times, in a manner reminiscent of coyote. Following each call it pauses for several seconds as though it is waiting for a response. In four or five leaps the cat descends the vertical bluff to a huge dark boulder by the trail. It moves around the far side of the boulder and without scraping, sniffing, rubbing, or apparent delay, it sprays the downslope side as it passes.

Again, he dared not leave. Would the leopard go up Tillisha Stream, or cross over and come out on the slope and cliffs opposite his vantage point?

8:30 A.M. [continued]

The leopard moves slowly west, crossing Tillisha Stream. It doesn't use the main trail; instead, it remains within a foot of the sheer escarpment edge. After walking a hundred feet it stops and with its ears cocked forward peers intently to the river below, as though it were stalking prey. Then the cat jumps and somehow clings to the steep slab rock and easily traverses down the hundred-foot cliff and onto the rockfall below. Although the cat's route down the cliff is done in such a seemingly routine manner, it would have been a major task for this biologist and probably one never attempted.

Two junipers at the base of the cliff caught its attention. It circled each of them, sniffing, spraying, standing on hind legs to smell among the branches. It looked fully occupied with those two trees, the terrain round about fairly rocky and open. Gary made his move. Eleven minutes to the tent and back with cameras, lenses, tripod, and film.

The cat was gone. He searched. He waited. An hour and a half went by and then he gave up, only slightly disappointed about the photographs, for he had learned what he needed to know about finding scent marks. The information would be the key to some of the study's most important findings.

Now that they had a better idea of what kind of features were likely candidates, they could use their noses quite effectively to sniff out the difference between a rain streak and a leopard spray. They found a treasure trove of scent-marked boulders and even an occasional tree trunk with scent or claw marks. Often they could even tell if the cat had been "cheek rubbing," rolling its face in its own or another cat's pungent scent, for sometimes a few frosty hairs were left clinging to rock or bark.

But their reputations with the villagers weren't improved by their stopping every few yards along the trails to sniff boulders.

"They think you're both crazy," I said. "Karma asked me, 'Why Ronney-Sah'b, Geddy-Sahb all time smelling rock?' "

Winter turned to spring while we were in Kathmandu; the wild peach trees decked themselves with pale pink blossoms, shrubs leafed almost overnight, the dun earth sprouted green with fragile shoots of herbs and grass. Seen from a distance, the slopes still wore their fall and winter shades of ocher. But we knew that we'd look up one day to find that tints of green and daubs of bloom had softly altered the mountains' harsh mood.

The winter had been so mild that the bharal never came down to feed along the river. We saw an occasional herd, but never the numbers of previous years. Snow leopard activity largely matched that of the ungulates; they roamed the high country, making themselves hard to catch, except for the hopeless "Dui."

A whole month passed under blue skies—short-sleeve days. Lizards basked on hot boulders, and our dough-white winter skins turned quickly to healthy-looking brown beneath a layer of Langu dust. No longer did we dread the moment when the sun sank behind the mountains.

The long johns went to Tillisha Cave, where it would be cold, even in summer. My hot-water bottle, with the hole I had "fixed" with glue and a patch, no longer threatened to spring a leak and get me evicted from the warm folds of our down sleeping bag. No more would I hear cries in the night from Rodney, "Don't turn over so fast, you're sucking in the freezing air!" No longer would he have to endure my iceberg feet pressed against his warm flesh. But the pee pot stayed in its corner near the door; not having to dash outside in the middle of the night was a luxury too good to give up.

At first all the others in camp had turned up their noses when they saw me emptying it over the bank each morning; but I noticed that when the nights got cold, the empty jars and coffee cans vanished one by one from the kitchen into each of their tents, and it wasn't long before the emptying of the pee pots became a campwide morning ritual.

Rod and Gary began working almost entirely at Pine Camp and Tillisha Cave. With the sheep staying high, Karan, too, made the journey to Tillisha. He and Sonam spent ten days exploring the grasslands and estimating the total number of sheep that made their living on the northern flanks of Tillisha Mountain.

Both tracking camps were supplied with a tent, stocks of food, and cooking utensils, and in the case of Pine Camp, a twenty-liter plastic jerry can full of water that would last two or three days, depending on how many people stayed at a time.

Two traps that could easily be put in and out of commission were set near Pine, activated only when someone was there. I would check the Base Camp traps early each morning; if we had a capture, whoever was at Pine would have to come down in a hurry.

If it weren't for the fact that walkie-talkies were prohibited, a few sets would have gone a long way toward solving two major problems: safety for anyone alone at a tracking camp for several days, and alerting Rod or Gary of a cat capture when they were away from Eding. But apart from the Nepalese Army and the police, no group or individuals except mountain climbing expeditions are given permits to have walkie-talkies, and even they must go through a rigid application process. Under the circumstances, our day-to-day logistics were often highly complicated.

Scheduled returns to Base Camp, for instance, had to be met; otherwise illness or injury was assumed, and a search would be mounted for the missing party. With careful planning, idle radio collars or colored flags could allow a little flexibility, but it was very limited: "A red flag on the dead tree west of Pine Camp means everything's okay and I'm staying a day or two longer." Such signals could easily be confused, especially when the "flag" was a T-shirt that had been on someone's back for a week!

That morning, Karma had the job of hauling a load of water to Pine Camp, a job that usually took half the day. The morning was warm, and he stopped to rest partway up the steep ridge that led to "The Eagle," a big bird-shaped boulder perched prominently on a small knoll. Surveying the scene below, he noticed movement at the far set of traps on Tillisha Terrace. A leopard was caught in the snare. Karma came leaping and shouting back to camp.

"Oh, no!" I cried, looking at my watch. "It's past ten o'clock. Rod will have stopped listening for our radio signal."

Karma headed off again for Pine Camp, as fast as he could go, hoping that Rod or Gary was in camp and not out somewhere mapping or running sign transects. Meanwhile, I got all the gear together, running back and forth from the tent to the storage shed to the rocks above the kitchen, where I could see the trapped, uncollared cat, praying it wouldn't escape, and biting my fingernails to the bone.

Karma found Rod in camp, preparing to go to sleep after spending the whole night monitoring "Tin."

The record they established that day would never be broken: an hour and a half for a round trip that normally took two hours just in the going. Rod, hollow-eyed, prepared to radio-collar his fourth snow leopard.

"At least it isn't 'Dui'!" he remarked, filling the syringe with a good, strong dose of ketamine. "But I'm following Gary's lead and not taking any chances, either with myself or with the leopard."

The cat lunged around, trying to get away, but never once growled or swiped at him. It was so completely sedated that we could have spent half an hour looking her over and taking photographs.

"This one *is* a female. She is *definitely* a female," Rod said as he examined and measured her. He looped a strap of webbing around her paws, slipped a birch branch through the loops, and he and Karma hoisted her up to be weighed. The scale read eighty-five pounds.

"She's a prime female," said Rod. "Definitely breeding age. She's just what I'd hoped for."

Later that spring, pregnant, she would be our first snow leopard—the first snow leopard in history—to take her own photo with the camera we had set up on Tillisha Terrace.

The bushes surrounding the trap site were hardly touched, certain evidence that "Char" had not been trapped long, that she had been traveling long after sunrise. We needed a better signal in case such a thing happened again. With binocs, Eding Camp could be seen from a point on the ridge above Pine Camp. In the future we would spread a yellow tarp on the ground to signify "Come down at once."

With Karan and Sonam again working from Eding, I took the next chance to join Rod and Gary on a trip to Tillisha Cave. I knew it was going to be a long slog up with less of a trail than on the southern side of the Langu. We all had heavy packs, Rod's and Gary's weighing probably more than sixty pounds each, but at least there wouldn't be anything to fall off of.

From Pine Camp we followed the knife-edge ridge until it melted into a deceivingly gentle-looking hump, covered in dense stands of thorny caragana. Sonam, wielding his kukri, had once cut something of a path through the bushes, but it was so steep that the loose earth made walking an exercise of one step forward and two back.

Rest stops were dictated by the marked points of the scrape transect more or less following our route. Any change—a new scrape or a rescrape—provided an excuse to stop and record the information. The higher we got, the harder the wind blew. After about three hours we branched off the vertical part. We stood in a gale on the peak of the humped ridge.

"See that small, dark cleft in the rock across the slope? That's Tillisha Cave," said Rod.

It was actually a large overhang, with two tents pitched in the middle, a stack of firewood, and a tiny stone fireplace. The whole rock band was surrounded by a solid mat of caragana—an especially deadly variety of awful thorny bugger—with slick, weedy branches and millions of needles, all pointing up. If I tried to step *on* the branches, they acted like a slide; if I tried to step *between* them, they grabbed my ankle and pulled it out from under me.

It was almost a shock to tumble one last time onto the threshold of Tillisha Cave to find the wind suddenly and magically cut off, to turn and face the breathtaking vista of the high Himalayas in their white coat. It wasn't long before I was holding a hot cup of coffee and doing an "I conquered the mountain" dance.

"I guess I'd better sit still," I said, joining Rod and Gary around what was left of the fire. "The coffee will run out through all my caragana punctures. I feel like a colander."

"Listen," said Rod. "One of the best things about Tillisha Cave is that since we're so high up, the river doesn't drown out all the other sounds. You can hear the snow cocks calling."

Both the Tibetan and Himalayan species of these large partridges lived in the rocks and grass of Tillisha Mountain. The dark bill and reddish neck-stripe distinguished the larger Himalayan birds from the smaller, yellow-billed Tibetan species. A variety of sounds drifted across the slope. Cackling and chuckling were mingled with whistles of three ascending notes, ending on a high, sharp "wheet." In the mornings the slopes resounded with their calls and gave Tillisha Cave a lovely and distinctive air.

We had three days to roam the grasslands above the tree line, but below the gray slate and rubble of the peak. It was exciting to explore the world at fifteen thousand feet!

We ranged over knobbly clumps of long, golden alpine sedge to the far eastern ridge, and looked down at the headwaters of Tillisha Stream. Far below us lay a world of gray and brown: oblique cliffs, grassland, and talus slopes. Tillisha Stream ran through the center of the broad valley that swept up and disappeared over a high pass between the peak of Tillisha Mountain and greater peaks behind Chaling La.

Deep chutes scored the rock faces. Boulders crashed, freed perhaps by melting ice. Frozen waterfalls hung silently from limestone lips high above the valley floor. Stark, deserted, the land looked empty but for a vulture circling on the high wind.

"It can't be as bleak as it looks," said Rod. "Bharal must graze, and leopards must at least pass through. It draws me like a magnet, though I can't imagine why. I feel as if I should see something special—perhaps a wild yak. If they still exist anywhere in Nepal, it would have to be in a place like this."

We would learn that the Dolphas themselves had never ventured into Tillisha Basin; the way in was too treacherous, even by their standards. But before the season's end the basin would give rise to an enigma so compelling as eventually to pit Rod and Gary mind and body against its harsh interior.

CHAPTER

23

Capture!—"Panch"

Rod and Gary had set their latest trap on the Tillisha Terrace bluff trail. Two days earlier "Dui" had, for a change, walked over it without even springing it.

"I don't know about that trap," I said. "If it can't even catch 'Dui,' I doubt if it will catch any *other* cat."

Early on the morning on April 30, I climbed the bluff near camp, where I could see five of the ten traps with the scope. As usual, I first did a quick search with the binocs, to look for any obvious bush-shaking or other signs of a trapped cat.

Hardly a bush or a blade of grass grew on the eroding bluff, and when I focused the binocs on the trap, the unmistakable form of a long-tailed snow leopard met my eye.

A rubbery rush began in my knees and quickly spread through my chest, my fingers, my brain. I fumbled with the scope's plastic screw-on caps, cursed the tripod for having three legs to fix just right before it would stand on the sloping bluff. My heart flopped wildly against my ribs.

The scope, three times more powerful than the binocs, revealed a woodsmoke- and charcoal-colored cat lying in a shallow depression formed by the trap site on the otherwise steep and crumbling trail.

"Here we go again," I said to myself as I looked long enough to confirm what I already knew. I left the scope and ran back to camp. Karma would have to hightail it to Pukchang to get Gary. He'd hang the spare collar on a bush along the way, but it was already eight-fifteen and we couldn't rely on him checking again soon. He and Rod were both due in Eding that day; if we were lucky they'd already be on the way.

In a near-repeat of "Char's" capture, I spent two hellish hours gathering the gear and cameras and running between the scope and a point where I could see the men when they came back over Eding Knoll. I had no receiver in camp, and I hadn't noticed if the cat was wearing a collar. Was this just another recapture?

When I went to check, I couldn't see the cat's head. It was lying facing away from me, lying still. Lying *absolutely* still—much too still for a leopard in a trap.

"Oh, no, it's dead," I said, adding, with the ridiculous illogic of panic, "strangled on the cable, or probably brained by the spring pan."

I moved uphill for a better angle, ponderously adjusting the tripod and refocusing the scope. The cat was sitting up, around its neck nothing but pale fur stippled with black.

"Get a grip on yourself, Darla. Maybe I should wash my hair," I thought. That would kill half an hour of this interminable waiting. But what if Rodney miraculously appeared? It was much too early to expect him, unless he had camped the previous night at Choyap. In any case, he wouldn't understand how I could be washing my hair with a leopard in the trap.

I stoked the fire. Gary and Karma would need a cup of tea after running all the way back. I could drink one now—and then check the cat again. Maybe by then *someone* would come.

When I next looked through the scope, the cat was gone.

"It got away," I said with moan, "even though it hadn't been struggling at all." A foot-tall ephedra plant stirred at the edge of the trail. Peering through the reedy clump beside the trap were two pointed ears and the dappled face of a leopard.

I was eventually delivered from the edge of hysteria by the sight of two figures moving quickly down the trail from Eding Knoll.

Gary had been a thousand feet above the river on the northern side of Pukchang and thought Karma's shouts were the "jimbu people" arriving for an early harvest. Fortunately, he decided to come down and secure his camp. He got his own dose of rubber legs when he found Karma there instead of the villagers.

It was the first day of good weather for weeks, and they were sweat-soaked and tired when they came into Eding. They caught their breath for a few minutes and off we went, sidestepping along the wobbly log bridge that soon was to be swept away by the rising river.

"Jabbing this cat is going to be tricky," said Gary uneasily as we boulder-hopped across Tillisha Stream. "I'll have to find a way up the bluff to the right of it, along the upper part where it's really unstable, and approach the cat from the trail above." His eyes sought out the route as he dropped his pack and began to unload the capture gear.

The leopard was trapped by the *hind* leg, which had never happened before and which made it even worse for Gary, since the cat had that much more swiping distance and ability with its forelegs.

He worked his way into a precarious position on the slippery bluff and wasted no time moving in for the jab. As I tried to photograph the scene from below, my view was obscured by flying dust as the cat desperately tried to avoid the outstretched stick in Gary's hand.

He got her the first time with a good dose of the drug. She chewed quietly on the metal stake as it began to take effect. She made no sound during the jabbing. Like "Char," she was out cold in a few minutes, eyes wide and muscles rigid. Except for the rising and falling of her chest, she looked more like a stuffed museum specimen than a living leopard.

At the steep trap site the tools, the people, and the cat kept slipping downhill.

"Let's move her down beside Tillisha Stream for weighing and measuring," said Gary.

"Good idea," I replied. "But the tape fell over the edge; we'll have to find something else to do the measuring with. How about this webbing?"

"It'll do," he said, "You can mark it with the laundry pen."

At forty-five pounds, "Panch" was the smallest leopard yet. Up close, her fur was less gray than pale yellowish-brown, especially along the back. Her markings were pronounced: very black ears, a downward streak at either side of her mouth, dense rosettes on her lower back.

We left her in the shade of the streamside trees and returned to camp. I forgot about the nearby active trap that Gary didn't know Rod had put in along the stream. We reviewed all the highlights of the day, starting with discovering the trapped cat and ending with deciphering the marks on the webbing indicating her body measurements.

We were still sitting on the big camp boulder when Karma announced, "Lo, sah'b," and Rod walked into camp, exhausted from the hard walk from Dhukyel over Tyson's Cliff, and starving, having run out of food the day before. Like a foraging langur, he'd found an old, broken package of noodles in the dust and dirt of the cave kitchen at Dhukyel and washed them in the Langu. That had been his dinner last night and breakfast this morning.

"Who are you monitoring?" he asked finally.

"No. 5," said Gary.

"Oh, you're testing the collar?" said Rod, oblivious to all the tranquilizing gear lying around. The signal was, of course, coming in loud and clear, and even Karma was laughing at Rod. All he could really think about was something to eat, and it took a few minutes before he was convinced that collar No. 5 was really on a cat.

The signal quickened with movement from the leopard, and I got really worried about that trap just upstream. In fact, most of her likely routes away from there led through a minefield of traps, all of which she probably had avoided in the past, if she was in fact the wary "Houdini" who had eluded us for so long. I took the scope and went to check.

Still lying where we'd left her, staring up at the trees, probably trying to get them in focus, she was surprisingly easy to see among the surrounding leaves and bushes with her long tail drooped over a low rock.

"Come and look," I called to Rod and Gary, and we spent a couple of hours watching and waiting for her to get up. When she finally did, she was still so wobbly it took her twenty minutes to go forty-five feet to the stream, where she crouched and remained drinking for ten minutes. She then lay down again near the water, concealed among the streamside boulders, and spent the night in the thick shrubs along the stream.

We expected her to move off during the night, as the other cats had done, but she stayed for two days. Rod went across the river, took a wash in Tillisha Stream, double-checked all the traps, and looked at the terrace sign transect, and through all that activity, she still stayed near the mouth of Tillisha Canyon.

We knew by her weight and the condition of her teeth that "Panch" was young. In the following weeks, radio-tracking presented a strong probability that she was in the final steps of becoming independent of her mother, and that her mother was none other than "Char."

Karma and I often made something special for the days when Rod or Gary were in Base Camp. Without a threat of snow to make wood-gathering difficult, we could bake things using the big, two-foot-diameter pot as an oven. We dug around in the treat box and found the makings for real bread with yeast, cookies, corn bread, cake, and most amazingly tasty pizza, with salami, canned olives, onions, and yak cheese.

We had our own pidgin language, Karma and I, a combination of English and Nepali that we picked up from one another in the long days we spent alone in Base Camp. We could understand each other fairly well on a basic level, though God knows what we were actually saying. I could barely make myself understood in the village and not at all in Kathmandu.

However much I enjoyed our kitchen banter, Karma would never replace my women friends. Even had I been fluent in Tibetan or Nepali, I would not have trusted Karma with thoughts I kept even from Rod. When I felt the need for a female confidante, I simply had to file it away until we went home, or write it in a letter for which the reply would be months in coming.

And, too, there was an element of danger in Karma and me spending so much time in Eding alone. Whether the danger was real or imagined, it seemed to materialize one evening after dinner when everyone else was away.

"*Ronney-Sahb, timro logne chha, ki chhaina, Didi?*" Is Rodney your husband or not? he asked. As he spoke, his cheek began to twitch.

I answered that he wasn't my husband but that he was very much my friend and that one day we would become husband and wife.

A long silence followed in which I was acutely aware of Karma's physical presence, the fact that he was young, healthy, and attractive and that he could be devilishly charming. "Could it be," I wondered, "that he's about to make a pass at me? I'm almost old enough to be his mother, but I'm also the only woman for miles around, and we are absolutely alone. What would be the consequences of an affair between the cook and the sah'b's woman? Would he tell all his friends? Rodney would murder me—not out of jealousy—I think, but rather for losing the villagers' respect. Why am I even thinking about this? There's no way I would allow it to happen. Most likely Karma is simply curious about American marriage customs."

Still, knowing his propensity to talk himself into trouble, I said good night and went to bed. At least I did have Rodney—companion, natural history instructor, friend, and lover all rolled into one. How much harder it must have been for the others. Though Gary said that Karan felt envious of Rod and me, neither he nor anyone else ever expressed it overtly to us. Gary confined his thoughts to the pages of his diary:

April 28, 1984

My guts continue to churn, my energy is low, my head and heart have not ceased to ache. My thoughts are with Roxy and Morgan, whom I long to see again; today the homesickness is paralyzing and uncontrollable. I realize that regardless of anything Roxy says to me, underneath she is bitter about my decision to join the study. I'll admit that a part of me will always regret leaving them, but I also realize that I would probably make the same decision given a second chance. But I wish they could know something of the life here. There's so much that Roxy would love about Nepal. Rod and Darla are so lucky; long after the fieldwork is done they will still have an almost endless reserve of common experiences.

We had talked before about Roxy and Morgan visiting Nepal, but the study would be over before we found the means to make it happen.

* * *

With Gary on ghost duty, Rod and I climbed up to Pine Camp to track "Panch." We stripped to shorts and T-shirts and sweltered in the blazing sun.

A lammergeier wheeled above our heads. Up close it was huge, with wings that might have spanned eight feet. It peered down at us through beady black eyes, cocking its head this way and that. Its big shadow ran before it on the ground, and the wind soughed through the feathers on its outstretched wings.

Another huge vulture, the Himalayan griffon, also circled Pine Camp. Crag martins, wall creepers, kestrels, and crows were among the other feathered visitors. Once Rod saw a flock of bar-headed geese, heard them honking high overhead as they migrated south for the spring.

For once, the shade of the "kitchen" juniper was welcome. We sat, languid, beneath its twisted old branches scattered with fat, dusty, brownish-purple berries, and wrote our notes.

Gary would join us in a day or two and we would all continue on to Tillisha Cave. It would be Gary's final expedition away from Base Camp for the season. At the end of May, after six months of fieldwork, he would leave for Kathmandu and go home to his family.

When we first heard the helicopter, we thought the heat had gone to our heads. For all the time we had spent in the Langu, we had never heard an engine of any kind, or seen a jet trail in the sky. The sudden thwocking of the helicopter's rotor carried over several miles; we couldn't see it, and couldn't even tell for sure which direction the sound was coming from. Then Rodney gasped and pointed toward the southern bank of the Langu.

High above the gorge, camouflaged against the forest backdrop of pine and birch, a big green army helicopter flew steadily, following the river course. We dove for our binoculars, too late for much of a view, as the machine flew over Pukchang, rounded the great bend of the Langu, and disappeared.

The silence rang—our voices lost in stunned amazement. That might have been the first helicopter ever to fly up the Langu. Minutes later it came back, flying directly over the river, just about equal in elevation to Pine Camp. We jumped up and down and waved our arms. Couldn't they see our blue Pine Camp tent? Couldn't they see the big tent and all the smaller ones at Base Camp?

"Land! Land, damnit!" yelled Rodney. "Give me a ride so I can do an aerial search for 'Ek' and 'Tin.'" There was no sign of the helicopter hesitating, or that its occupants had seen either camp. In minutes it had covered, in both directions, country that would easily take us two weeks of walking.

We dropped to the ground, limp with astonishment and disappointment, feeling peculiarly bereft at our "abandonment." Who was it? What were they doing? We could think of only one possible explanation. A new national park, Shey-Phoksundo, was being established by the Department of National Parks and Wildlife Conservation. It would encompass most of Dolpo District and extend west to include the Langu. They might have been surveying the boundaries.

Gary came up the following day. "Karma and I were down by the cable bridge when the 'copter flew over," he said. "I don't think whoever was inside saw us, but if they did, they didn't try to let us know."

Gary brought the gear for setting up a remote photo station on the grasslands around Tillisha. We hoped to get the bharal to photograph themselves. At least eighty animals grazed the slopes from Dhukyel to Tillisha, merging and breaking into smaller groups and reforming in a constant, gradual shuffle of sheep. Herds often would use a particular "bowl" where we thought we could set up the camera to get a nice shot.

"We'll entice them," said Gary, "by baiting the area in front of the camera with this Tibetan rock salt I bought in Dolphu. If they like it, maybe they'll make a habit of visiting the bowl."

While Rod and Gary went looking for "Tin"—and "Ek" (though we had given up hope of hearing from him again), I would watch over the photo station from a vantage point on the near ridgeline, with the remote switch box at the ready to trip the camera in case the sheep came.

"I'll wait until they're in just the right position, push the button, and get the ultimate close-up bharal photo, with spectacular mountains in the background," I said confidently.

Meanwhile, Karma would scour the grasslands in the other direction for whatever deadwood he could find among the scarce patches of low-growing alpine juniper. Gary's work on the kerosene stoves had been only marginally successful. The Jumla kerosene was so watered down and dirty that the stoves continued to clog up and quit.

I spent the whole first day sitting in a small hollow below the ridge, writing letters for Gary to take out, and watching thirty-five sheep slowly circle the bowl. They ate grass, lay around, and ruminated—but never got quite close enough to find the salt. Perhaps they saw the camera box sitting beside a rock, smelled our scent on it, or simply didn't like the looks of it.

The following afternoon, as we were all returning to the cave together, we surprised a group of five female bharal with their near-yearling lambs. They came from above us, and it was unclear if we were the cause of their alarm or what. When we saw them, they were running downslope, right toward us. They stopped suddenly, only a few yards away, and stood perfectly still, watching us.

"Put your pack down, slowly, and get your camera," whispered Rod. But before I could bend my arm, they all started running again, literally thundering past us, disappearing over the knoll below. We searched the terrain for any sign of a leopard. If there was one, it was well hidden among all the dents and depressions and rocks above us.

That was the closest our cameras, including the photo station, ever got to a live bharal.

CHAPTER

24

The Den

Rod took out all the traps in May, after Gary left for home. He couldn't track three leopards and stay close enough to camp to be available for a capture. We had never caught a cat so late in the season, and the lack of activity along the terrace transect was a good indication that we weren't likely to.

While Rod tracked "Panch" in the grasslands behind Pine Camp, I stayed in Eding with Sonam, tracking "Char." Sonam took it for granted that I would never leave him alone in camp overnight. While we could joke with Karma, offer him bribes, and tease him about his ways, Sonam, for all his physical strength and daring, was emotionally fragile. Unlike Karma, he seemed never to question, and certainly never to challenge, the forces that shaped his life. He had the trust and innocence of a child, and we hadn't the heart to trifle with him.

Had I been better at pinpointing "Char's" signal, we might have spent several days watching her at a kill on the slopes above Tillisha Terrace. We would have seen her as she moved the fifty yards between the carcass of a female bharal and the shade of a juniper, where she rested during the heat of the day. She must have run back and forth, chasing off crows and vultures, though there couldn't have been too many birds, or Sonam and I would have seen them circling and known there was a kill.

I had the direction right. I knew her signal was coming from about the midpoint of Tillisha Terrace. It was the elevation that threw me. It simply never occurred to me that she could be so close to camp, or that she would *stay* so close.

Rod came down from Pine Camp the day that "Char" moved off, crossing Tillisha Canyon and heading for the grassland.

"Oh, hell, I should go back up, but I can't face it so soon," he said. "I'm filthy and I want a bath. Where's the soap?" he asked, rummaging around in the corner of the tent.

We went across the river and submerged ourselves in the clear, cool water of Tillisha Stream, and then up onto the terrace to check the scrape transect. Our noses told us that nearby something was dead, and it wasn't long before we had located what was left of "Char's" kill.

All along, Rod and Gary had been greatly discouraged by the rarity of finding *any* kill remains, much less fresh ones. We almost never saw the vultures intently circling or landing, and Rod finally resorted to offering a bounty. Any villager or staff member who found a kill would get paid, depending on the freshness of the carcass, up to 250 rupees. For a while there was a lively new spirit of competition as everyone kept a sharp eye skyward. Off would go the bounty hunters, all the hired help in camp, at the slightest hint of a gathering of vultures. But always they had come back tired, tattered, and defeated.

For the first time we had fresh remains of a kill made by one of our collared cats. Nothing was left but the head, forelegs, stomach contents, a little skin, and small piles of hair. The head, with one horn missing, had been picked clean by the "invisible" birds. What time of day "Char" had made the kill, what kind of throat bite she had used, and how much she had eaten at a time, especially the first meal, were all questions that would remain unanswered. Still, relatively speaking, these remains were a gold mine of information.

The cat left five huge, messy scats, lots of tracks, and five or six bedding sites as she followed the shade around a juniper and a peach tree. She had deeply gouged the juniper, probably sharpening her claws.

We tried not to breathe in either the rotten smell or the hundreds of flies crawling in our eyes and noses while we took notes and made measurements.

Rod may have missed a chance to fill in some gaps in his data, but perhaps it's just as well that "Char" enjoyed this ample feast, for unbeknownst to us she was then only days away from denning up and giving birth. It would be many weeks before she got to eat again at her leisure.

When we got back to camp late that evening, Sonam was bursting with a surprise to top off the day. Our errant rooster had run away when he'd tried to catch it for the pot. Despite Sonam's reputation as a hunter, he wasn't very good at hurling rocks at a chicken; perhaps he didn't find the activity very sporting. He'd missed the rooster coming and going, but he'd left it with no doubt about his intentions. It hadn't shown its face in camp since it ran squawking down the trail toward Dolphu.

Sonam felt really bad; it was our last chicken, and maybe a fox or a jungle cat would get the treat that was meant for us. He made a trap out of string and a long twig bent just so. When we walked into camp, there was the rooster, hanging upside down from the branch by a string around its leg. "Oh, sah'b," Sonam declared, nearly exploding with pride and relief, "sure tonight, sah'b, Didi, I, chicken eat!"

June began with the hottest days we'd ever known in the Langu, ninety degrees in the shade and surely 110 in the sun, though we never risked breaking the thermometer to find out.

I guess we were lucky that the migration of the fleas took as long as it did. Up until that spring, Eding Camp had been relatively flea-free, except for short periods when the Dolphas came. But when the hot weather arrived, there wasn't a spot in camp where we could sit without feeling their quick pings. They even jumped into our plates of food.

Insect repellent was powerless against them, and we determined to bring something next time that would do the trick—DDT, if it came to that. They had even made their way to Pine Camp.

The hot weather also brought a new batch of flies, sluggish and clingy, attracted to any patch of bare, salty skin. They found our lips especially appealing. Trying to work in the tent, Rodney went on afternoon rampages, slapping hopelessly with a homemade fly swatter, outnumbered five hundred to one.

Sonam thought Rod's tantrums were funny. His attitude was, Why bother to kill them? Tomorrow there'll be just as many.

We thought of Gary, hopefully by now in Kathmandu, probably drinking a bottle of ice-cold beer. We put some lemonade powder into a canteen and filled it with cold water from Tillisha Stream, staving off thoughts of "civilization" with three weeks of work still ahead of us.

Rod and Sonam hacked a new camp out of the hillside above Pukchang Cave, high enough to pick up signals from collared cats. Like Pine Camp, the new Pukchang High Camp had no water supply, and Sonam would have to haul it from Eding. The hike was longer but much less steep than the way to Pine. All along the way the hillsides were covered with blooming plants; my collection was growing almost faster than I could handle. But the jimbu, lush and nearly ready for harvesting before the heat wave, was now shriveled up and dead.

Karma came back on June 11, having seen Gary fly out on the third, on the first plane to fly for nearly two weeks because of the heavy smog.

Karma also reported that all the kitchen equipment we had stored at Dhukyel had been stolen: a pressure cooker, pots, jerry cans, utensils.

"I guess it was irresistible," I said. "All those things are so hard to get, and expensive for the villagers."

But Rod's feelings were hurt, and he was angry. "I had the idea that they thought more of us than that," he said. "We were obviously using the gear, and it was important to our well-being. Anyway, we can't ignore the theft; if we don't make some sort of protest, we'll be in for worse trouble. We must try to find the thief—or at least to get our things back."

Karma had an idea. Tenzing Thakpa's father, an old man bent by some deforming disease, was a jhankri, a shaman. Perhaps Sonam could take him a little money from Ronney-Sah'b and ask him to use his powers to look into our problem. It seemed like a good idea to approach it the way the villagers might if it were one of them who had been robbed.

Even if it didn't work, perhaps it would give the thief a sleepless night or two.

Almost overnight, the weather changed to scattered light showers, lots of clouds, and mist hanging on the peaks. "Char" was spending all her time in one small area, raising the good possibility that she was denning.

We had one more trip to make to Tillisha, to collect alpine plants, hide the gear and remaining food as best we could against foraging Dolphas, and for Rod to mark the transects for next season's work.

We camped overnight at Pine, and from the ridge above, Rod fixed "Dui" in the same spot he'd been located previously, up in Tillisha Basin. The bouncing signal was weak and hard to fix precisely, but what worried us most was that it was "inactive" and continued to be over the three hours Rod monitored it—just as the cat had been the last time. Had the leopard shed its radio collar? Or worse, had it died?

Early the next morning we began the long climb to Tillisha Cave. Karma was less than enthusiastic about having to move the half-dozen loads to Rod's proposed hiding place in the cleft of some rocks *above* the cave. Karma wanted to investigate the possibilities *below* the cave, which would make his work considerably easier. Rod thought that any of the small caves below Tillisha would be too obvious for hiding places, but Karma was determined to see for himself. We watched him move, surefooted across the slick, brushy slope, and then suddenly veer off, for some reason, downhill and out of sight. As we moved slowly up the hump of the ridge his voice drifted up, but none of the words was intelligible over the distance except *na,* Tibetan for bharal.

We came to a big, fresh, sloppy leopard scat, with a scrape beside it so fresh the blades of grass were still bent over. Had Karma found a kill site? The transect followed the ridge above our trail, and while Rod went to look for more new signs, I made may way over the "samurai" caragana to the camp and a hot cup of coffee.

We wanted to get everything done quickly, in a day if we could, and while I waited for the water to boil, I organized the plant-pressing gear and clipped some plants near the cave. Karma came up beaming from ear to ear.

"I, veddy good eye, Didi," he said, "I see big died bharal, sabu not eat."

Rod was slipping and sliding across the slope, and Karma could hardly wait for him to reach the cave. He was quivering with excitement over the top bounty he had just earned, bringing his dream of owning a radio that much closer, and for the red-meat orgy on his horizon.

On the slope just across the dry gully lay a dead bharal, its brown hide just visible in the long grass. It was so fresh the flies had barely touched it. We must have scared the cat away, for it had hardly eaten a mouthful from the sheep's rump.

It was a full-grown male bearing big, curving horns. Rod counted eight and a half rings, one for each year of the bharal's life. Without the scale we could only estimate its weight, at a minimum of 120 pounds.

We followed a swath of disturbed grass and bushes well above the spot where the animal lay. Tufts of leopard fur and bharal hair clung to grass and bushes.

The sheep had put up a great struggle for its life. It was clear that the victor, a leopard of some fifty pounds, had brought down an animal nearly three times its weight. Rod, exploring further, discovered where the cat had approached and made its final rush at a small herd of grazing sheep.

The cat had leaped upon its victim, riding it until it finally fell and presumably presented its neck for the fatal suffocating bite. There were deep holes in its throat and cuts and scrapes all over its body. Its ballooning stomach protruded through a hole in its belly.

From Pine Camp, Rod had picked up a weak signal from "Panch," placing her west of our present location, more toward Dhukyel.

"Now I wish I hadn't left the receiver at Pine," he said. "I don't *think* 'Panch' was here; her signal should have been stronger, but I can't be positive. Anyway, it was a young, determined cat that killed this bharal, and I feel bad about ruining its meal."

Probably while we were eating crunchy granola and drinking tea at Pine Camp, the young snow leopard was getting breakfast the hard way, only to lose it to the likes of us—one of whom was intent upon skinning it, carving it up, and carting off whatever he could carry. We argued over who had a right to the carcass, us or the cat.

From Karma's point of view, anyone would have to be crazy not to take advantage of such an opportunity. In a land where hunger lurks, and especially in this year of borderline famine, he simply couldn't fathom the idea of leaving even one pound to the flies and vultures. He was fully convinced that our pervading human smell would keep the cat from coming back, even if we left it a whole meaty leg. Rod and I thought of the young leopard going hungry.

"Could it starve to death because of us?" I asked.

"Probably not," he replied. "If it were that hungry, it would also be weak; it wouldn't have been able to bring the sheep down in the first place."

If we'd had the gear with us to set up a remote camera, Rod might have been more insistent that we leave the carcass intact. In the end, Karma got his way, partly because Rod felt that an autopsy would provide useful information. When it was done, Karma had a good sixty pounds of "Grade A" bharal meat. But Rodney drew the line at taking the whole thing. Not only did it seem grossly unfair to the cat, which had worked so hard for its meal, but already we had a serious problem of what to do with sixty pounds of meat.

Karma would have to go back to Eding early in the morning and work quickly to get it hung to dry before it spoiled in the heat. He was supposed to carry a load of equipment from Tillisha Cave, items we couldn't dare leave behind. Now he would be completely loaded with bharal, and he would have to make another trip up.

We disagreed, too, about where to hide the camp gear. Karma had found a deep, low cave, one so deep and dark that ice still lay in the recesses. No one could ever camp there, but it was also undoubtedly well known to the Dolphas, and the first place they would look. Karma argued that if the villagers went to all the trouble of getting to Tillisha on the off-chance that we'd left anything behind, they'd find it no matter where we hid it. They'd scour the grasslands. He was probably right, but the thought of giving in was maddening.

"Who's in charge here, anyway?" said Rod.

He had treated the camp staff in the Western manner, rather than the Asian one of a master/servant relationship. We could never adjust to or feel comfortable with playing the part of the master. But just now it felt a little like Karma was taking advantage, that he was seeing dollar signs (or in this case rupee signs) in the bharal meat and didn't really care what happened to our equipment. His English vocabulary was only just workable, but he could still speak with keen, persuasive power. He would have made a killing as a used-car salesman.

Karma got the gear stashed and headed off down the hill early the next morning, almost staggering under his load. Rod and I finished the plant collection and made our way down in the afternoon, carrying heavy packs, collecting plants as we went. We fell often on the steep, loose trail, landing on the caragana, puncturing holes in our beloved Therm-a-Rest mattresses, and turning our ankles. We arrived exhausted at Pine Camp, not intending to proceed another step.

While I brewed a pot of tea, Rod checked the radio, getting no signal from "Panch" and locating "Dui" still inactive in Tillisha Basin.

The wind began to rage in intense gusts bursting over the ridge, blasting through the kitchen tarp, tearing at the blue tent. The tent was in bad shape to begin with; they aren't made to withstand six continuous months in such extremes of weather. One of four aluminum poles, bowed to form the tent's dome shape, had snapped, ripping a jagged hole in the top of the fly sheet.

We had tried to mend the pole, using duct tape and a wrapper cut from a tin can, but it snapped like a piece of plastic. The tent drooped where the pole was missing, its tattered fly sheet flapping and tearing more as the wind picked up.

"We'll get soaked if it rains," I said.

"You're right," Rod replied. "Let's go down."

We unloaded some of the things from our packs, Rod stuffed the heavy plant press into his, and we set off, leaving the tent to the fates, for neither of us had the energy to unpitch it.

We had our fill of bharal curry over the following days. As a special treat, Karma took a morning to make *mo-mos,* tender and tasty morsels of noodle-wrapped meat.

"Eventually, with good behavior and good cooking like that, he may collect his bounty," said Rod—making sure Karma was out of earshot!

"Char" hadn't moved. No kill would have kept her there so long. It was obvious that after something like six weeks of freedom from "Panch," she had given birth to another litter of cubs, in the rocks high above Tillisha East Terrace. For about two days she stayed in an area not much bigger than a football field. Then she began to make daily forays, at first returning frequently to the den to nurse her cubs. Gradually she stayed away longer, until she made a kill, and then she traveled once a day from the den to the kill.

The temptation to go up there was almost overwhelming. The area of the den was higher than Pine Camp, and like Pine Camp, there would be no water. From the looks of the place through the scope, it seemed to offer even fewer prospects for a campsite than the ridge above Pine Camp.

"Lets assume we *could* find a place and that we could haul water up," Rod said, thinking out loud. "There's still the problem of finding the den site without disturbing 'Char.' She could move the cubs, or she could abandon them, or she *could* even attack me to protect her young, especially if I was to stumble upon her."

I looked through the scope at the area he had pointed out. "There's such a jumble of broken rock and boulders, it seems like it would be easy enough to get too close accidently."

If we were lucky enough to see her coming or going as we searched with the scope, then Rod could possibly go up cautiously to a point where she would tolerate his presence. By spending long hours of quiet observation, he might get close enough for photographs. But that could take weeks, and we had only days before leaving for Jumla.

There was no way we could get enough food to extend the field season for the month or six weeks until the cubs would emerge from the den. We would have to be content with what we could learn by delaying for just a few days: valuable first-ever information on "Char's" activity pattern, time spent in the den as opposed to time spent hunting.

Rod made a final hike to Pine Camp before it was taken down and packed up. He spent several hours fixing "Char's" den site, but he got no signal at all from "Dui." Half of him was glad not to get a signal; the other half was aware that the collar could simply have quit, even though the batteries *should* still be good.

Then Rod pitched a tent at Eding Knoll and held a radio-tracking and scope-searching vigil, while Karma and I began sorting, listing, and packing our things. When that was done, Karma went to Dolphu to arrange porters. He came back with Jickchor, to help him carry down the gear from the tracking camps. We hoped that Jickchor, seeing there was nothing left in the cave, would pass the word around the village. At Pine Camp we left one locked metal trunk, containing mostly extra pasta meals and other food supplies.

His vigil at Eding Knoll gave Rod a good idea of how "Char" divided her time between her need to feed herself and the need to nurse her cubs, but he was not lucky enough to catch her in the eye of the spotting scope.

How many cubs she had would remain a mystery. All we could hope was that they would survive until we came back and that "Char's" radio collar kept going.

CHAPTER

25

High Trail to Jumla

The route to Jumla over the mountains behind Wangri was known locally as the Chaudabese Trail. Its three passes over fifteen thousand feet were usually under deep snow, but this late in the summer the way was open, and we looked forward to the change of scene. Lying on our sleeping bags, we retraced the route marked on our maps.

"In getting to Tillisha Cave," Rod pointed out, "we gain five thousand feet of altitude in the space of two miles. To get over Maralung La, the first of the Chaudabese passes, we will gain *8,500* feet. But you'll be glad to know that we'll have some twelve miles in which to do that. After leaving Wangri, we won't see a single village for three or four days until we get way down the Chaudabese Valley on the other side. There'll probably be shelters for summer yakherders, but I have no idea what to expect in terms of wildlife or what the weather will be like."

"Or what it's like at nearly seventeen thousand feet, either," I replied. "But anything is better than the Mugu Trail for the tenth time. I guess we could always hitch a ride on a yak!"

The twenty-two porters kept up a good pace, but when we got to Dhukyel it took two hours to get them and their loads over the cable. The men had long since overcome their fear, and they loved the bridge.

Whereas I had once wondered how the women got the seat sling on over their skirts and aprons, I now saw how they managed to tuck the hems in and pull them down so that their legs were covered at least to the knee. The men, very kindly—and lecherously—tried to help, getting smacked a lot for their efforts. When each woman was ready, the men would pull her across to midstream and leave her dangling over the water while they negotiated for favors. When they thought she had done her share of yelling for mercy, they brought her the rest of the way to safety.

When the boys Orkin and young Thondup got their turn they each put on a sling, clipped on to the pulley, and rode together, clowning all the way across. But when the grown men did it, one riding piggyback on the other, with nothing for him to hold on to to keep from falling, Rod had to be a spoilsport and lay down a new set of laws—laws that would be overlooked as soon as our backs were turned. "If they really want us to leave the cables after we're gone," he said, "they aren't doing a very good job of convincing me that they'll use them safely, or with good judgment. Sooner or later someone's bound to fall in the river, and I doubt if anyone could survive that when the Langu's in flood."

As soon as they were across they all went searching for our stolen gear. Tenzing Thakpa's father had performed his ceremony, with the result that the culprit "could have been someone who had worked for us," but he wasn't sure. He instructed Karma to place a prayer flag high above the Langu on either side, where they could "see" the canyon and watch for the thief to act again. He must also do a *puja,* a prayer ritual, throwing grains of barley as an offering; then he might find the missing items after three days of looking around Dhukyel.

Karma had put one flag at Eding Knoll and the other near Eagle Rock, on the way to Pine Camp, and had done the puja. Then, when he and Jickchor were on their way back to Eding, they had hunted around at Dhukyel and Jickchor had found a small stash of sugar, a bar of soap, and a spoon. Karma was sure that the rest of it would turn up.

"All porter help; everybody one day looking," he said. "Same one people, three day looking." But nothing more was found.

Gary had brought some fireworks from Kathmandu, "thunderflashers" that made a loud bang, thinking they might serve as signaling devices between camps. They hadn't proven very effective, except as an amusing way to scare the daylights out of the porters huddled around the campfire cooking chapatis. "BLAM!" went the bomb, and the circle of Bhotes jumped six inches off the ground, still sitting with their legs crossed.

At Dhukyel a young porter came to us asking if there were any "booms" left. He needed one for his "kill the thief" puja. He had made a stone effigy, and set it up among the rocks on the bank of the river. On one of our white enamel plates he had arranged little pieces of all our best food: cheese, biscuits, nuts, raisins, and little piles of the most precious thing of all: our tiny supply of sugar.

All twenty-six of us stood in a circle while the food was "blessed"; then we passed the plate around, each person taking a morsel until it was almost all gone. The crumbs were scattered beneath the trees—for the god of the "thief ceremony," I guess.

Next, we each picked up a rock from the riverbank as Karma ran down and lit the fuse of the "boom" at the foot of the effigy. When the blast came, everyone threw their rock at the flying fragments of the shattered "thief."

The whole thing was repeated again when we reached the chorten nearest Dolphu with our last bomb.

"A fine performance," I said to Rod. "And I'll bet it was a lot of hocus-pocus, treats, and a good time at our expense!"

"Well, whatever, it was worth the fun," he said. "But if the actual thief is among us, he or she has certainly remained very cool."

It did seem to us that though this rather questionable show of concern had been made, no one really took the theft very seriously. But, in fact, Tenzing Thakpa's father's statement that the suspect could be someone who worked for us made more of an impression than we thought. We had not heard the end of the Dhukyel theft.

When we were settled on Thondup's rooftop, Tsewong's wife called us to her house. She had prepared yogurt, boiled eggs, and chang. The food was the very best she had to offer—she had saved the eggs for days in anticipation of our coming.

Now that Tsewong was gone, she and her teenaged son, Thondup, were alone. They had never been very well off; now they would have a real struggle to get enough crops in to feed them for a year. Thondup had come to carry a load for Gary, but only from Eding to Dolphu, for though that was their only way of paying us back, he was needed with greater urgency to help with the planting.

"Oh, my God," said Rod, expressing the horror with which we both realized that she thought we expected her to repay the 150 rupees borrowed when Tsewong was dying.

"Tsewong wife, every time rain," said Karma, pointing to his eye with a slender brown finger to indicate that she was always crying. "Food is nothing, money is nothing. What to do?"

That Tsewong's middle-aged wife, worried and grieving, was "raining" seemed to me a perfectly apt description. If only we had known, we would long ago have told her that with Tsewong's death, the money was forgotten. We wanted neither the ninety rupees Thondup would earn as Gary's porter, nor the equivalent of their debt in food, which would be enough potatoes to feed two people for a large part of the winter.

Unlike Sonam's house, where the chang came from a twenty-gallon jug, she had only enough to fill our bowls twice. Over and over she apologized, tears running freely down her face, for the poor quality of her hospitality. We did our best to show that we appreciated her gifts, and we made certain she knew beyond any doubt that she owed us no debt whatsoever.

Wangri, half the size of Dolphu, was lush by comparison. Forests of pine and birch grew almost at our fingertips, and a lively stream, splashing down from the heights, ran past the village. Unfamiliar flowering plants grew in profusion, scenting the humid air.

With most of the twenty-three loads left stored in Dolphu, we would need only five yaks to carry our remaining gear to Jumla. Three men would go along to tend the animals, another to carry a light kitchen load.

To our Langu-jaded eyes, the trail out of Wangri was lovely, following the clear, fast stream, with forests on either side, as it meandered through a shaggy carpet of wildflowers.

We spent the first night at a summer yak pasture just at the edge of the tree line, where the men would find their animals and get them ready to go to work.

In the morning we found out something about yaks. We had read of how reluctant they could be to submit to the wooden saddles and bulging duffel bags they were expected to carry. What we didn't know was that once the loading is accomplished, they undergo a transformation. They get serious about walking, charging single-mindedly up the trail like locomotives. The steeper it is, the faster they go. We couldn't have kept up with them if our lives had depended on it.

Each day we would have to climb a pass; they ranged in height from 15,272 feet to 16,932 feet. The twenty-five-mile journey would take five or six days.

From the yak pasture, the trail led up a treeless valley of rolling alpine grassland and followed Wangri's river, which was still overhung in places with thick slabs of grit-flecked ice. We ascended a high plateau, its edge lined with chortens. I thought at first, somewhat jubilantly, that it was the pass, and how easily and painlessly we had reached it. But beyond the chortens lay a long meadow and beyond the meadow, like an exclamation point, rose Maralung La, a mountain whose peak was lost in the clouds. Rough pinnacles surrounded the peak, and blue glaciers plunged toward the valley floor. Vibrant alpine blooms flashed among the green meadow grasses at our feet.

We stopped to eat a quick snack where the valley narrowed and the path cut steeply up the mountain's flank. Up and up we climbed, with the air growing thinner, our lungs heaving, the yaks going faster, and gray clouds descending slowly around us. The vegetation grew sparse and eventually disappeared. We crunched along on gray fragments of slaty scree, far behind our yaks out of sight in the mist ahead. Up and up and up, one foot in front of the other, Rod and I stood alone on the mountaintop.

We reached the pass as sheets of rain began to pour, and we stumbled without a rest down the other side over massive heaps of stone left by the retreating glacier that had covered the mountain long ago. Left behind, I moved slowly following the yaks' trail of dung for an hour, from boulder to boulder in a heavy fog. My glasses steamed over and slid down my wet nose, and my fancy Gore-tex rain jacket leaked like a sieve. Rodney waited far below, down where the meadow grass began again and where the rain was lighter.

"Are you all right?" he asked, rubbing my cold hands between his warm ones. "I'm freezing cold, soaking wet, and dog tired," I replied, and still we had several miles to go down the valley before we found our companions in a meager rock shelter, the only possible camping place for miles around.

I sat on a rock, watching numbly as Karma and Rod pitched our tent on a knoll beside the rock shelter. I shook with the cold and wondered if this was what hypothermia felt like. One of the Wangri men untied the hard-knotted laces of my sodden shoes while I watched mute, and Rod, for once without asking where they were, found dry clothes and jackets in the duffels. With a cup of tea in a warm sleeping bag, I was soon recovered enough to look at our surroundings and join the others in the rocks for dinner.

Our yaks browsed happily nearby, snorting like domestic hogs. (Their Latin name, *Bos grunniens,* means, appropriately enough, "grunting cow.") Karma said that today's walk had been relatively short and added, "Tomorrow, Kang La, little bit long way—maybe veddy windle." It's always very "windle" on the peaks of the Himalayas. At almost any time of day you can look up and see the snow plumes flying from the summits like enormous windblown flags.

The next day, Rod and I got an hour's head start on the hairy steam engines. We took frequent rest stops, and the way up seemed easier. Mist and clouds obscured our surroundings, but there was no rain. The final pitch led up a snow-covered glacier lying in the saddle of two peaks. Looking back, the glacier seemed to plunge off into darkness. Lowering clouds of ash-white, black, and charcoal hung above the abyss. Plodding relentlessly through the snow, our caravan of yaks appeared over the glacier's lip. Despite the stupendous view that probably lay hidden to our sight beyond the clouds, we weren't sorry to have come this way.

We let the yaks pass us by and waited for their dust to settle. The other side was a different world. A series of vast grassy bowls faced with

gold-colored stone descended the mountainside like an ornamental fountain in a giant's garden. The last bowl opened upon a wide green meadow
lush with the most outrageous flowers yet: blue knee-high poppies, pink
primulas, red bistorts, blue gentians, and purple louseworts.

On and on we went through a near-pristine land. The faint path and
undisturbed pastures were testaments to the fact that man had touched the
high country of the Chaudabese only lightly.

Karma had hoped to get over the third pass, Dongari, in the afternoon,
but upon our reaching the rock shelter at the base of the ascent there was
unanimous agreement that it was a bad idea. The tents were pitched just
as the thunder rolled and the rain spilled.

As he looked toward tomorrow's pass, Karma noticed movement on
the trail. Along the low contour of the hillside walked a pack of *dhole*—
nine sandy-red wild dogs with black-dipped tails. Looking much like fine
big coyotes, dhole are fairly common in parts of India but rare in the
mountains of Nepal. This was the only sighting of *any* wildlife on the
whole journey, though the Wangris said there were bharal throughout
the range.

Snow leopards, too, were certainly to be found among the untouched
massifs and grasslands through which we walked, but Rod remarked
more than once how hard they would be to study: The winters would
be impossible, leaving just the few months of summer and late fall in
which to gather data.

He had pointed out the other difficulties as we walked along. "Where
would you put a trap on all this sweeping grassland?" he said. "How
would you find pugmarks, or scats, or scrapes? The rain would quickly
wash them all away."

Karma brought the morning tea through a gray drizzle to our droop-
ing tent, followed shortly by heaping bowls of gray, glutinous oatmeal.
We did our best to stuff it down, pocketing the last half package of
biscuits to get us over the pass. We wouldn't have another meal before
we reached Maharigaon, on the other side of the mountain, late in the
evening.

Again we set off before the yaks were loaded, and we walked up

through intermittent rain into the familiar crumbled flagstone that signified the pass was near. The crest was flat, a starkly beautiful "moonscape"
with three clear lakes of pale green liquid sunk into the slate-gray rock.
The path descended from one high green plateau to another. Down and
down and down we went and the path became a trail, complete with
edges and built-in steps, winding through forest thick with birdsong and
sticky monsoon heat.

We came to Maharigaon, the end of the road for the yaks. There the
Wangris quickly untied the loads, dumping them in the wet grass and
sending the gasping beasts lunging back up into the cool alpine grassland.
They would join other herds of off-duty yaks to graze unfettered until
the men came to find them.

The yak men, as tired as the rest of us from three days of mountain-
walking, then took up the double loads and marched on down the trail
past busy villages and fields of verdant vegetables and grain. If we had
been unsure whether the location of the Langu meant that its villagers
dwelt in the "rain shadow" of the Kanjiroba and Sisne Himal, all doubt
was erased by the relative abundance, variety, and healthy condition of
the Chaudabese Valley's crops. As we walked along, the monsoon rain
fell steadily, soaking the fields and leaking slowly through the seams of
my jacket.

Our evening camp site was provided by a farmer and his family: shelter
for the porters; a rooftop for the tents; firewood; new apples; and a
handful of exquisite green peas, fresh off the vine. Total charge, thirty
rupees—less than two dollars.

By the time we reached Jumla two days later, the weather had cleared
and our hopes were high for a rice shuttle, even though the RNAC's
passenger service was stopped for the season.

Judy and Jenny greeted us warmly. Pouring coffee, Judy said, "The
radio at the airstrip has been out of commission for several weeks. We
never know what might be scheduled. You'll just have to go out there
and wait; a rice shuttle might come in anytime between six in the
morning and five in the evening."

For six days, we more or less lived at the airstrip, while not a drop
of rain fell on the Jumla Valley.

The thing that really kept us from getting on our feet, hiring some Jumli porters, and walking was the thought of how awful it would be if we got half an hour down the valley and a plane flew in over our heads. We could never get back in time to catch it.

It was the U.N. Development Project's Twin Otter that saved us, bringing in supplies for the school. Early in the morning of our seventh day at the airstrip, we heard the engines and looked up to see the blue plane coming in for the typically abrupt, noisy, and dusty landing. The plane would be returning empty to Nepalganj, and yes, there was room for two people and a few duffel bags.

Two weeks later I was sitting at my sewing machine making muslin bags for the snow leopard scats that Rod and Gary had collected. They needed to separate the soft matter in each scat from the solids to find out what the cat had eaten. The muslin would act like a sieve. Into each bag they tucked one complete specimen, sewed up the end, and with a marking pen wrote the number of the scat and when and where it had been found. The bag joined others in a galvanized tub of water where they soaked, far from the house, for several days prior to being sneaked into Gary's sister's washing machine while she was out at work. Several cycles later the bags were transferred to the dryer, all the organic matter having been washed away, leaving only whatever hair, hoof, bone, and feather fragments might have been left from several hundred snow leopard meals—and Gary's sister none the wiser about the use to which her machines had been put!

Part

4

November 1984–July 1985

CHAPTER

26

Hunters

Five months passed between the summer day when we flew out of Jumla and the fall day when we again walked into Eding Camp. But we were at home for only two and a half of those months. At the end of the study, when we added up all our time, it seemed unbelievable that of the study's forty-four months, seven were spent in Kathmandu waiting for things to happen and nearly five and a half months were occupied in walking into and out of the Langu Gorge.

We were behind schedule when Rod, Karan, and I took the Sky Van to Jumla in mid-November 1984, loaded with food and gear for our final field season in the Langu. Gary would work at home on project tasks and make up for some of the lost time with his family, joining us at Eding in January of the new year.

"Are you ready for this?" Rod asked me as we stepped again onto the Jumla airstrip.

"I hope so," I replied. "Eight whole months in the gorge without a break is a long time—longer than we've ever spent before. Knowing how we get after only four or five months out there, it's a good thing we've got that full treat box!"

Each season, the ratio of vital gear and staple foods to luxury items like chocolate bars and Kool-Aid had shifted a little more in favor of our taste buds; this time we tucked enough M & M's, smoked oysters, and plastic water bottles full of brandy into our always overweight duffel bags that we would need a whole extra yak to get the treat box into the Langu.

Karma was at the airstrip to meet us, pointing out rather gloatingly that he had been waiting for us for nearly a month.

"Whadappened, sah'b?" he said. "Twenty-six day, every time plane is coming—sah'b, Didi is nothing."

Rod answered his question, "The money crop was no good this year. The farmers plowed their land, the rains came, but all the dollar trees died." Karma gave Rodney such a funny look that for a moment I almost thought he'd believed him.

We were enough ahead of the first winter storms to take the high route again. But now the Chaudabese River was low and we could take the shorter, one-pass trail. Karma had assembled most of our crew from last summer—and twenty-nine yaks.

"I'm not so sure about this," I said to Rod. "I don't know if I'll live through another trek over the Chaudabese."

"You can do it," he urged. "It can't be as hard as the three-pass route. Think of the great new views we'll see. And no grubby teahouses, staring children, or barking dogs."

He had a point. In fact, the difficulties of the previous summer had receded, leaving only images of bright flowers and magnificent heights. I wanted to see the mountains again, to see what had lay hidden last summer behind the low monsoon clouds.

Though the nights would be cold, we were in for a sun-filled adventure, marked by the serene beauty of the deep and narrow Chaudabese Canyon, where the trail ran close beside the clear mountain river. The infectious, happy mood of our companions, combined with the glorious, untrammeled country we passed through, made the trek the most spectacular and enjoyable we had ever experienced.

The yaks were led by "Golduk the Amazing," a huge, brown, ugly, hornless bull with a pure strength and power that clearly came to him unaltered from his wild yak ancestors. "Thakpa the Prime" commanded only slightly less respect from the Wangri men.

" 'Thakpa' is everything a yak should be," said Rod. He had long horns curving forward; white eye patches in a thick mat of shaggy black and white fur; and a moplike, bushy tail. Decorative tassels of long, red-dyed yak hair had been woven into his halter.

Every man, woman, and child of Wangri was waiting for us in the fields where we would camp, with warm and happy greetings and bottles of chang to cheer the weary travelers.

We stayed the following day, despite Rod's protests. The yak men insisted that the animals needed a rest day before crossing the Langu and climbing the hill to Dolphu.

We made the rounds of Wangri's leading households. Sitting around the hearth of Dorje, the yak men's leader, we ate eggs deep-fried in mustard oil, drank chang, and met his aged father. He claimed to be slightly younger than Thondup's blind mother, but he could still walk to Dolphu and back.

Dawa had invited us next, but to get to his house we had to pass Guru's door. She tugged at Karan's arm, insisting that we come inside, and it was clear that we would have been extremely rude not to accept. Soon we were seated by her fire, with her three sons getting out the silver-and-wooden chang bowls and passing boiled eggs.

At Dawa's house there was no chang and no way to convince Dawa that we were already so full of chang, and everything else, that we were quite happy just to sit and talk.

What was it about these people that made them seem so full of warmth and harmony, so much more contented and free of tension than the Dolphas? Karan explained that Wangri, in contrast with Dolphu, was a village undivided by factions. It seemed, too, that Wangri's smaller size was an advantage: fewer mouths to feed on the same amount of land. True, here the winter snow was slow to melt, whereas in Dolphu it seldom lay on the ground for more than a week; but unlike Dolphu, there was plenty of wood to warm the Wangris through the cold months. Otherwise their houses were essentially the same, their possessions just about equal, their troubles no different. We felt that they were more accepting of us, and we wished, in some ways, that we had been able to deal with Wangri as the principal village.

By the time our social rounds were finished, so were we. Lurching back to our tent, we fell asleep instantly, forgoing our chicken dinner!

The yaks thought their work was done; in the morning they were feisty and unwilling to be loaded down again with green duffels. One was sick, and another had uprooted a horn in a fight.

Disappointed that we had no yak medicine in any of the duffels, the Wangris slashed the ear of the sick one so the "bad blood" could drain out. The other would live without its horn, but its value would be much reduced. The two were taken out of service, their loads carried to Dolphu by the families of their owners.

Since the yaks could not go beyond Dolphu, Rod wanted to take the porters to Eding in two separate groups, leaving a day apart.

"Twenty-nine yak loads, with Dolphu potatoes added in, means seventy-five people loads," he pointed out. "That's half the adult population of the village. They'll devastate Dhukyel and Eding Camps with their cookfires, they'll cut all the nearby trees and bushes for wood, and just think about seventy-five morning turd heaps scattered all over our base camp. You know you can't get them to use the latrine. At least if they go in two groups it'll be easier to keep an eye on everyone and everything."

Our problems over the latrine were not confined to the locals. Karan and all the camp staff found the idea of using a pit to be completely disgusting and offensive to their religious and/or ritual customs. But at least they walked a good distance from camp; the Bhotes, used to having dogs and chickens to help keep the village byways "tidy," made little effort to go very far away.

But there turned out to be a more pressing reason for going in one huge group, and going soon. Thondup had drawn Karan aside and quietly explained that since we were over a month late, the villagers thought we weren't coming back. To our utter amazement, he admitted that there was a hunting party out after bharal somewhere up in the gorge. He had decided that it was better if we heard it from him, rather than finding out on our own by catching the hunters at it. Rod was astounded.

"*How* are they hunting?" he demanded. "With guns, or with spears? If they kill one of our collared cats—or *any* snow leopard, for that matter—there's going to be hell to pay! If they thought I gave them trouble before, they haven't seen anything yet!"

"But Rodney," said Karan, "we must think that there is some reason why Thondup would confess this serious business. I am sure that none of the other villagers know he has warned us."

Was Thondup protecting Sonam against impending accusations of theft? We had left at least ten loads of food and gear hidden near Tillisha Cave and on the terrace across from Eding. Even if Karma had tried to dissuade the villagers from looking, all of our things could be found with a little effort; the river was low and could be easily bridged with our stored logs. Though we had never singled anyone out, Sonam and Jickchor were both possible suspects in the Dhukyel case, and they knew enough about our haunts and habits to make them prime suspects again if any of our gear was missing. But Sonam was at home. Shyly and with great pride he and his wife had presented their tiny new daughter to us as we sat at their hearth. We had not seen Jickchor, and we suspected that he might be found among the hunting party. Had he completely duped Karma last summer? Should we cease to trust even Karma? Either way, it seemed highly likely that the hunters were going to bag more than a few bharal.

Our troubles were further compounded by Karma Lama. He had recently learned of plans for the Langu to be included in the new Shey-Phoksundo National Park, and he had gotten everyone in Dolphu, as well as everyone in Wangri, all upset about the park and how it would affect them. He had convinced them all that the Snow Leopard Project was responsible for the park being created in the first place, and they took out all of their anger on Rod and Karan.

The precise park boundaries were still in question, but whether or not Dolphu and Wangri were included, the villagers were certain that the next step would be eviction from their villages and relocation out of the mountains. Even if they were allowed to stay, they were worried about what would happen to their rights over livestock grazing, woodcutting, and jimbu harvesting in the gorge. Without those rights, how could they live?

Karan put on his "liaison officer" hat, a role he assumed with enthusiasm, and tried to convince Thondup that the Snow Leopard Project had no part in the formation of the national park—that it had been planned long before we came. But since no one else in the government was as familiar with the Langu and its needs as the Snow Leopard Project, we could act as village advocates. There was little worry, he said, that the villages would be forced to leave. With something like twenty villages in the proposed park boundaries, it would be impractical if not impossible to find alternative homes and land for everyone. And they needn't lose their livelihoods if they were willing to abide by certain rules. The government was acting to protect endangered wildlife, but at the same time it would encourage better land use practices. He cited Kimri's dry spring as an example of how deforestation and overgrazing could lead to changes in the environment that would be more likely to cause abandonment of a village than designation as a national park.

Karan and Rod encouraged the two villages to collaborate on a letter to Kathmandu stating their collective concerns about the new park.

We hadn't yet seen Karma Lama, and Rod inquired after his health. He was in Gum, they said, on Panchyat business.

When the loads were sorted, weighed, and reassembled the next morning, with slightly lighter ones set aside for the women, Karan had an idea about how to minimize the business of assigning them. He would hold a lottery.

First he took a pen and paper and wrote out little numbered tickets, wadding them up and placing them into two bowls, one for the women and one for the men. Then he took a black laundry marker and numbered each load to correspond with the tickets. It seemed like a good idea until he discovered that hardly anyone could read his Nepali numbers. One by one he would have to walk the porters to their assigned loads.

It was four hours of pandemonium. Every time he asked someone to choose a number, ten or twelve people grabbed. They all reasoned, illogically, that if they were last, they'd get the heaviest loads.

The loads were all leaned against the wall in a long line, and when a number was picked, seventy-five porters plus assorted onlookers followed Karan to find the load, crowding and shouting and laughing—back and forth went the mass of people, like a slow-motion basketball game with Karan the ball.

Long after we were on the trail, Karan discovered that several of the men had made their wives pick their number so they could get a woman-size load!

During all this exciting activity, "Crazy People" was nowhere to be seen. He was hibernating, they said; so far he'd been asleep for seven days.

When everyone finally had their load, no one wanted to go. *"Pug-daina,"* they said, meaning, "There's not enough time." Thondup backed up the villagers, and we suspected they were trying to delay long enough to get a message to the hunters to make themselves scarce.

Rod and I picked up our backpacks and told Karma that either he would have to come with us to carry pots and some food or he'd better find someone else to do it.

"I'm going," said Rod. "I don't care if the rest of you come or not." He started to walk down the log ladder off the roof and onto the trail, but Karma called him back. We hadn't had the send-off chang ceremony, and it wouldn't do for Thondup to let us go without it. The porters gave in and promised to leave right away, so we descended into the murky darkness of Thondup's living room.

We made it to Shimbu that night, which was only slightly better than going nowhere. "The seventy-five" spent the whole night sitting up around a big fire and telling dirty stories. Early in the morning most of them set off for Dhukyel.

As Rod and I prepared to leave, we heard loud voices down below where the porters had camped. Karma Lama had returned from Gum and sent a messenger to recall all the porters to Dolphu on "urgent business."

"Let him wait," said Rod, " 'The seventy-five' have an obligation to us first." Only a verbal message had been sent, and Karan pointed out that it was an insult for Karma Lama not to have written a note. We suspected it was all just a ruse to stir up trouble. If the matter was really so urgent, he could come to *us*. But the porters were afraid of crossing him, and two men, one from each village, went back with the messenger to see what it was all about.

Our group reached Dhukyel early to rebuild the log bridge. The hunters had already placed two of the logs haphazardly across the midstream boulders. While the porters finished the job, Rod and I investigated the terrace for leopard sign. All we found were a few broken bamboo spears, a pile of roots used for making glue to mix with the poison and smear on the speartips, and fresh Bhote tracks.

Just before dinner, the messenger returned, saying that two representatives weren't good enough, that the police were in Dolphu, and that they'd all better get themselves back at once. The shouting, with all seventy-three joining in, lasted a long time. The presence of police was taken seriously, however much they were unloved. The result was that one member from each family among us was elected to return, a compromise between responsibility to us and the consequences of crossing Karma Lama.

No one wanted to go. It would be dark long before they reached the village, but the judgment of the older men prevailed, and twenty porters left at about 5:00 P.M.

At 7:00 P.M., nineteen people returned. The messenger had admitted, somewhere beyond Shimbu, that the information about the police was a lie. Fortunately, they were already over the Shimbu Cliff or the messenger might have "found the short way down." All but one of the porters got so mad that they turned around and came all the way back, climbing over the cliff by feel.

"Good!" said Rodney. "One point for our side!"

We reached Eding Camp on December 3. The last of the bridges had to be rebuilt to cross over below camp, and four men waded the icy river in an impressive show of fortitude to place the long logs. "The seventy-two" waited in rowdy, hungry impatience for it to be done.

"I hope they all go away when they've had their lunch," said Rod.

There's plenty of time for them to get back to Dhukyel." But soon it became obvious that they planned their biggest party for that evening.

Eding looked like a seedy refugee center, with fires dotting the flat river terrace, surrounded by sooty, dark-clad Bhotes with their blankets draped over their heads like hoods, stirring bubbling potfuls of potatoes and slapping chapatis into flat, plate-size disks.

The porter payoff took forever, with Rod, Karan, and Karma counting out and handing over each wage packet, writing the name and amount in the budget book. Back in Kathmandu, we had spent hours at the bank, sorting through the paper money—a daypack full of cash that would have to last the whole season—making sure every rupee was in good condition. If the locals found even a tiny hole or rip in any bill, they would reject it. Inevitably, wear and tear took their toll once we were on the road, and my job was to wield the Magic-tape dispenser, patching up the money. We could count ourselves lucky that the paper was acceptable at all. Not so long ago only coins were considered legal tender in Nepal's outlying districts. Had that still been so, our daypack of money would have taken up at least a trunk, and we'd have needed several people just to carry it!

The gear we had left hidden around Eding was untouched, but Rod came back from Pine Camp with bad news.

"The metal trunk has been vandalized; everything is gone except a few backpacking meals. They didn't even close the damn lid. Whatever was left, the mice made short work of it. Where's Karma, the guy who was so *sure* the villagers wouldn't touch our stuff?" Karma came out of the kitchen to see what was going on. He ended up wishing he'd stayed inside.

Missing were a twenty-liter jerry can, a fuel bottle for the emergency stove, string, glue, needles and thread, trap cable, dried fruit and nuts, and other small items identifiable and useful. A month's worth of food was gone or ruined by the mice, and the trunk was in bad shape for future use.

Still, we could manage without those things; we had taken the risk of leaving them out in the open. The stuff we had hidden at Tillisha was a different story. Along with leftover food, we had stored a jerry can of kerosene; tranquilizing gear; and vital clothing, including Rod's and Gary's heavy winter boots. If those things were gone, it would be bad news for future work in the grasslands.

"I *should* make Karma pay for it," said Rod. "He was so sure no one would bother our things. But what's the point? He can't replace the missing gear. Obviously, the 'killing the thief' ceremony was no deterrent."

From Pine Camp Rod had received a signal from "Dui," inactive over several hours, coming from the same place in Tillisha Basin that he had located it before.

"I don't know why I didn't pick it up just before we left last summer," he said, "but now I'm back to thinking that the cat has either died or shed the collar. I can't go in there alone, and by the time Gary arrives, there'll be too much snow. We'll just have to hope the collar doesn't quit."

Early the next morning, Rod and Karma set off for Tillisha Cave. Karma returned by himself two days later, relieved to report that if the villagers had looked, they hadn't found his hiding place.

I tracked "Char" as she moved into Tillisha Canyon. Checking the terrace path for tracks, I found a single set leading *away* from the canyon. They did not belong to "Char," and we were no closer to knowing the fate of her family. Returning to camp, I found that we had visitors: Dolphu Cinon, and the infamous Jickchor, a man so high on our "most wanted" list that I could hardly believe my eyes.

"What in the world is *he* doing here?" I asked Karan.

"He's badly injured; they have come to ask for medicine," he replied.

The story went that they had been at Kimding cutting *marang,* pinewood with a high pitch content that makes bright candles and long-burning torches. A piece of wood had flown from the log they were working on, hitting Jickchor in the lower leg and splitting it open. It was a terrible wound, a five-inch gash with his muscle protruding from the hole. They had sewed about an inch and a half of it closed, using

God-knows-what kind of needle and a piece of string from Cinon's chuba. The leg was swollen from the knee down.

They'd been alone at Kimding, and rather than going home, Cinon had carried him here.

Jickchor lay on the ground near the big camp boulder; a film of dirty sweat made his face look gray. He averted his eyes when I looked at him hard, torn between concern and anger at what certainly seemed to be damning evidence at Pine Camp.

"Karan," I said, "how could a flying chip of pinewood cut through his pant leg all the way down to the bone? More likely it was a hunting accident, an ax cut. I'll bet they're lying about cutting marang. I think we should get a few questions answered before we leap to fetch the first aid kit; this is as good a time as any to get to the bottom of the Dhukyel theft, the Pine Camp theft, and any thefts that may be in the planning stages. If we get satisfactory answers, we *might* consider giving away our precious drugs to someone who probably doesn't deserve them." The good old eye-for-an-eye approach.

As a Hindu, one might have expected Karan to be reluctant to interfere in any way with Jickchor's karma (fate), but no, he firmly believed that we had to save the man's leg first and *then* ask questions.

"He is seriously injured," said Karan. "And he is in great pain. We must help him; it is the only human thing to do."

I saw the sweat beading on Jickchor's brow. Suppressing my anger and bitterness, I went to get what we would need from the medical trunk. "Damnit," I muttered to myself, "why does Karan have to choose this particular moment to be so vehemently compassionate? Now we'll never find out if Jickchor's guilty. He might at least have *tried* it my way."

When we began to clean the wound, carefully removing the filthy string, we could see that it would be a long time healing and that he would need antibiotics to fight the infection. He certainly wouldn't be going anywhere very soon. My hard-hearted attitude softened as he winced when I scrubbed the wound with soap and water. I gave him one of our strongest painkillers; soon he would be sound asleep on his blankets in the kitchen.

* * *

By December 18 we had four traps and two photo stations in operation; and Karan and Sonam began setting a new kind of "Dolphu rope-and-tree-branch" traps for bharal, hoping to catch several so Karan could dart and mark them with Day-Glo orange collars.

Jickchor's brother and Yangyap arrived, bringing food for Jickchor and Cinon, who had run out and were "borrowing" from us. They also brought a bottle of chang, payment for the "doctor."

"How did they know that Jickchor and Cinon were here if they had been alone at Kimding?" I asked Karan. I didn't get a reply.

Cinon and Yangyap went back to Dolphu, leaving Jickchor's brother to look after him. A day or two later I heard a commotion coming from the kitchen. There was such a wailing and carrying on that I thought Jickchor had suffered an attack of remorse, even though he had told Karan that he "knew nothing" of the Pine Camp theft, swearing so upon his mother and his children. Wanting to be in on any impromptu confessions, I hurried to the kitchen. I found Jickchor's mother standing before him.

Apparently she had been sure that Cinon and Yangyap were simply sparing her the worst when they'd returned to Dolphu and told her he was fine, that his leg was getting better, and that he would be coming home just as soon as he could walk the distance. She'd come to get the body. By the time I arrived at the kitchen door she had Jickchor weeping, too, and puddles were beginning to form on the dirt floor. The Bhotes have a rhythmic and rather beautiful way of crying that seems to gather all the earth's primordial sadness into the misery of one person. Jickchor hardly seemed embarrassed at all that his wrinkled old mother had come to save him.

They all left on December 20, Jickchor walking with a limp but with his wound mending nicely. As he left, Karan remarked, "He's a lucky man. He might have lost his leg, isn't it? In any case, our medicine saved him at least six months of pain and disability."

On a low river terrace just downstream from Eding we found the hunters' main camp. Scattered about were fresh bharal horns, bits of skin and hair, and flat rocks where they had mixed the poison and coated the tips of their bamboo spears. The men had made a halfhearted attempt to hide the evidence with pine branches, and their trail with dead bushes. But they had built a chorten and hung bits of red, blue, and white cloth from twigs inserted in the top of the shrine. If that hadn't given them away, their big sausage turds deposited all along the riverbank would have done the job.

CHAPTER

27

Langu Christmas

Over the summer, Rod and Gary had worked out a new idea for monitoring boulders scent-sprayed by the snow leopards. They wanted to know if the cats marked in response to already-sprayed sites; how often they did it; how the scent marks might relate to other sign along the transects, such as scrapes, scats, and raked trees; and how long the scent might last in the environment.

Part of the problem they had had in finding spray sites was that the musky scent did not usually leave a stain, except on a few sites that were heavily re-marked. Even when they could smell that a particular boulder had been sprayed, their noses could tell them only limited information. They had an ascending scale to note the strength of the scent—"1" was very weak, "4" was very strong.

"But we really need to know when a site has just been resprayed," Rod explained. "We might know that a particular cat walked along the transect on a particular day. We can check the boulders an hour after the cat went past and smell a strong scent on one or more of them. But some of those sites already have strong '4' scent marks, and our human noses are simply not sensitive enough to distinguish between hours-old and days-old sprays.

"So we're going to mark a selection of scent-sprayed boulders with small squares of yellow crepe paper, to match the rock as nearly as possible, and stuck on with clear tape. When a leopard shoots its spray onto that rock, the crepe paper will be bleached where the liquid hit it. *Voilà!* Instantly recognizable fresh-sprayed sites and new data, never before collected, on marking behavior."

The plan meant a lot of marking and measuring and note-taking, even though we had improvised and photocopied stacks of forms to keep track of the sites. But the strips of yellow crepe paper proved very effective. The sprayed scent made clearly bleached streaks so that, assuming no rain had fallen, it was easy to see when a site was marked by a cat.

"I wonder, though, about the crepe paper," said Rod. "Do these little yellow squares actually attract the cats, or would they have done it anyway? For that matter, we are probably affecting their behavior along Tillisha Terrace just by being at Eding."

Another plan Rod and Gary had worked out during the summer concerned luring cats to the vicinity of our camps during the mating season. We had been given a zoo tape recording of captive snow leopard mating calls and vocalizations during copulation. We also had a tape recorder and a small amplifier that could be operated with rechargeable batteries plugged into our solar panel. We thought for sure that any wild leopard hearing the cries of its kin, either in the throes of mating or else looking to be, would come running to find out who was making all the noise.

We needed to test the equipment, and Rod chose a moonless night, crisp and dark, not letting on to our campmates what he was up to. He waited until after dinner, when Karan was in his tent and Karma and Sonam were talking by the fire in the kitchen.

He snuck out of our tent and crept down by the river below camp. I waited inside, pretending to be going to sleep. Soon there came a short "yowl" in the night. No reaction from Karan's tent or the kitchen. Then another, more prolonged snow leopard call, loud and clear. That got some action.

"Ho ... Rodney ... Rodney ..." came from Karan's unlit tent. Karma and Sonam poured from the kitchen.

"Ronney ... Ronney-Sahb ... *sabu* ... Ronney ... *sabu chha* !"

275

Of course, Rodney wasn't in the tent, and when Karma and Sonam came running to the door, I had to think fast.

"Rodney went to the latrine," I said, trying hard to look surprised and keep a straight face.

Then, from farther upstream came another good yowl. The light went on in Karan's tent. Karma and Sonam pointed excitedly to the terrace, both talking at once, convinced that the cat was up on Tillisha Terrace.

The speaker was a cheap one but the recording sounded so good that almost anyone would have been fooled. I couldn't help laughing. Sonam and Karma were completely taken in, but Karan had not uttered a single comment beyond his first "Ho . . . Rodney . . . Rodney . . ."

"Where *is* Rodney?" I said, trying to cover myself. "He must be getting a big surprise squatting there with his pants down, in the pitch dark, with a leopard crying out practically at his feet."

When the yowls started coming up the path right into camp, the light went off in Karan's tent. Karma and Sonam began to chuckle just a tiny bit nervously.

"Karma, go and look by the big boulder," I said. "Here's a flashlight, okay?"

"I'm not sure," he said with a little grin, the muscle jumping in his cheek. Sonam thought the leopard must have used our log bridge to cross the river, but he looked very puzzled and more than a little frightened— what with ghosts and all about at night.

Then Rod walked into the circle of light cast by the candle in our tent, the Sony slung around his neck, the speaker "yowling" in his hand. For a moment Karma and Sonam outdid the speaker with their howls of amazement and delight. They made Rod reenact the whole thing, starting from the first yowl.

Christmas, like the previous three days, dawned steely-gray, threatening but never delivering snow. Karma brought the day's first treat to the tents—steaming cups of "real" coffee made with beans brought specially from home. We tuned the shortwave to the Voice of America and sang along with "White Christmas"—hahaha! When we tired of the radio's poor reception, there was always "Gary's Song," composed last winter as the holidays approached, to the tune of "The Christmas Song":

> Yak meat roasting on an open fire,
> Yeti nipping at your nose,
> Buddhist chants being sung by a choir
> And Bhotes dressed up like Eskimos . . .

Late in the afternoon, Santa Claus arrived, in the form of Sonam's brother-in-law. He brought from the Chaudabese Valley a ten-liter jug of rakshi, hoping we would buy it. He couldn't have known that, being Christmas, we would have a hard time declining.

We'd been letting the chickens gorge for a month, keeping the crows from getting their share of the leftovers. The two chickens that Karma chose to relieve of their heads were relatively fat, and once plucked and cut up, Western style, they marinated all day in teriyaki sauce in anticipation of the evening barbecue. Served up with baked potatoes, cauliflower with cheese, and Hain's herbed rice, and followed by instant deluxe cheesecake by Jell-O, it was considered a spectacular meal by all.

As a post-Christmas bonus, Rod recontacted "Panch" for the first time of the season, on the twenty-seventh, near the river opposite Pukchang.

The snow finally came on December 30, fitfully at first and then socking in for New Year's Day. But at the end there was less than six inches on the ground—nothing to speak of! We thought of the Sierras and what a three-day December storm would accomplish at ten thousand feet! And we thought of our snowbound first Dolphu winter. The snow melted quickly off the south-facing slopes.

"Good," said Rod. "I can get in at least one more run on the three Tillisha Ridge transects before winter closes off the high country."

When he passed by Pine Camp on the way up, he stopped at the tent to get out the leopard receiver and try for "Dui" and the other collared cats. The tent was a mess. Everything had been rifled, and the earphones were gone.

"Oh, no," he said with a sigh. "How could the Dolphas have been here again without our knowing?" But there was a pack of cigarettes lying on the ground, with a few of them scattered about. No self-respecting Dolpha would leave those behind.

He began to search beyond the tent, along the steep northern slope. Lying in the scrubby rhododendron was one of our "book-size" solar panels. Small tracks led down the hillside. Following them, Rod found strewn along the trail a ten-pack AA battery recharger (minus the plug, which had been chewed off), assorted Ziploc bags, and a roll of colored flagging tape.

He lost the tracks and, widening the search, discovered a denhole in a pile of rocks. He knew it was a denhole because a lot of our equipment was stuck in the entrance. The earphones, plainly too big to go in, had been severely modified by the den's owner. All the wiring had been chewed through and the plug chewed off. There were tooth punctures in a neat row all around the plastic-covered foam earpads, and still they wouldn't fit through the hole. Stuck alongside them was a roll of brown duct tape, three AA batteries, a Ziploc bag containing a bottle of seam seal, and one foil wine "bladder" used for storing water. Inside the den, out of reach, Rod could see another bladder glinting in the sun.

As if Dolphu hunters, mice, and crows were not enough, now we had a robber-weasel sharing space at Pine Camp. It wasn't as if we could just run down to Radio Shack and pick up some new earphones, assorted plugs, and electrical wires. We would just have to fix these.

"Where's the pliers?" asked Rod as he pawed through the toolbox.

It took us half a day, sitting with scissors, a pocket knife, the pliers, and a roll of electrical tape to reattach all the wires. And when we were done, our lumpy, untidy repair job looked hopeless. We hung a radio collar on the peach tree for a test.

"They're absolutely destroyed—I'm sure they'll never work again," Rod said with a groan as he plugged them into the receiver. "They look like a dog's breakfast."

"Beep, beep, beep, beep," came through the weasel-air-conditioned earpads.

"Well, I'll be damned," he said, beaming. "They *work*! Wait till Gary sees *this*!"

CHAPTER

28

Pugmarks in the Snow

Two storms followed on the heels of the New Year's snow, making us really begin to wonder if we were in for a repeat of the Tongdom Gomba days. Karan decided to leave for Jumla two weeks ahead of schedule. He was getting married in March, and he didn't want to be snowbound in Eding.

The marriage had been arranged by the two sets of parents the previous year, in accordance with the Eastern custom of forming alliances to enhance the family fortunes. As the couple lived together and came to know one another, love might develop between them, and it often did in arranged marriages. But the foremost consideration was to keep the family strong. Karan had *seen* his bride-to-be, surreptitiously, from a distance, but they had not had as much as an hour's conversation. He seemed happy enough, but many younger Nepalese, influenced by Western attitudes, were beginning to rebel against tradition, demanding marriages based on love. Their actions often brought grief to their families, who saw it as another step toward the annihilation of their culture.

Between Karan's family astrologer and that of his future wife, an auspicious wedding date had been chosen. Karan had much to do in preparation, and he wanted to catch the January 17 plane out of Jumla, the one that Gary was due to fly in on from Kathmandu. Taking Karma, who would return with Gary, he left Eding on January 9.

"I will be back as soon as possible," he promised Rod, "providing everything is all right." He said the last part with a glance at me and a funny little laugh. I took it to be a reference to the nuptials—particularly the wedding night.

"Who could blame him for being nervous?" I thought. How would I feel if, on my wedding night, the man beside me in bed was a virtual stranger?

If we thought the idea of such a marriage was odd and rather awful, what must Karan, Karma, and the Dolphas have thought about the arrangement that Rod and I had entered into—and without our parents being involved at all?

We didn't hear from Karan again until early May.

With Rod at Pine Camp, I took fresh batteries for the photo stations and crossed the river to Tillisha Stream. When I'd filled my water bottle with icy-clear melted snow, I walked upstream to check the trap sites.

There was something odd about the "enclosure trap," a regular snare loosely fenced with pine and poplar branches. In the sloppy snow on top of Rod's "handmade" leopard scrape I could see what looked like a cat track. Sure enough, a line of tracks led from the stream and into the enclosure—where we had suspended a chicken wing to entice a cat—missing the trap at the entrance coming and going. The leopard had jumped the stream on boulders covered with snow and ice. I followed the trail upstream along the bank. The snow was patchy along the streambed, melted off the bigger rocks, and the cat had walked on the dry spots wherever it could.

Cat? . . . "Wait a minute," my brain said to me, "there're *two* sets of tracks here. And one set is considerably smaller than the other." I had no measuring tape, but it was suddenly clear that I was following a trail left the night before by a mother and her cub. What's more, Rod had picked up "Char's" signal the previous day high on the ridge above Tillisha Terrace. She could have come down in the wee hours while we were sleeping.

I followed the trail's winding course, skimming like a bird over the uneven ground, buoyed by the thrill of discovery. Again the cats crossed over, using boulders and a fallen log. The boulders were six feet apart, their rounded tops covered with a white film of ice. Disappointed, I knew I'd never make it without a drenching in the freezing stream.

I started back, hoping against hope that Rod would return early *and* that he'd located "Char" in the canyon, to prove that these were indeed her tracks. It wasn't likely; if anything, a signal would delay him. I was afraid to climb the bluff to Tillisha Terrace alone to change the photo station batteries. The trail was icy and too slick.

Crunching along, headed for camp, I heard a shout from the cliff trail. Rodney! I waved to him to hurry. He made a gesture that was unmistakably, "Big? And little?" When I nodded yes vigorously, he began running down the trail.

"What have you found?" he asked excitedly.

"Oh, I think it's 'Char's' tracks—and she has a cub with her! Come and see. What did *you* find?"

"From the ridge I could see tracks crisscrossing at the bottom of the canyon, way up. I picked up 'Char,' so I knew it was her, but I couldn't tell how many sets of cub tracks."

While he took care of the photo station, I returned to camp for the cameras and film. By the time I got back, he'd determined that I was wrong.

"There isn't a set of cub tracks here—there are *two* sets!"

"Char" had padded down the bluff trail from the cliffs above, stopping off at the big spray boulder. Without respraying, she rubbed her cheeks in the scent, leaving hairs clinging to the rock.

The cubs had stuck their front feet out and snowplowed down the bluff in one long slide. "Char" continued up the trail, approached the photo station, rescraped a site not two feet from the camera, and proceeded over the pressure pad with her backside to the camera, leaving a nice pugmark squarely on the pad. Meanwhile, the cubs made their own trail, missing the photo station by a wide margin.

We followed all the pugmarks in the snow, taking measurements and photographs, sketching diagrams, and writing notes. "Char's" cubs would now be seven and a half months old, based on the radio-tracking data from last summer, when her activity and travel pattern first indicated that she was denning.

We could not know how many cubs "Char" had to begin with, but two probably was an average number in the wild; and the fact that she had successfully raised these to the age of seven and a half months said plenty about her skills as a provider.

We had cooked and eaten our dinner and gone to bed, glad for the peace and solitude, and were listening to "Margaret Howard's Letterbox" on BBC when there was a noise outside.

At first all we heard was a low rumble, a sound like thunder rolling at a great distance. But the noise quickly built, very close by, into a roaring avalanche. The great landslide by Eding Knoll was coming down. Rod jumped up and stood in the doorway of the tent, obscuring my view.

"Oh, my God! Jeezus, I don't believe it! The whole mountain must be caving in!" he shouted, frozen to the spot with amazement.

"Let me see," I pleaded, squeezing between his arm and the tent flap. I gasped as a huge cloud of flying snow and earth rose to engulf the canyon, the tent's nylon wall ruffling in the wake of wind and dust.

"What are we doing standing here?" I yelled, "We're going to get buried!"

"If we were going to get buried," he said, "it would have happened already. Besides, where are you going to run to? You haven't got any shoes on, and you'll freeze out there in your long johns." A second, smaller avalanche followed, tumbling quickly down the steep incline. The cloud slowly settled, and all was still for several minutes.

Shivering, we went back to bed, lying rigid, unsure if the continued thumping came from our hearts or the slopes outside.

In the morning we went onto Tillisha Terrace, opposite the landslide, to survey the damage. A huge section—tons of soil and snow between the pine forest and the original slide—had come down. From some thirteen hundred feet above the river, the avalanche had destroyed everything in its path, obliterating the trail we had worn across the lower third and spreading brown dust and rocks to within two hundred yards of camp.

Rocks continued to fall as we looked for bharal, wondering if the Eding herd had been on the landslide when it went. If any of its members had been trapped in the mud and rubble, they were undoubtedly buried deep. Just east of Eding Knoll we spotted the herd—the bulk of it, in any case—grazing peacefully.

"Could the sheep have made the whole thing go like that?" I asked Rod.

"I doubt it," he replied. "I expect it was the freezing and expanding of moisture in the rocks. I hope it's through for a while."

Eding Knoll and Pukchang would be out of bounds for some time, and I wished, not for the first time, that there was some other way to get upstream on the Eding side of the river.

All through January, the days practically alternated between sunshine and snowfall, the sort of weather sure to delay Jumla flights and Gary and Karma's journey to Eding.

Turning on the radio one morning, I picked up "Char's" strong signal on the Langu's bank opposite camp. It was a "5" signal, as loud and clear as they get. The cat, with her cubs, probably was within my line of sight, but the beeps, bouncing off all the surrounding cliffs, were impossible to pinpoint; I knew only that she was very close by. Was she on Tillisha Terrace, near the canyon mouth? Or on the trail to Pine Camp? Search as I might, all I could see were rocks and bushes. You would think that three leopards traveling together would be easy to spot, but I had no luck that day.

Rod returned from Pukchang in late afternoon, having monitored their progress toward Eding, and also the activity of "Panch" on the Pukchang North cliffs.

"Char" and her cubs had walked along the Tillisha Terrace transect. The mother and one cub walked directly over the photo station pressure pad, *facing* the camera. (We would not find out until the following July that the roll contained only photos of our knees where we had tested the setup, and several black frames.)

They descended the bluff more or less on the trail, then crossed the stream and came the short distance out of the canyon to continue along

283

the Langu, finally climbing high above the river to the west of Pine Camp. They used our trail for part of the way, and "Char" tripped the streamside trap.

"She probably jumped about a mile," said Rod. "And then it looks like she attacked this boulder where the snare is attached." He pointed out one very distorted cub track on the slope above the trap. "It's pure speculation, but I would say this small cat thought its mother had lost her mind. Look how it suddenly sprang off the trail with its toes all spread—it was probably scared out of its wits!"

We agreed it was probably just as well we didn't catch her. Judging by her attitude toward the boulder, she might have been especially dangerous and determined to protect her young.

"I don't know *what* she would do if we caught one of *them,*" Rod said.

"After your experience with 'Dui,' I replied, "I for one will be quite happy if what 'Char' would do *remains* a mystery. Still, wouldn't it be really something to catch a baby? We could measure and weigh and look at it, and take pictures of it."

"Remember," he said, "They're eight months old now—not so small anymore. I bet they'd almost come up to your knee."

We were getting concerned about Gary and Karma being so overdue. There was such a range of possible reasons that it was useless to speculate, but we did it anyway. Two weeks weren't really *that* much; after all, we were nearly a *month* late. But it was not knowing that was so awful, the underlying tension of anticipation that made each day seem an eternity. We could have used some carrier pigeons.

With the continuing beautiful weather, our spirits sank lower and lower as each evening brought no sign of our missing friends. I decided to go with Sonam to Dolphu to join the celebration of "Second Lhosar," a minor holiday of feasting and drinking. The trail had been too danger-ous to go for "First Lhosar." Now the snow was gone and we could make it in a day. It would be a break from the awful waiting, and a traveling villager might have some news from Jumla.

Sonam and I left on February 19, planning to be back on the twenty-first. Rod stayed behind to work.

We arrived in Dolphu at about six o'clock. As we passed the spring outside the village, a boy shouted that Gary and Karma were in Jumla, waiting for two loads that hadn't come from Kathmandu. He said something about planes.

Thondup was just returning to the house with a basketful of freshly butchered goat; Sonam's mother and his wife were pressing mustard seeds for oil in wooden troughs; the old blind grandma was rocking a basket containing her now four-month-old great-granddaughter. There were big smiles and happy greetings all around. "Everything okay? Was the trail difficult?" Sonam's mother clasped my hands to her forehead—just the way I'd seen the Bhote women do among their friends and those they especially respected. "Well, that was worth the whole journey," I said to myself as I returned her gesture.

Sonam and I went onto the roof to pitch my tent, and Lundup came by. He and Sonam talked. Sonam turned to me and said, "Geddy-Sah'b coming."

"What?" said I. "When? Where is he?"

"*Ahile.*" Now. "Five minute coming." He was grinning broadly. On the trail from Eding he'd repeatedly said, "Maybe today coming." He'd said it at least a hundred times, and we'd laughed. I didn't believe him now.

But it was true. I could see two porters on the path below the house, and then Gary walked around the corner. In seconds we were again trading hugs, to the villagers' delight. Suddenly the weeks of worry were over, and hours later we were still talking in torrents.

"A plane crashed some months back, in eastern Nepal," he explained. "So the RNAC instituted new regulations: Because of high afternoon winds, no landings would be allowed at STOL [short takeoff and landing] airstrips after eleven in the morning."

"I'm glad they decided to do that," I said. "The wind at Jumla can be really scary."

"Right," replied Gary. "However, the Jumla flight, which you know used to take off from Kathmandu at seven o'clock A.M., was rescheduled for ten o'clock A.M. Since the flight takes an hour and a half, there was no way the plane could land before eleven. *You* figure it out!"

For weeks, the Jumla airstrip had rested in the sun, the dust unruffled by anything bigger than a rangy cow.

"The discrepancy got sorted out," Gary went on, "because we took off on February 6, and here I am."

Gary went a little ahead when we got near our camp the next evening and found Rod recharging batteries on the solar panel. Rod's surprise was doubled because he'd been down the trail earlier, and when he didn't see us coming by four o'clock, thought for sure that Sonam and I had stayed another day in Dolphu.

They were already hard at work the next morning as I rushed to finish my long letter home for one of the porters to take back to Jumla, from where it would go to Kathmandu in the United Missions mailbag and finally to the United States.

"Char" and her family returned to the cliffs behind Pine Camp, taking Rod up for the night at a minimum. Gary went upstream and established our fourth tracking camp at Nisan Phu—"bush place," named for the hunting shelter built of poplar beams and juniper.

A two-hour walk beyond Pukchang High Camp, Nisan Phu would allow for more accurate locations on "Panch," who seemed to be ranging easterly. Perhaps "Panch" was looking for turf farther removed from her mother and the cubs, though they, too, used the upper reaches of the Langu. The country around Ruka Canyon was so extraordinarily rugged that it could take two days' travel, one way, to locate the cats when they roamed beyond Pukchang North.

More than ever we could have used a helicopter, but at nearly a thousand dollars per hour of flying time, our budget couldn't cover the cost. In Kathmandu, Gary had discovered that the one we had seen last summer had been chartered by a group of Canadian land-use planners, whose subsequent maps would prove immensely helpful to us.

We now had tracking camps situated throughout the study area such that we could cover approximately fifty square miles of territory, all along the riverfront and both the inner Tillisha and Dhukyel basins. Although there were areas that we could never get to on foot—such as the headwaters of Dhukyel Canyon, and the northern reaches where the Langu made its great bend—we were able to pick up radio signals from a wide enough area that the boundaries of the collared cats' ranges could be traced with acceptable accuracy. The enormous degree of range overlap among the cats and the way they shared the territory, as shown by this tracking data, were to be among the study's most unexpected and important findings.

CHAPTER

29

The Phantom of Lobur

In the middle of April, while Gary was on ghost duty at Eding, I got my season's first trip to the "windle" but lovely Pine Camp.

For two heavenly days there wasn't a cloud in the sky; at noon the wind was only a welcome stirring of the hot air. "Char" was in range, and I monitored her activity while Rod did sign transects in the broken country west of camp.

I made a list of items needed to restock the food trunk, and as I finished I happened to look up at the gully in the grasslands where "Char" and her young had spent the previous day. Vultures were circling. And landing. My binoculars revealed crows as well, all concentrating on the same spot.

"Rodney," I called, "there's something going on up in that gully. Come up here and have a look."

He came quickly, his powerful binoculars slung around his neck. "The birds are landing out of sight in the gully," he said. "I can't tell for sure, but I'll bet it's a kill."

It was an hour's journey through thick stands of stickers, and there was virtually nothing left of the kill, an adult female bharal, but skin and bones. There was no sign of a chase; it looked like the cats had caught the sheep completely by surprise. Just below the kill site was a rock outcrop where the cats rested during the day. The rock was big enough to block most of the signal and cause it to bounce all during my monitoring on the seventeenth, even though the effective rock face was no higher than three and a quarter feet. Rod could find definite evidence of only one cub, but the tracking medium was especially poor. The kill had been made sometime on the seventeenth, and they left the site on the morning of the eighteenth. Even if there were only two cats now, it didn't take them long to consume a whole sheep.

The kill was made in very open, exposed subalpine scrub, with almost nothing to afford cover for a stalk, proving that it takes very little to hide a cat and to make its radio signal highly erratic.

"You've earned yourself the bounty," said Rod, "if we still have ten bucks left when we get to Kathmandu!"

Karma told us he had loaned some money to Jickchor to buy two yaks from Dolpo. Both yaks had bitten the dust within two weeks of arrival at their new home, and Jickchor still owed Karma 230 rupees.

We shouldn't have been surprised when Karma made a potato run near the end of April and hired Jickchor to carry them to Eding. Presumably Jickchor had agreed to turn over his "porter charge" as part of the debt repayment. But Karma should have realized that having Jickchor in our midst would not sit well. The fact that he had come to us when he was hurt had not erased our suspicions over the missing gear.

That conflict was forgotten, however, in the face of a much more immediate one. Jickchor walked into our kitchen carrying the carcass of a female tahr, still warm and whole but for a tiny patch of meat eaten from just behind the left front leg. The potatoes were on Karma's back.

"What's going on?" Rod asked, looking at Karma.

"Good news, sah'b," Karma replied, his cheek twitching. Descending Tyson's Cliff, the two of them had interrupted a leopard's dinner. They had seen the tahr lying on a small ledge some way off the trail, and the cat, alerted by seeing or smelling the men, making a hasty exit up Muga Canyon.

"Oh, shit," Rod said with a groan. "Why didn't you leave it alone? The cat will come back, find its kill gone, and leave. All that great information is lost. Why didn't you tell us before you took the tahr away?"

"Too dipcul, sah'b," he replied. "Sun is going. Muga too much long way."

Karma *must* have remembered Rod giving him the flagging tape and asking him to mark any kill he found, and not to move it before Rod or Gary had a chance to look at it. His cheek gave him away. But Jickchor must have argued very convincingly to get him to take the carcass. A whole, fresh tahr was a prize find, by far the locals' favorite meat, wild or domestic.

Rodney, without hiding his disappointment, let it be known that he would want the beast returned to Tyson's Cliff in the morning, to reproduce the scene for photographs and to set up a camera station with the remote switch box.

Karma argued that according to Dolphu tradition, any animal found the way the tahr had been found had to be shared equally by the finders. He implied that it belonged to Jickchor and him, and it wasn't Rodney's place to tell them what to do with it. Rod and Gary were furious.

"Who the hell is he working for, Jickchor or us?" asked Gary. "It's bad enough that we have to give Jickchor a share of the bounty. And Karma's going to get it all anyway. Just what is he playing at?"

Rod tried to explain calmly that we needed to get a leopard photograph, and that to do so, enough meat to keep a cat at the site through a night and a day must be put out as bait. The head and skin had to go along as well to make it look convincing. Even though there wasn't much chance of luring *that* cat back, another one might come along.

Karma understood the words, but what did he know of our world of glossy magazines and scientific journals, computerized data analysis, and conservation? He just wanted the meat.

In the morning, Jickchor lugged the body back up the Lobur side of Tyson's Cliff to just below the ladder-and-roped section, then cut across to where several small ledges formed well-used resting sites for tahr.

The kill had been made about halfway up the cliff on a narrow "leopard trail" that led along the western cliffs of Muga Canyon. Scrapes of varying ages attested to its regular use, and fresh tracks in the dust confirmed that it had been used the previous night.

Seeing that the leopard obviously had been back looking for its meal, Rod got angry all over again that Karma and Jickchor hadn't left it there.

"It'll never come back again tonight," he said. "*Damn* the luck!"

There was so little sign of a chase or a struggle that it appeared the cat had managed to sneak *really* close before pouncing. How it kept from falling over the cliff during the kill was a mystery.

Karma and Jickchor hadn't wanted to struggle getting the carcass down the cliff so they had thrown it over the edge—a fall of about a hundred feet—then picked it up at the bottom. That probably explained how both horns got broken.

We finished with the photography and inspection of the site and took the thing back to camp to perform an autopsy. Along with its horns, it had a broken neck, seven broken ribs, a smashed skull, and extensive internal injuries and bleeding. Some of the damage might have occurred after death when they dumped it over the cliff, but we would never know what injuries the cat had inflicted.

By the time the autopsy was finished, Rod and Gary were swearing in long, slow, elaborate, and graphic sentences.

There were no rake marks on the tahr's body at all, though Rod had found gashes on the Tillisha bharal around the rump where the cat had made its first attempts to catch it. There were only three very small punctures on the tahr's throat, two of which had barely broken the skin. (On the Tillisha sheep and the older carcasses they had found larger, deeper holes where the cat had held the neck and strangled its prey.) The small punctures and lack of rake marks, along with the relatively undisturbed kill site, could have meant that the chase took place above the cliff.

"It could have fallen over and was already dead or dying when the cat got to it," Gary said. "I could wring both of your necks," he added, speaking to Jickchor and Karma, who were sitting nearby, waiting impatiently for Rod and Gary to finish with their examination so they could take the portions that would not be used at the bait site.

They both came out well off. Jickchor would go home with a treat for his family or, if he chose to sell the meat, soon would have a little cash. With the bounty, he could repay most of his debt to Karma. Karma would end up not only with all of the bounty but also would get to sink his teeth into a decent-size feast of tahr. But still they sulked.

We went back up the cliff the following morning to set up two photo stations. There were no fresh tracks, and it was obvious that the leopard had not returned. We placed the carcass, minus the choice cuts of meat, on the ledge trail against the cliff, partially sheltered by an old juniper.

"I hope a leopard finds it before the vultures do," I said as we set the cameras so I could trip them with one of the two switches on the box that National Geographic had given us. My job would be more or less to live on the ridge opposite the cliff and keep a lookout for any leopard that might come upon the tahr. I was also equipped with spotting scope, binoculars, and a 35mm camera with a 400mm lens.

I found a nice hiding place beneath a young pine tree on the edge of Muga Canyon opposite Tyson's Cliff. Muga Stream ran five hundred feet below my ridgeline perch. With the spotting scope I could see the general area where the bait was tied down, but branches of the juniper were in the way. I would have to rely on seeing movement to know if a leopard had come. Another problem was the ever-present wind, whipping up by midafternoon to a steady blast.

While I sat sentry over the camera station, Rod and Gary would at last make the expedition into Tillisha Basin to look for "Dui."

"We'll use the cave as a base," Rod explained, "and cross over the grassland to the ridge overlooking Tillisha Basin. It looks pretty steep and difficult, but if there's a way down over the edge, we should be able to find a small ledge or knoll where we can pitch the two small tents and camp. I hope we don't have to go all the way to the bottom of the basin."

From the radio signal, they were certain the collar was about halfway down into the basin; the search would be that much harder if they had to work from the very bottom. They would be gone about ten days, more if the weather continued so unsettled.

I had just finished my lunch of dried fruit and crackers, on my first day as "lookout," when I looked up the ridge behind my perch to see a herd of tahr on the slope above. Few photographs existed of Himalayan tahr in their native habitat. Now, midday sunlight glared on the canyon's features, and the wind was at maximum blast. I tried to stay hidden as I tried to find a good position from which to shoot, one where the tripod and camera and I wouldn't tumble over the cliff.

One by one, grazing and browsing on leaves, the animals disappeared behind the ridge. I moved back down to my perch and checked the bait site. The tahr reappeared, not two hundred feet away. Now I was shooting into the shadows. One female grazed toward me, oblivious even though I was standing up, maneuvering the camera and tripod. She finally looked up at me, did a double take, and fled, taking the others with her. That was it for the day.

I packed up and started back to camp. There in the dirt, fifty feet away from my perch, big cat tracks led along the slope. For a minute I was stunned. Could it be that while I was straining my eyes to see a leopard all that morning, one was walking around right behind me?

Looking closer, I could see rain beads in the tracks; it must have come along the previous night. Nearby, the cat had left a scrape, and that had been rained on, too.

The tracks were heading west-east, away from Muga Canyon. Could this cat have found the bait, eaten it, and continued on its way the previous evening or night? Or was it on my side of the canyon all day, watching me? If that was the case, how could the tahr have been so unconcerned?

The next morning I awoke full of excitement and anticipation. Would I see a leopard? Creeping to the lookout, binocs in hand for a quick overview, I found the bait site as quiet and still as the morning air. I put the scope on the tripod, focused on the bait site, and watched for many minutes, seeing no sign of movement or any change in the surroundings.

Several times during the day vultures circled overhead, dropping low, knowing something was there but apparently unable to find what must by now be a very smelly carcass. A storm blew up in the afternoon and there was rain at the river level, snow on Tillisha. Not a very promising outlook for Rod and Gary.

On May 1, I got to the lookout at seven-thirty, scanned the bait site, the face of Lobur, the slopes above, and the hill on my side. I poured coffee and sat down to do a more intensive search of the visible terrain. Movement to my left caught my eye. Three hundred feet away, a snow leopard, with its back to me, was walking slowly over the ridge.

I jumped to get the scope off the tripod and the camera on it. My fingers felt paralyzed and my heart slammed in my chest. How long had the cat been there in plain sight, creeping slowly away from me? No doubt since I arrived fifteen minutes earlier.

"Please, please, come back," I prayed as I fumbled with the camera. The sun was just beginning to hit the ridge.

I set the f-stop and shutter speed and focused on the spot where the cat disappeared. And I waited, looking all around, up and down the ridge.

There it is! About 150 feet farther up, standing on the edge, looking at me. QUICK! Move the camera up, get it framed. Get it focused. Migod, it's perfect, beautiful. But overexposed—the sun's fully up. Stop it down, QUICK! Too late. Too LATE! It's disappearing—over the edge. Take it anyway, knowing it's no good. Nothing but a tail. Oh, no. It can't be. I've missed it. The chance of a lifetime. It was so *close*. Maybe it'll come back. . . .

Ten eternal minutes passed, and suddenly three tahr appeared on the crest of the hill. They were on the move, lunging downslope, doubling back in a zigzagging race, disappearing again behind the ridge into the canyon. I looked in vain for a leopard giving chase.

It was all over then. Had I been on Tyson's Cliff, I could have seen the whole area where the cat disappeared and where it had apparently found the herd of tahr.

I sat down to let my sweat and tears dry, numbed and nauseated. I had it all, everything I needed to get the picture, everything but speed and skill. Had I been just *one second* faster . . .

For three more days I sat beneath the pine tree. Again, one morning I found fresh leopard tracks on "my" trail, very near the lookout, headed in that direction. They were the same size as the other ones. There was never any action at the bait site; only the crows had found it. It was time to go and have a look.

Karma went with me. There were fresh scrapes on the ledge trail below the meat, but the rain had washed away any tracks. The carcass was untouched except by the crows and flies. Karma pulled back the skin, then sprang back, horrified by the seething mass of maggots. We cleaned the rain spots off the camera lenses and left the stinking bait as it was.

In the afternoon I went to change the Tillisha Terrace photo station batteries. I'd picked up "Char's" signal the night before and thought she might have gone along the terrace and tripped the camera. I discovered that she hadn't walked over the pressure pad, but she had come down the bluff trail to cross the stream. That there were fresh tracks of her and *two* cubs, proving she still had both her young, lifted my sunken spirits.

Rod returned to Eding late that evening. "We spent the whole time at the cave, hemmed in by snow," he said. "We couldn't even cross the grassland, much less descend the backside of the mountain. We did some mapping and habitat sampling but we'll never get into that bowl unless we have nearly a week of straight sun."

Later, in our dark tent, Rod listened as I relived my encounter with the leopard. His warm, weather-roughened hands and gentle loving erased my wretched sense of failure.

CHAPTER

30

Two Against the Mountain

Karan arrived back in Dolphu on May 3. He sent three porters from the village to get his food and equipment and a letter to Rod explaining that, since the river was up, he would not cross Tyson's Cliff to come to Eding but would instead establish a camp at the Dolphas' summer yak pasture and observe the bharal above the village.

He was married on March 8, but his return to the field had been delayed by various project-related problems. He had been accepted as a Ph.D. candidate at Tribhuvan University, with the bharal study as his thesis topic. His choice of study areas revived the earlier dissension, though Rod would cease insisting that he try to climb the cliff. Sadly, there would be little further communication between the two camps, and we would get no details of his home leave and how the ceremonies went, although he did tell Rod that his wife was very beautiful and that he loved being married.

Rod and Gary left on June 5 to try one last time to get into Tillisha Basin. Again, they worked from the cave, where temperatures hovered around zero.

They carried food, a kerosene cookstove, tents, and extra clothing.

Searching through the scope and binocs, they had thought they could find a way across a band of cliffs on the backside of Tillisha's peak, at about seventeen thousand feet. It took five hours to climb from the cave, and by the time they reached the cliffs, they began to despair at their luck in pathfinding; swirling mist and clouds became thicker as the day wore on. From the rubble on the peak above them, rocks loosened and fell, missing them by inches.

Earlier, Gary had stashed a supply of backpacking meals in the rocks below the peak; now they found only a few remains of wrappings and plenty of weasel droppings. They would have to ration what little they had brought with them; there was no time to return to the cave. With the clouds becoming denser, they had to find the way over the cliffs—and soon.

On the point of giving up, Rod found a narrow ledge, barely big enough for two boots side by side, that traversed the mountainside, offering a way across the jumble of rock and scree. For about one hundred yards they dodged a hail of falling stones, wondering how often the slope was swept by a major rockfall. Even getting hit by a pebble could be serious. Should they continue? Was the risk too great? They thought of all the questions waiting to be answered and knew they had no choice.

They made a rough bivouac camp on a knoll still wet from recently melted snow. Their water came from a bank nearby. The stove, clogged by impure kerosene, refused to burn despite even Gary's attempts to fix it. So they lived on dried fruit, nuts, cold milk, and granola for the three-day round-trip from Tillisha Cave.

From the knoll they picked up "Char," transmitting from the basin in a broad sweep of grassland half a mile away. Just for the hell of it, Rod took a look along the bearing through his binocs.

"Oh, my God, Gary!" he called. "I've got 'Char'—and there're two cubs with her!"

"Char," whom we had tried so hard for so long to glimpse, was sauntering along, with her big year-old cubs doing everything *but* saunter beside her. They romped. They chased one another, rolling and tumbling down the steep hillside. They stalked imaginary sheep. They leaped and charged, playing as if they were baby kittens while their mother padded along, well aware of the small herd of bharal on the slopes above. If she was hungry, too bad; none of these bharal would become leopard food, thanks to the cubs!

They were too far away and there wasn't enough light to photograph, so Rod and Gary simply watched, enraptured, until it got too dark to see.

"I wonder how on earth 'Char' has managed to raise those two," Rod said. "They must bungle at least half her attempts at hunting!"

"I don't know," Gary replied. "But she's managed somehow; they look healthy and strong to me. Otherwise they wouldn't be playing so vigorously."

Such play would be important in the cubs' development—honing their skills for the serious work of learning to hunt for themselves. In another year or so they would be on their own, establishing their turf around Tillisha Mountain or elsewhere.

At first light, Rod and Gary set off to look for the collar. Later, Rod remarked that it was the longest and hardest day in his life. They climbed down two thousand feet, all the way to the basin's bottom, seeking the best of several dangerous routes. Then they covered the hummocky grassland, up the valley, then zigzagging across it, zeroing in. As they got closer, the signal bounce increased. They had it down to an area of several hundred square yards, which they began to cover yard by yard until the signal became consistently loud no matter which way the antenna faced.

They found the collar lying on an open grassy slope above jumbled boulders of a glacial moraine near the confluence of a side drainage with Tillisha Stream. It had been lying there for almost a year. Excitedly, Rod and Gary examined it; the nuts and bolts that held it around the leopard's neck were still intact, and the belting was in good condition.

"This isn't the kind of place where a sick cat would choose to die," Rod remarked to Gary.

"Right," Gary replied. "And if he had been injured badly enough to die on the spot, why is there no sign? What about vultures? There's no way they could have broken a dead cat's neck and carried the collar here."

Rod frowned. "It certainly doesn't seem likely, does it? Let's make a thorough search of the area." There were no bones, hair, or skin belonging to a leopard anywhere around.

They took a break for lunch and puzzled over the collar. Stuck to the band was a mudlike substance they agreed was the stomach contents of a bharal, dried and hardened with the passage of time. "Let's expand our search farther downslope and examine every boulder of the moraine," said Rod.

"We'd better start now," Gary replied. "There are hundreds of them."

Later that afternoon Gary found the only shred of reasonable evidence: Beneath a boulder several hundred yards downslope of where the collar was found, out of sight of prying vulture eyes, were the skin and bones of a fully grown male bharal, judged to have died around the time "Dui's" last active signal was received. The best theory seemed to be that "Dui" had killed the sheep and somehow managed to hook a horn or hoof. There were deep scratches in the collar; if he was desperate enough, he could have pulled it off.

"I think we can presume that 'Dui' is still alive," said Rod as they began the long walk back along the valley and made the steep, two-thousand-foot ascent back to their camp. There was no fire to toast their weary bodies, no coffee to warm their bellies, but they were immensely satisfied with their day's work. They had been privileged to see a new and spectacular Tibetan plateaulike landscape, one that was in marked contrast to the main canyon. If the Dolphu villagers had told the truth, no other humans had ever walked the ground they had covered that day. Even the villagers considered it too difficult.

The mystery still remained as to what really happened to "Dui," but they were happy enough to imagine that he still wandered over his old haunts; perhaps we had even seen his tracks in the dust of Tillisha Terrace.

Back at Tillisha Cave, Rod picked up "Panch." As he walked over the grassland her signal came in better and better, finally beeping in a clear, loud line of sight. It was almost too much to hope that this cat, too, would show itself in the final hours of the study. But that is what she did. Some three hundred yards below, at the edge of a drop-off, "Panch" was lying down, watching Rod.

She lay absolutely still, hardly moving a muscle for two and a half hours. Finally, at dusk, she moved a few feet to recline under a bush. The last Rod saw of "Panch" was her tail, protruding from the branches in the fast-fading light.

CHAPTER

31

Kingdom of the Cloud Dwellers

Beneath the late June sun we worked on Thondup's rooftop, setting aside the few items of still-usable gear that we could leave behind as gifts. The clothing, containers, metal trunks, ropes, and tools made a very small pile, not nearly enough to give every family something of value. There were several tents remaining of the fifteen we had worn out over the years, all in appallingly bad condition, with broken poles and zippers, holes in the floors and roofs. But they were coveted by every villager.

An argument broke out between two of the men over an old beat-up pair of leather boots, and we saw how desperately they wanted things we would have thrown away as beyond repair anywhere else. In the "Amrika" of their imaginations we were rich beyond belief and could easily replace all the things we had brought to the Langu. It wasn't so; we could not buy replacements, and we could not be certain of any future donations. But there was no denying the vast material disparity between our lives and theirs, and I was torn, painfully aware that our gifts were so inadequate.

Several of the women climbed the ladder to Thondup's rooftop, joining the other villagers watching us prepare to leave. Some brought boiled eggs, others just handshakes and well-wishes.

Those we had come to know best—Sonam's family, Tsewong's wife,

301

Tenzing Thakpa, and even Jickchor—all invited us to their hearths for a farewell bowl of chang. Without them, we could never have lived in the gorge. They had done their best to look after our needs, helping us in spite of some good reasons not to and pressure from Karma Lama and his supporters. Some had caused us a great deal of trouble as well, but it hardly seemed important anymore. We wanted them to know how much they had come to mean to us and that we would never forget them.

I looked into Sonam's expressive face, his eyes deep and black in the firelight from his father's hearth. What would he say to me, if he could? He held my gaze for long minutes, and I drifted off, thinking of the thread that connected this family to the world outside.

Twenty years before, his father, as a young man, had been an essential guide to John Tyson, leading his group into the gorge. A six-foot section of the aluminum ladder that Tyson had used to bridge the Langu still stood in Thondup's yard.

Thondup had known another Westerner, Dr. Barry Bishop, a mountaineer and now Vice Chairman of the National Geographic Society's Committee for Research and Exploration. Barry and his family had spent fifteen months in Jumla in the early 1970s, studying the area's anthropology. On the wall of his office in Washington, D.C., hung a photograph of a Bhote trader, a man he had noticed in the bazaar one day, who went on to become his chief informant on Dolphu. Barry had forgotten his name, but we recognized Thondup.

What would attest to our time with the Bhotes? How had we affected their culture, their hopes and expectations? Will they eventually go the way of other vanishing Third World cultures, becoming homogenized into a "Western" Asia preoccupied with money and status? Long before we arrived they were acquiring Hindu names and rejecting their distinctive homemade clothing. Now Sonam's big wish was for a cassette recorder just like Lopsang's.

If we had temporarily accelerated their Westernization, perhaps we also had had a positive influence, demonstrating that the Langu's snow leopards were a unique and valuable resource, now and for future generations. We had proven that the snow leopard is worth more to them alive than it is dead, as a ten-dollar pelt on the black market. We had come to the Langu to see snow leopards; if we hadn't found them, we soon would have gone away. Instead, because the villagers had not eliminated them or their wild prey, Dolphu and Wangri had had four years of steady income in a time when famine might have taken a heavy toll. But would they ever really abandon their appetite for the hunt?

I felt certain, at that moment, that a new thread was being spun, that the path of their lives would intertwine with ours as we continued to work in our way on the issues that concern them. But I felt just as strong a certainty that the villagers will do what they must to adapt to new realities, for they are, when it comes down to it, creative and capable rulers of their own cloud-kingdom.

Sonam's young son, Thakpa, climbed into his lap. Almost five years old, he had beaten the odds that keep thirty-five out of every thousand Nepalese children from making it to their fourth birthday. Would that sweet little boy one day walk into the gorge and know the magic of seeing a wild snow leopard? Would he grow up to share a fragment of his life and his world with a visiting stranger, picking up the invisible thread that stretched from Dolphu to England and Washington, D.C? My heart began to break, for I knew there was little chance that I would ever learn the answers to those questions.

We emerged from Thondup's house into the bright sunlight and shouldered our packs, ready to go down the notched ladder off the rooftop and onto the trail. Sonam's mother tugged at Rodney's shoulder. She held a small dish of precious yak butter. Reaching up, she smeared a fingerful of the butter first onto Rod's temple and then Gary's. Turning to me, she put a dab on the top of my head, all the while mumbling a low chant. Normally she would do this for the members of her family departing on a journey. Now, like those who would accompany us to Jumla as porters, a prayer had been given for our safe passage, too.

As we walked along the village path breathing in the dung smell and the humid green fragrance of summer, it seemed out of the question that it could be for the last time. If I thought that I would never again see the place that had so touched our lives, the leaving would have been unbearable. And yet I knew, too, that if the choice to leave were suddenly eliminated, if we knew that we could never go home, it would be a different story.

"I wonder what would happen," Rod had said, "if we had to live here for the rest of our lives. Once we got adjusted to the idea and accepted it, would we be any better than the Dolphas at making a living? Working side by side with them, herding yaks and farming, would we be any better at using the land wisely? How long would pass before we, too, stopped caring much about what happens to the snow leopards?"

The whole notion raised the hair on my arms, and I turned my thoughts to tangible realities. I must not forget the gnarled peach trees with their rough bark, the cackling call of wild chukor partridges hidden in the grass, the smooth feel of red-stained mud on the village chortens, the way the terraced fields hug the hillside. I must remember how funny Jickchor looked jumping rope and how tightly little Thakpa's fingers curved around a piece of meat.

I lingered at the edge of the village, letting the porters file past. Rod and Gary were already out of sight, and Karma, too, had dashed ahead, singing a high, girlish song of happiness to be on his way home. At least I wouldn't have to face *that* parting yet; I'd have a week on the trail to get used to the idea of not seeing Karma anymore. I wouldn't be hearing his cheery "Good morning, Didi," when he brought tea to our tent. There'd be no more tight corners I could help him out of. Most of all, I would miss his crooked smiles.

The Langu roared far below as I walked up through the greening fields, keeping to paths along the edges. Rod and Gary waited on a stone bench beside Murki La's chorten, where colored scraps of tattered cloth fluttered in the wind. We sat together looking back across the hillside to the village, just visible on the ridgeline. Rodney took my hand, linking our fingers.

"Do you remember the first time you saw this view?" he asked. "Can you remember your impressions, with all the kids running around, none of us knowing what the future held?"

"It seemed that we still had so far to *go*," I replied. "All the way across those fields. Now it seems like no distance at all, with everything that has happened. Perhaps it's just a dream; perhaps I'm about to wake up in a flash of smoke in some office twelve thousand miles on the other side of the world."

"In a few weeks we'll be plunging back into another whole reality," Rod said. "I'm looking forward to it. We could go on with the fieldwork here for years, but you have to draw the line somewhere."

Gary bent to tie his shoe. "There's a mountain of data waiting to be sorted out and analyzed. And I've got to get a job, fast."

"Still, I guess I'll always get a feeling of unfinished business whenever I think of the Langu," Rod said. "We may have learned something about snow leopards, but there still is so much here to unravel."

"We've made a beginning," Gary replied. "And I feel really good about what we've been able to accomplish. It would be interesting, now, to compare what we know of the Langu to some other areas where people have had more of an impact on the habitat."

Rod looked at me and said, "I think he's hooked."

"That makes three of us," I replied.

Reluctantly, we left the easy old bench of worn stone and turned our backs on Dolphu, setting our boots for the last time on the long, winding Jumla Trail.

EPILOGUE

No one could have guessed that this book would be four years in the making—four years *after* we returned from the Langu. It's a fact that I am grateful not to have known at the beginning. I did not want to return immediately to work as a secretary following our Nepal adventure. I had long since realized that the diaries I had kept and the letters I had written home could be turned into a book. My family, Rod, and our many friends and associates had offered ample encouragement.

Rod and Gary wanted, above all else, to continue working with snow leopards and the preservation of their habitat. The first step would be analysis of the Langu data and production of the study results. And that, too, took far longer than we would have guessed.

The overriding necessity was to earn a salary. Rod and Gary went back to work as part-time consultants. I took temporary word-processing jobs, and all of us experienced extremes of frustration at the slow pace of our primary work.

Rod and I rented a bungalow with a second bedroom for the desks and two computers. Once we were settled, our friends would ask, "If your relationship can survive four years in the Langu, it can survive anything. Why don't you get married?"

We had found in the Langu a harmony that went far beyond our early concerns over whether we might end as lovers or enemies. But I could sense that while the Langu had a nurturing force along with its power to erode and destroy, that force concealed a danger of its own. We had come to terms with the gorge so happily that the test was no longer whether we could handle its rigors, but rather how we would function in the world that lay outside. From now on our reality would not lie at the bottom of the isolated Langu Gorge, but rather in the San Francisco Bay Area, one of the most costly, heavily congested, and yet desirable regions in the United States. Our recent experience had been in a land where "struggle" means the elemental battle against hunger, but now we would be facing a different sort of struggle, in a society pervaded by overconsumption, waste, and selfishness. We might not like the circumstances, but we would have to come to terms with them, along with America's rushing pace and strong, often ruthless competition.

We knew it wasn't that the United States had changed; it was our point of view that was different. I thought of our American missionary friends in Jumla, some of whom had chosen to live all their productive lives in the Third World, where at least they could see that they were making a difference. Could we hope to ever see as much?

Having chosen to stay, we knew it was possible that a greater emotional effort would be required of us than even the Langu had asked. Aside from the Muries, who seemingly flourished no matter where they happened to live, we knew of enough couples who had worked and lived together successfully for long periods in the wilderness, only to part when they returned to the "real world." We had to assume that the day-to-day pressures of modern life caused those bonds to be broken, and we could hope only that the Langu had instilled enough inner peace and self-confidence in us to protect our personal bonds while we worked out the practical problems that lay ahead.

At the time of this writing, we still face a future that is in many ways uncertain. There is no clear path to achieving the life we envision for ourselves and the Snow Leopard Project. We started out breaking new ground, and so we continue. The Appendix that follows describes some of our study findings. It also highlights the issues that must be addressed if snow leopards—and Asia's unique mountain wildlife, habitat, and people—are to be protected from the onslaught of modern civilization and environmental degradation.

But however unsure the future looks, some things seem certain: The bonds of love and friendship remain secure. The joy, beauty, and strength we found in Nepal, personally and as a team, are lasting legacies that will serve us well in the years ahead.

APPENDIX

Preserving the Snow Leopard

by Rodney Jackson

Over the past few years I have presented slide shows to audiences in places as far-flung as Kathmandu and New York City. As the slides flash past on the screen, I find myself reliving our adventures—something I never tire of. Did I really see "Char" and her two cubs? Was the Langu really so incredibly rugged? The presentation ends with a snow leopard track in deep snow, high on a mountain pass. The audience applauds, then it is question time. I always am amazed to find how similar the questions are: After asking how we managed to survive "those terrible winters," most people want to know, "What will happen to snow leopards?" "Did you learn enough to help protect them from extinction?" "How many are left in the wild?" These, after all, were the threads that brought us to the Langu in the first place.

Looking back, it is easy to appreciate the rewards for those long hours spent trying to take notes in the frigid morning air, or nudging myself to stay awake during an all-night tracking session. We managed to gather the most detailed scientific information ever on snow leopards and their natural history. Like most scientists, we had speculated freely on the meaning of our observations, wondering where the "mounds of data" would lead us. Would those impartial weapons of science—statistics and number-crunching—support our hypotheses? Now, after so many

311

months of transcribing notes, hunched over a computer, or fighting recalcitrant software, a picture of this rare cat's life has indeed emerged, often to confirm the suspicions Gary and I had in the field. It took almost two years to make a dent in the data and to report our findings, with both of us working on other jobs to pay rent and grocery bills.

We found that the snow leopard exhibits many of the traits of other solitary cats like its cousin the common leopard, or even the tiger. For example, snow leopards were continually on the move seeking new resting sites each day, unless on a kill. Although not adverse to moving about during the middle of the day, snow leopards are crepuscular—most active around dawn or dusk. Typically they would spend the heat of the day resting beside a jumbled pile of boulders or a shady cliff ledge. They particularly favored prominent places, and well-defined landscape features such as cliffs or sharp ridges. Toward evening they might lie on top of a massive boulder, blending into the speckled sandstone, barely visible from even a few yards away. There they could scan the terrain below for herds of blue sheep, their favorite prey item.

There is a saying among mountain people: Where there are blue sheep or bharal, you will find the snow leopard. Both live above the tree line, and the ecology of predator and prey is linked by more than a common distribution. The bharal, described by biologist George Schaller as "an aberrant goat with sheeplike affinities," is a superb rock climber, though it prefers nearby rolling terrain. One British hunter wrote that bharal seem to "delight in good grazing ground in the immediate vicinity of rocky fastnesses." Since life among cliffs tends to discourage coursing predators like the wolf, it is not surprising that snow leopards are the main predator of the species—after man, of course.

Our telemetry locations showed that snow leopards prefer deeply dissected terrain broken by cliffs, ridges, and gullies. In prime habitat like the Langu, cliffs are situated close to the rolling sheep pastures. Such a spatial relationship presumably offers benefits to snow leopards in terms of the detection, stalking, and successful capture of prey. Although our information is very limited, it appears that most attempts at stalking seem to end in failure for various reasons. The Langu cats appeared to make large kills about once every ten to fifteen days or so; as "Char" found out, providing enough for two hungry mouths can be very demanding. The area she roamed over appeared to increase in size as her cubs' appetite for meat grew!

Although they depend heavily upon bharal, snow leopards are opportunistic predators, taking anything in size from a young yak to a diminutive musk deer, from the resplendent *danphe* (Impeyan pheasant) to the ever-busy pika or social marmot.

We refuted a number of popular myths. Contrary to the conclusions of some zoo studies, there is no evidence to suggest that snow leopards mate for life or share in the raising of their young. They live a lifetime of solitude except for the brief mating season or the nearly two years when they are being raised by their mother. Mating occurs from January through March, a time when eerie "yowls" may echo through the late evening or night darkness, evoking thoughts of mountain demons. Could this be the yeti mountaineers and Sherpas have made world-famous? Yowling is a long-distance vocalization that aids in animals locating one another. The young are born just over three months later. As in zoos, a litter size of two or three probably applies in the wild. Availability of prey, as well as den raiding in areas of heavier human population, are factors that affect cub survival. In zoos, the cats can live to be eighteen; in the wild, an animal of eight or ten years may be considered old.

But it was the high number of resident cats, obviously solitary, sharing a small area that most intrigued Gary and me. We had expected snow leopards to have large home ranges and that adult males or females would exclude adults of the same sex from their turf. Not only did the radio-tracking indicate that the ranges of all cats—male and female—overlapped almost entirely, but also that at least four leopards shared the same general centers of activity, to which they returned at frequent intervals. They would spend up to 60 percent of their time in an area less than 20 percent of their total home range. Admittedly most of our tagged snow leopards were relatively young and just entering the reproductively active phases of their life, but the fact that even *preferred use areas* overlapped completely puzzled us! We learned that their visits were staggered, so that on any given day a particular leopard was more than a mile apart from another individual. By avoiding direct contact with others, the potential for fights that could result in serious injury or death is minimized. And well spaced, they would improve their chances at hunting wary prey. Since they were avoiding contact with one another, how did each know where the others were?

One of the clues lay in the elaborate marking behavior of snow leopards. Although they are solitary by nature, they are not asocial. To examine this behavior, we established a "sign transect" that followed a common route used by leopards in moving through the core area. I wrote, in the July–August 1987 issue of *Animal Kingdom:*

From our sign transects it soon became apparent that the cats were marking in response to each other. On one 750-yard transect we cataloged more than 100 scrapes of varying ages and visibility. The intensity of marking peaked during the mating season, from January through March, when nearly half of the fresh scrapings were remarkings of existing scrapes.

Individuals of both sexes repeatedly visited and marked the same rocks; their sign was especially prolific in regularly traveled areas. Prominent topographic features such as large outcrops or promontories were more likely to be marked and visited again. We found numerous places that appeared to have been marked by several generations, judging from the distinct sculpturing—tufts of bunchgrass growing on pedestals and surrounded by as many as 24 scrapes.

We think the snow leopards were able to share their habitat to such a degree because of the relatively dense bharal population, the brokenness of the terrain, and the fact that they visit common areas at different times. It also seems likely that the cats' elaborate scent-marking system does not serve a territorial purpose; instead, it probably serves to maintain familiarity and distance between individuals, and to attract pairs during the brief mating season. At least two factors appear to foster this pattern of shared land use. One is the species' solitary nature. Another is the snow leopards' common travel corridors: All cats are equally constrained by plunging gorges and high, prey-poor peaks and ridges. Perhaps not coincidentally, preferred *core* areas were located around the confluence of the Tillisha Gorge with the Langu River, where bharal were profuse.

_____

I haven't answered the "sixty-million-dollar question" of how many snow leopards are left. Here I freely admit I have absolutely no idea, not that we failed to ponder the question. Major obstacles stand in the way of estimating population sizes. Occupying a vast range in the mountains of India, Pakistan, Afghanistan, Nepal, Bhutan, Tibet, Mongolia, China, and the Soviet Union, snow leopards inhabit some of the most inhospitable or remote terrain on earth. Surveys undertaken so far by Asian or foreign biologists are spotty, and extrapolating freely from them can be misleading, as each investigator applies a different "hit or miss" methodology. I can say that the species appears to be more numerous in the Langu and several other places than previously thought to be the case.

A deeper, more serious question faces the conservationist: What is to be done about the increasing number of hardy mountain people who are going to bed with hungry bellies? How can we possibly expect a Bhote in Dolphu, a Chitrali in Pakistan, or a Golok in Qinghai to care about snow leopards and blue sheep if they or their children are swamped by poverty and want? Unless we can find ways of improving their standard of living, wildlife conservation faces a dismal future. Conservation must be better integrated with development. For example, we need to find ways whereby benefits from tourism dollars can find their way into the pockets of the very people who have to share the same space, or who are being asked to tolerate leopards and wolves taking valuable livestock. Wildlife simply has to pay its way, regrettable as that might sound to some. Today's world is becoming increasingly pragmatic, utilitarian, and uncompromising about the remaining wildlands it harbors.

Snow leopards stand as a flagship species at the apex of the food chain, and they require relatively large amounts of land to survive. Calculations based on generally accepted theory indicate that *at least* fifty breeding pairs are required to sustain genetic variability in the population over the long haul; thus, unless you are talking about a "snow leopard heaven" like the Langu Valley, at least two thousand to five thousand square miles of preserve are needed. Very few Himalayan parks are this size or can be made so. As snow leopard populations become increasingly fragmented and isolated by areas much altered by man, so they become more subject to possible inbreeding—unless there is periodic movement of individuals between separated reserves to replenish lost variability. For snow leopards to cope with change on an evolutionary time scale, the species must retain as much variability and plasticity as possible. Since we have few options for setting up any more national parks, we have to find ways of ensuring the land between parks can be used by transient snow leopards, or can support sparse populations of the cat. The only other alternative to avoid extinction is to promote artificial breeding exchanges and loans among separate parks, like zoos routinely undertake. Knowing the difficulties we had catching snow leopards, I wince at the difficulties inherent in such an alternative.

Anyway, people are a fact of life within nearly all Himalayan national parks. The survival of wildlife and their habitat depends upon the good-will and aspirations of the local people. The sooner we embrace them in the solution, the better. I firmly believe that man, his livestock, and large predators can coexist, if somewhat precariously. Of course, we have to ensure that snow leopards have sufficient natural prey so they will not turn to livestock so often. Snow leopards that do so literally sign their death warrant; for the peasant the only choice usually is retribution. We should be finding ways of reducing his dependence on the land, given its poor soils, harsh climate, and limited productivity. Could he or his wife guide tourists or make cultural handicrafts for a livelihood? Could wealthy foreigners pay large fees to hunt trophy blue sheep or argali under strict control? Should I dream that tourists visiting a national park in the high Himalayas may one day be able to view snow leopards over their kill of a Himalayan tahr or blue sheep, as today's tourist views tigers in the lowland jungles of India and Nepal?

Since our return to "civilization," Gary, Darla, and I have all traveled down new trails in a mutual quest to find ways to better protect both the wildlife and the ancient human cultures of the Himalayas. A new profession is emerging—that of conservation biology—and I hope that

Gary and I can be among its pioneers. We want to continue our work, focusing more on status and habitat evaluation surveys, ways of reducing predator/livestock conflicts, and ways of rehabilitating overgrazed alpine habitats. To obtain a broader perspective of the problems as well as the range of possible solutions, we need to visit snow leopard areas in India, Pakistan, and China. We are now grappling with the reality of raising funds to accomplish these goals. Unless our financial base is reasonably secure, we cannot have more than a meager involvement; and with our loyalty split between or among two or more other jobs, we can hardly effectively explore the possibilities for strengthening bonds between conservation and development.

We have joined forces with an institution whose goals are entirely mutual with our own: the International Snow Leopard Trust (ISLT), 16463 Southeast 35th Street, Bellevue, WA 98008. Since its formation in 1981, the ISLT has coordinated research on the conservation and management of the snow leopard and its high mountain habitat, providing contact among researchers working with captive and wild snow leopards. The ISLT also has prepared an educational program on mountain wildlife for Asian villagers and schoolchildren. In conjunction with the government of India, it sponsored the Fifth International Snow Leopard Symposium, held in 1986 in Srinagar. An ambitious conservation plan was passed by symposium delegates from Europe, Asia, and North America, addressing the issue of a global strategy for survival of the snow leopard and its habitat. Priorities were placed on increasing our understanding of the snow leopard's ecology, on identifying viable montane habitats in need of protection or rehabilitation, on including local human needs and involvement in any resulting decisions, and on the snow leopard as a keystone species.

The skeptic may ask, "Why protect snow leopards?" For one thing, the snow leopard stands as a sensitive indicator or barometer of a healthy mountain environment. Where forage is more productive, so domestic sheep and yaks will weigh more and succumb less to disease. People will have more milk and meat; fewer animals will be lost to snow leopards, which will in turn have blue sheep to prey upon. For another, the snow leopard stands as a vital symbol of Asia's mountains—in scientific jargon, a "charismatic megaspecies." By protecting this species, home for others is assured.

Himalayan mountain fauna are remarkably resilient, and with proper management they can return. Can the same be said for the unique cultures of the people who share the "roof of the world" with the snow leopard? As I fall asleep at night, knowing that the sun is just rising over Dolphu, I think of the women bent to the hearth blowing on their morning cookfires, the men and children stirring in their blankets. It is winter now, and soon the snow leopards will be calling. "Panch" is out there, maybe. She should be. Will she find a mate this year? And what about her mother, "Char"? For those of us who have seen the wild snow leopard, there can be no other wish than this: Long may these exquisite creatures roam the cliffs and valleys, and long may they gaze across the wide, untrammeled vistas of their lofty mountain realm.

GLOSSARY

bhakra	Nepali for domestic goat.
bharal	Indian (accepted international name) for wild blue sheep *Pseudois nayaur*. Nepalese name is *naur*.
Bhot	Tibet.
Bhotes	Tibetans; also "Bhotia."
blue sheep	Common English term for *Pseudois nayaur*.
caragana	Highly thorny pea plant, prolific throughout our study area.
chang	Home-brewed beer made from barley or rice.
chapati	Flat disk of unleavened bread.
chiya	Nepali for tea.
chorten	Buddhist shrine.
chough	Crowlike bird.
chuba	Long, loose upper garment worn as a shirt, jacket, or robe by the Bhotes. It is usually bloused and tied at the waist, and objects can be carried in the folds.
chumba	Novitiate lama.
cotoneaster	Shrub with small, dark, shiny leaves and small white flowers.
dal	Lentils, cooked as soup or sauce.
dal-bhaat	Meal of rice with *dal,* vegetables, or meat sauce.
danphe	Nepali for Impeyan pheasant, the Nepalese national bird of nine colors.
dhole	Wild dog.
DNPWC	Department of National Parks and Wildlife Conservation, His Majesty's Government of Nepal.
doko	Large conical carrying basket used throughout Nepal.
gomba	Buddhist temple.
jhankri	Shaman; one who conducts religious or healing ceremonies using ritual, trance, and possession to influence the spirits.
jimbu	Wild, chivelike herb with the flavor of garlic; a prized cash crop growing only in the mountains.

319

karma	Tibetan for star; also a Hindu term that loosely corresponds to destiny.
kata	White ceremonial scarf significant in the Buddhist religion.
khola	River.
kukri	Curved, daggerlike knife made famous by the British Army's Gurkha regiment.
la	Tibetan for mountain pass.
lama	Buddhist priest.
lammergeier	Large Asian vulture.
langur	Species of primate.
lekh	Nepali for hill, or mountain pass.
Lhosar	Tibetan New Year.
marang	Pinewood with a high pitch content; used for candles and torches.
mo-mo	Meat-filled pasta resembling large ravioli.
monsoon	Rainy season.
mukyia	Bhote village headman (hereditary; serves alongside the elected *pradan panch*).
na	Tibetan for bharal, or blue sheep.
nema	Tibetan for sun.
nun	Salt.
Panchyat	"Council of Five," Nepal's governmental system of representation.
Panthera uncia	Latin name for snow leopard.
pradan panch	Village representative, comparable to our mayor.
pugmark	Footprint.
puja	Prayer ritual.
rakshi	Home-distilled liquor.
RNAC	Royal Nepal Airlines Corporation.
roti	Bread.

scat	Feces.
scrape	Mark left by snow leopards and other big cats, made by scuffing the ground with their hind paws.
sirdar	Foreman of a group of workers, porters, etc.
tahr	Wild goat of the Himalayas (Himalayan tahr), *Hemitragus jemlahicus.*
topi	Hat.
transect	Predetermined ground measurement along which geographical, botanical, zoological, or other data are recorded.
tsampa	Roasted wheat or barley flour.
tumpline	Leather forehead strap used for load-carrying.
Uncia	See *Panthera uncia.*
yeti	The "missing link," known in the United States as Big Foot or the Abominable Snowman.

BIBLIOGRAPHY

Books

Anderson, John Gottberg, ed. *Insight Guide to Nepal.* Englewood Cliffs, N.J.: Prentice-Hall, 1985.

Aziz, Barbara Nimri. *Tibetan Frontier Families.* New Delhi: Vikas Publishing House, 1978.

Bezruchka, Stephen. *A Guide to Trekking in Nepal.* Seattle: The Mountaineers, 1981.

Bird, Isabella. *A Lady's Life in the Rocky Mountains.* London: Virago Press, 1982.

Blum, Arlene. *Annapurna: A Woman's Place.* San Francisco: Sierra Club Books, 1980.

Chorlton, Windsor, et al. *Cloud Dwellers of the Himalayas.* Amsterdam: Time-Life Books, 1982.

Fleming, Robert L., Jr. *Birds of Nepal,* 2nd ed. Kathmandu: Avalok Publishers.

Ganhar, J. N. *The Wildlife of Ladakh.* Srinagar: Haramukh Publications, 1979.

Govinda, Lama Anagarika. *The Way of the White Clouds.* Boulder, Colo.: Shambhala Publications, 1970.

Gurung, Harka. *Vignettes of Nepal.* Kathmandu: Sajha Prakashan, 1980.

Matthiessen, Peter. *The Snow Leopard.* New York: The Viking Press, 1978.

Murie, Margaret E. *Two In The Far North.* Anchorage: Alaska Northwest Publishing Company, 1978.

Polunin, Oleg, and Adam Stainton. *Flowers of the Himalaya.* Delhi: Oxford University Press, 1984.

Rieffel, Robert. *Nepal Namaste.* Kathmandu: Sahayogi Press, 1978.

Rowell, Galen. *Many People Come, Looking, Looking.* Seattle: The Mountaineers, 1980.

―――. *Mountains of the Middle Kingdom.* San Francisco: Sierra Club Books, 1983.

Sakya, Karna. *Dolpo, The World Behind the Himalayas.* Kathmandu: Jore Ganesh Press, 1978.

Schaller, George B. *Mountain Monarchs.* Chicago: University of Chicago Press, 1977.

―――. *Stones of Silence.* New York: The Viking Press, 1980.

Snellgrove, David. *Himalayan Pilgrimage.* Boulder, Colo.: Prajna Press, 1981.

Swift, Hugh. *The Trekker's Guide to the Himalaya and Karakoram.* San Francisco: Sierra Club Books, 1982.

BIBLIOGRAPHY

Taber, Barbara, and Marilyn Anderson. *Backstrap Weaving*. New York: Watson-Guptill Publications, 1975.

von Furer-Haimendorf, Christoph. *Himalayan Traders*. New York: St. Martin's Press, 1975.

Wilkerson, James A., ed. *Medicine for Mountaineering*, 2nd ed. Seattle: The Mountaineers, 1975.

Articles and Papers

Ahlborn, Gary, and Rodney Jackson. "Marking in Free-Ranging Snow Leopards in West Nepal: A Preliminary Assessment," Proceedings of Fifth International Snow Leopard Symposium, Srinagar, India, 1986, in press.

Bishop, Lila M. and Barry C. "Karnali, Roadless World of Western Nepal," *National Geographic,* November 1971, pp. 656–89.

Fox, Joseph L.; Satya P. Sinha; Raghunandan S. Chundawat; and Pallav K. Das. "A Field Survey of Snow Leopard Presence and Habitat Use in Northwestern India," Proceedings of Fifth International Snow Leopard Symposium, Srinagar, India, 1986, in press.

His Majesty's Government of Nepal, in conjunction with the International Union for Conservation of Nature and Natural Resources (IUCN). "National Conservation Strategy for Nepal: A Prospectus," February 1983.

Jackson, Rodney. "Aboriginal hunting in west Nepal with reference to musk deer (*Moschus moschiferus moschiferus*) and snow leopard (*Panthera uncia*)," *Biological Conservation,* vol. 16 (1), pp. 63–72.

———. "Threatened Cats of Asia, Snow Leopard," *Wildlife,* September 1978, pp. 403–5.

——— and Darla Hillard. "Tracking the Elusive Snow Leopard," *National Geographic,* June 1986, pp. 793–809.

———. "Snow Cats of Langu Gorge." *Animal Kingdom,* July/August 1987, pp. 45–53.

——— and Gary Ahlborn. "Observations on the Ecology of Snow Leopard (*Panthera uncia*) in West Nepal," Proceedings of Fifth International Snow Leopard Symposium, Srinagar, India, 1986, in press.

Mallon, David P. "The Snow Leopard in Ladakh," *Int. Ped. Book of Snow Leopards,* vol. 4, 1984, pp. 23–37.

Martorell, Reynaldo; Joanne Leslie; and Peter R. Moock. "Characteristics and Determinants of Child Nutritional Status in Nepal," *The American Journal of Clinical Nutrition,* vol. 39, January 1984, pp. 74–86.

Moock, Peter R., and Joanne Leslie. "Childhood Malnutrition and Schooling in the Terai Region of Nepal," *Journal of Development Economics,* vol. 20, 1986, pp. 33–52, published by Elsevier B.V., North Holland, Amsterdam.

Schaller, George B. "Imperiled Phantom of Asian Peaks," *National Geographic,* November 1971, pp. 702–7.

———. "On Meeting a Snow Leopard," *Animal Kingdom,* February 1972, pp. 7–13.

Sherpa, Mingma Norbu, and Madan Kumar Oli. "Nar-Phu Valley Wildlife Habitat Survey," unpublished report submitted to King Mahendra Trust for Nature Conservation.

Sitwell, N. "The Snow Leopard in Pakistan," *Animals,* London, vol. 14., 1972, pp. 256–9.

Tyson, John. "Exploring Nepal's Remote West," *The Geographical Magazine,* London, vol. 35, no. 9, January 1963, pp. 532–46.

———. "Return to Kanjiroba, 1969," *The Alpine Journal,* vol. 75, no. 319, 1970, pp. 114–23.

Valli, Eric. "Life in Dolpo reflects rugged simplicity—as it has for centuries," *Smithsonian,* November 1985, pp. 128–43.

Wemmer, Chris, and Mel Sunquist. "Felid Reintroductions: Economic and Energetic Considerations," Proceedings of Fifth International Snow Leopard Symposium, Srinagar, India, 1986, in press.

Ziskin, Joel F. "Trek to Nepal's Sacred Crystal Mountain," *National Geographic,* April 1977, pp. 500–17.

INDEX

327

INDEX

INDEX

INDEX

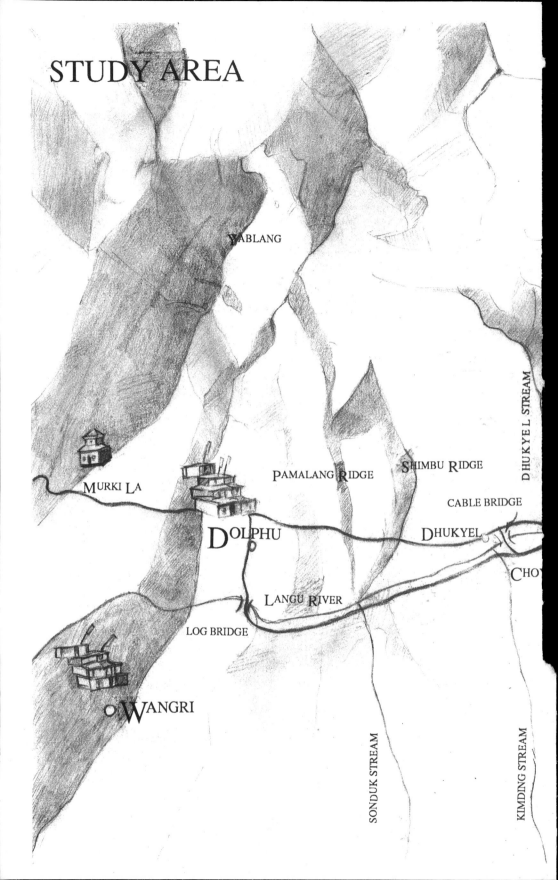

STUDY AREA

YABLANG

MURKI LA

DOLPHU

PAMALANG RIDGE

SHIMBU RIDGE

DHUKYEL STREAM

CABLE BRIDGE

DHUKYEL

CHO

LANGU RIVER

LOG BRIDGE

WANGRI

SONDUK STREAM

KIMDING STREAM